DIVERSE EARLY CHILDHOOD EDUCATION POLICIES AND PRACTICES

Diverse Early Childhood Education Policies and Practices explores issues in early childhood education and teacher preparation in five Asian countries: India, Singapore, China, Sri Lanka, and the Maldives. Some observed classrooms in these countries reflect influences that are simultaneously indigenous and colonial, local and global. By highlighting the diverse and often hybrid classroom pedagogies at work in these 21st-century Asian classrooms, the discussions in this book take into consideration the influence of globalization on local policies and practices, and the challenge educators face when they are expected to reconcile different and sometimes conflicting cultural and pedagogical worldviews.

Through a research-driven analysis of key issues such as recent revisions to national early childhood education policies, perceptions on "play-based and child-centered" pedagogy, curriculum and learning materials, and an emphasis on the teaching of values, this book illuminates the diversity of the observed classrooms as well as current trends in early childhood education in parts of Asia. The cross-national perspective serves to expand and diversify the global discourse of early childhood education and teacher education.

Amita Gupta is an Associate Professor of Education in the Department of Teaching, Learning and Culture at The City College of New York, USA and is on the doctoral faculty at the CUNY Graduate Center.

DIVERSE EARLY CHILDHOOD EDUCATION POLICIES AND PRACTICES

Voices and Images from Five Countries in Asia

Amita Gupta

Routledge
Taylor & Francis Group

NEW YORK AND LONDON

First published 2014
by Routledge
711 Third Avenue, New York, NY 10017

and by Routledge
2 Park Square, Milton Park, Abingdon, Oxon OX14 4RN

Routledge is an imprint of the Taylor & Francis Group, an informa business

Library of Congress Cataloging-in-Publication Data
Gupta, Amita, 1959–
Diverse early childhood education policies and practices : voices and images from five countries in Asia / Amita Gupta.
    pages cm
Includes bibliographical references and index.
1. Early childhood education—Asia. 2. Teachers—Training of—Asia.
3. Education and state—Asia. I. Title.
LB1139.3.A78G86 2014
372.21095—dc23   2013043626

ISBN: 978-0-415-85803-8 (hbk)
ISBN: 978-0-203-79784-6 (ebk)

Typeset in 10/12 Bembo
by codeMantra

To
Usha & Harimohan for everything they have taught me
Nihaar & Naman for everything they are

CONTENTS

LIST OF FIGURES

ACKNOWLEDGMENTS

The completion of this book marks another milestone in the research inquiry I undertook many years ago. The journey started with my research project as a doctoral student and the resulting dissertation that explored issues in early education and teacher education in India. Thereafter, the road led me into the larger region of South Asia where I undertook a collaborative exploration of the historical development of schooling and education in all of South Asia. And with the study underlying this book, I launched into an inquiry that took me further into Asia. My journey proves to be mystifying and never-ending, for the further I go, the more I discover how little is known about the context of education. There is still much to be explored and discovered.

Numerous individuals in my professional and personal life have helped to make this book possible, and I wish to thank all of them from my heart:

Parts of this study in India, Sri Lanka, and the Maldives were completed during my stay there as a Fulbright Regional Research Scholar. I wish to acknowledge the Fulbright Foundation and the wonderful people who staffed the Fulbright country offices for these countries. Their warmth and help were invaluable and much appreciated during the research process.

I wish to acknowledge all the schools, universities, colleges of education, and policy institutions in India, Singapore, Sri Lanka, China, and the Maldives for opening their doors to me.

To those who shared their professional perspectives and enlightened me in so many ways—teachers, teacher educators, deans, heads of departments, policy makers, school administrators, and early childhood consultants committed to the cause of early education—I wish to offer very special thanks: Asha Singh, Anita Madan, Amita Tandon, Abha Sahgal, Prof. G.C. Upadhyaya, Prachi Kalra, Rekha Sen, Rita Paes, Prof. P.K. Sahoo, Suzana Andrade, Pooja Thakur, Surabhi, Dr Thakur and his colleagues from the KV's, Carissa, Saroj Khurana, Seema, Melinda Parker, Vidya Mulay, Ali Fawaz Shareef, Hassan Mohamed, Azra Abdulraheem, Shamila Abdullah, Leela Ahmed, Asim Sattar, Swarna Jayaweera, Chitrangani Abhayadeva, Kamala Peiris, Elsie Kottawele, Chandra Gunawardene, Dr. Wanniigama, Samudra Sanarath, Manjula Vithanapathirana, Srini De Zoysa, Indrani Telegala, Yamuna Perera, Wilfred Perera, Diedre Thiogarajah, Pat de Rose, Sirene May Lim, Audrey Lim, Vashima Goyal, Belinda, Vijaya, Betty Sim, Sharon, Pushpa, Ng Pak Tee, Joshua Ka Ho Mok, Xu Xiaozhou, Wei Li, Mei, and many others who made this research possible.

To Alex Masulis, my editor at Routledge, a big thanks for his encouragement and his support in turning my research into this book.

Thanks also to my colleagues and wonderful students at the City College of New York for cheering me on.

And as always, my deepest gratitude to all the special people in my life—family and circle of friends—for filling my life with love and joy, for cheering me on, and for keeping the dream alive.

PREFACE

> There is a very puzzling contrast—really an awesome disconnect—between the breathtaking diversity of schoolchildren and the uniformity, homogenization, and regimentation of classroom practices.
>
> Genishi & Dyson, 2009, p. 4

As we make our way through the second decade of the 21st century, the phrase "the world is a changed place" sounds like a stale cliché. And yet, we continue to be startled by how completely our lives have been transformed in the last 20 years and how rapidly the world continues to change before our very eyes. Anyone with just a cell phone can attest to the fact that it has become almost impossible to keep pace with how quickly technology changes. And the lives of those who live in urban hubs are governed with so many more devices! Technology has quickened the pace of globalization. Although globalization is an age-old phenomenon that started with the very first trade routes and conquests in the history of the world, it is the pace of today's trade that is new, as is the nature and definition of conquests. The effects of global forces move with lightning speed today, and information and ideas can be shared the world over in real time. The challenge now is for policy discourse to be able to keep pace with the rapid changes in the world.

This book is about early childhood education, and before I proceed any further I wish to clarify that in the United States the term *early childhood education* refers to the education of children between the ages of birth and 8 years. This range includes school levels up to Grade 2. In Asia, the terms used more often are kindergarten or preschool or pre-primary education for children until the age of 5 years, and primary education for children over that. Technically, then, my study on early childhood education includes preschool or pre-primary, as well as early primary grades. The terms *early childhood, preschool* and *pre-primary* have been used interchangeably throughout this book. Another clarification regards the various terms being used in countries in Asia to refer to this field: Early

Childhood Education (ECE), Early Childhood Care and Education (ECCE), and Early Childhood Care and Development (ECCD). These terms will also be used interchangeably in the book.

Recently in the United States there has been an increasing critique on early childhood education and early childhood teacher education, accompanied by an increase in the emphasis on standardization through the emergence of the Common Core standards and the new state certification requirements for teachers. Simultaneously, there has been a rapid emergence and expansion of early-years education in the developing world, including Asia, Latin America, and Africa. A paucity of a robust body of published research on diverse perspectives in early childhood education and teacher education begs us to be open-minded when exploring the field in a global context. Much of the mainstream published literature on early childhood education is written from a Western perspective that is based mostly on an understanding of the development of young children who live in the Euro-American West. But early childhood classroom practices in many non-Western communities demonstrate complex interplays between teaching and learning that have evolved within the context of an amalgam of indigenous, cultural, colonial, global, and local influences. This often leads to hybrid pedagogies in classrooms, as opposed to either/or approaches closely aligned with specific early childhood models.

Sustaining a locally relevant, yet globally competitive, educational discourse is one such challenge faced by countries around the world today. At both personal and professional levels, I have had numerous opportunities to observe, teach in early childhood classrooms, and participate in educational conversations and dialogues within the United States and Asia in a very bicultural and cross-cultural manner. As an early childhood educator who has worked and continues to work with early childhood teachers and teacher educators in the United States and Asia, I have been privy to discussions about pedagogy and policy in both parts of the world for the last 25 years. I have observed how nation governments have been recommending policy changes to adjust and address the gaps within their respective educational systems in order to keep up and be more aligned with an increasingly connected world. During my bi-annual trips to New Delhi, I have met educators in India who expressed dismay at and frustration with the academic rigor of their schools and the absence of an emphasis on nurturing children's creativity, imagination, and sociocultural development. At the same time, during the course of my professional work in New York, I have encountered arguments that have highlighted the low ranking of U.S. students on the international field and the need to increase academic rigor in U.S. schools. With much interest I have watched policy makers trying to fill in existing gaps within their educational systems: Asian educational systems moving to embrace child-centered pedagogies in policy and attempting to implement the same in practice, and U.S. educational policy reforms striving to achieve higher academic standards and an increasingly test-driven pedagogy to compete with international standards.

Within the last two decades, and more so within the past 8 to10 years, countries such as China, India, Singapore, Sri Lanka, and the Maldives, among many others, have examined their educational policies and made fundamental changes in early childhood education. A strong impetus for this change has been the widespread ratification of the Convention on the Rights of the Child (CRC) and Education for All (EFA) led by world organizations such as the United Nations and the World Bank. The goal that was initiated in Jomtien in 1990 was further reiterated and emphasized in the 2000 Dakar Framework for Action, which set the goal of achieving EFA by 2015. The very first goal of the Framework for Action is expanding and improving comprehensive early childhood care and education. And thus the 2015 deadline for EFA has profoundly impacted the work of several governments, private sectors, and NGOs in the field of early education during the past 12 years. The need for a professional, nationally organized field of early childhood education has been a high priority on the policy agendas of nation governments around the world. The current spotlight on early childhood education even in the developed world has been catalyzed by recent research conducted by economists that demonstrate the long term economic benefits of quality preschool education.

My research study included interviews and school observations that I conducted in India, Sri Lanka, Singapore, China, and the Maldives. The purpose of the study was to examine how changes in national early childhood education policies in Asia are being reflected, or not, in local early childhood classrooms, while recognizing the vast diversity of schools in each of these countries. This book is the result of the findings from that study. It is a book for teachers, teacher educators. and policy makers. The chief concern of this work is to present glimpses of current trends and directions of pre-primary education and teacher education in some parts of Asia, and to reflect on the lessons that teachers and teacher educators everywhere can learn from these experiences.

Globalization has created the need for new benchmarks with regard to the knowledge, skills, and attitudes that the next generation everywhere will have to be familiar with in order to function effectively and efficiently in any given society. And there is no doubt that every society is becoming increasingly diverse and multicultural. Teachers thus have to learn not only about cultural awareness but cultural empathy. As early childhood education and teacher education are currently being systematically reformed and coherently organized at national levels across the world, the United States can be inspired by efforts underway in other countries to reexamine its own early childhood education by keeping in sight both policy and pedagogy. On the other hand, the United States has an established record of research on early childhood education, and countries such as India and China have learned how to take research findings and translate them into practice, producing some stellar examples of "inventive, creative early childhood pedagogy" (Stewart & Kagan, 2005, p. 243).

As is to be expected in increasingly globalized world systems of schooling, there are practices that are informed by multiple sources both global and local. During the course of the study, many questions arose about local practices being colonized and influenced by Western and global trends. The discussions in this book converge onto the phenomenon of educational hybridity or pedagogical hybridity within teacher education and how this hybridity is navigated. Rather than idealizing or rejecting global or local traditions, I wish to engage the reader in a process of rethinking teaching by moving toward the creation of a more explicit and conscious synthesis of culturally diverse pedagogical views. I wish to urge policy makers and practitioners to make decisions regarding young children within the third space of cultural and pedagogical hybridity.

Chapter Overviews

This book is based on field observations and narratives related to early child-hood education, grounded in the work of teachers, teacher educators, and policy makers in Asia. The descriptions help shed light on examples of classroom design and school structure, curriculum and learning materials, government policies and initiatives, efforts and initiatives at the grass-roots levels by private enterprises and NGOs, and general trends in early childhood education. The book will present images and descriptions of the above issues in early childhood education in India, China, Sri Lanka, the Maldives, and Singapore, and will serve as springboards for further discussions on pedagogy and teacher preparation within cultural contexts.

Chapter 1 introduces the book with a narrative account of existing tensions between the dominant discourse and local practices in non-Western school settings. The chapter emphasizes the interfacing of local and global elements in the creation of a hybrid space in some classroom practices in Asia, and urges the development and expansion of a third space in theory based on research conducted in the local context. A discussion on the conceptual frameworks utilized in the study follows, with an overview of the current global spotlight on early childhood education. The chapter ends with a brief overview of the research methodology underlying this study.

Chapter 2 seeks to familiarize the reader with the overarching context of the study—the demographic, geopolitical, and sociocultural-philosophical features of the Asian contexts within which data was collected. Included in the profile for each country is the attempt to trace the early childhood education policy shifts that have occurred in these countries in recent decades. These shifts in national policy discourses demonstrate the intentions to change the nature of education from the traditionally didactic to a more progressive pedagogical approach.

Chapter 3 focuses more closely on this policy shift from a traditional approach to a play-based and child-centered pedagogy. The chapter begins with the definition of a "child-centered" pedagogy as constructed within the progressive education framework in the West. It further includes a description and discussion of where, how, and to what extent the policy changes in Asia are or are not being reflected in local classroom practices with regard to teachers' perceptions of play, the classroom environment, and curriculum planning.

Chapter 4 highlights the widespread emphasis observed in the teaching of character, citizenship, and cultural values in schools across Asia. Descriptions of school environments and classrooms are accompanied by a discussion to highlight how many of the curriculum decisions made and values taught in the classrooms were reflective of larger national and cultural values in these societies.

Chapter 5 includes a detailed description of classroom curriculums and materials that are specifically made by teachers and that not only reflect local cultures and lifestyles, but also present instances of how the local is juxtaposed with the global. The discussion highlights the concept of cultural and pedagogical hybridity that works to support the development of skills needed to navigate and succeed in the 21st-century world.

Chapter 6 draws the reader's attention to institutional partnerships for teaching and learning, and provides three examples of uncommon partnerships that were observed between schools and other institutions and organizations: a technology-based partnership between a teacher education institute and a primary school; a digital web-based partnership on reflexive teaching between a teacher education institute and community preschools; and a citywide media partnership between schools and local newspapers. The discussion addresses the highly competitive and crowded environments in urban Asia and how children may be best prepared to succeed in such societies.

Chapter 7 presents current and important issues in the domain of early childhood teacher education. A detailed account of the current systems of teacher education in each of these countries is not within the scope of this book. Instead, the chapter focuses on voices from the field as practitioners and policy makers articulate concerns about the preparation of pre-primary and primary grades teachers in Asia.

Chapter 8 concludes the book with a summary of the main themes that emerged in these instances of non-Western systems of education in Asia; reflections on the value of learning about, and from, the practices of teachers around the world; and recommendations for expanding and diversifying the discourse of early childhood education and teacher education to be more reflective of the majority world.

Most importantly, I wish to remind the reader that my descriptions of classroom and school practices within various contexts are specific to those particular environments that I observed. It is imperative that these accounts not be generalized and understood as being the norm or standard across the countries in which they are situated. Each of the five countries presents a wide diversity in terms of the early childhood settings found there. The purpose of this book is not to present a system of early childhood education as being representative of the national system in any of these countries. Rather, my aim is to describe policy debates and instances of schooling and classroom practices at particular institutions, as moments in time and as windows into some of the current thinking underlying early education in Asia.

1
INTRODUCTION: EXPANDING THE DISCOURSE FOR EARLY CHILDHOOD EDUCATION AND TEACHER EDUCATION

This chapter highlights the critical relationships among knowledge, power, and voice and questions the underlying assumptions that contribute to the construction of a dominant discourse in education. Voices that are heard most often assume power and privilege over those that go unheard. Critical theories maintain that the dominant ideas underlying the discourse of early childhood education have largely developed from theories of learning and child development that emerged in the cultures of the "West."[1] Before I proceed any further, I wish to emphasize that even though the "Western/non-Western" dichotomy is a false one, these terms are used to acknowledge the ethnocentric assumptions and stereotypes already present in cultural worldviews when different groups of people conceptualize and accept ideas on how children learn and grow. Cross-cultural research has indeed consistently highlighted the different constructions of childhood within diverse social, political, and cultural contexts (Cannella, 1997; Bloch, 1992; Kessler, 1991, 1992; Delpit, 1995; Katz, 1996; Viruru, 2001; Trawick-Smith, 2006; Gupta, 2006; Tobin et al., 2009; Marfo & Biersteker, 2011; Brooker, 2011). However, for the longest time, it has been the Western voice and knowledge that have dominated the early childhood educational discourse. Emerging diversities regarding images of children and childhood have thus worked to create a tension between the Western discourse of early childhood education and teacher education theory, and the cultural worldviews of the non-West.

In urging an examination of worldviews that constitute the "other," it is important to note that the emphasis in this book is, as Tikly (1999) notes, about repositioning the local and the global in relation to each other such that multiple worldviews become reflected in the scholarship that defines childhood and child development. Globalization in its various forms has now made the world a much smaller place, and educators the world over often find themselves face to face with ethnic, religious, linguistic, racial, and other differences in their classrooms, schools, and neighborhoods. Human livelihood and ways of life the world over have become interregional, interethnic, interreligious, intercultural, international, and thus increasingly interdependent. The field of educational research would benefit by the inclusion of perspectives on the educational philosophies, pedagogies, and practices of the non-West and the global South, thus allowing the knowledge matrix to resemble cultural truths in a clearer and more accurate way.

This then begs the question of how the "voice" of pedagogy and educational theory can be made more inclusive and multilayered. A good place to start is by asking what it is that sustains the status quo of educational and teacher education theory and what prevents it from incorporating a more expansive knowledge base. Referring to the important ways in which indigenous knowledge could contribute to the educational experience of all students, Semali & Kincheloe note that "because of the rules of evidence and the dominant rules of epistemologies of Western knowledge production, such understandings are deemed irrelevant by the academic gatekeepers" (Semali & Kincheloe, 1999, p. 15). An example from the field of early childhood education can illustrate this point. In early childhood education, the dominant discourse on child development is based on the view that children develop in a universal, linear sequence that all children must undergo to achieve maturity. To question these ideas about child development is discouraged, and this naturally rejects other perspectives on how children grow and learn (Viruru, 2005). To illustrate further, in the non-Western worldview of Native Americans, the aim of traditional education was to strive toward learning how to achieve harmony in one's physical, mental, and spiritual realms (Locust, 1988 as cited in Reagan, 2005). Thus traditional Native American ideas about education and childrearing became intimately linked to ideas on good health and the responsibility of the individual for his or her own health.

Another example is seen in the traditional view of education in Africa, which included the following goals: development of latent physical skills; development of character; inculcation of respect for elders and those in positions of authority; development of intellectual skills; acquisition of specific vocational skills and respect for honest labor; development of a sense of belonging and participation in family and community affairs; understanding, appreciating, and promoting the community's cultural heritage (Fafunwa, 1974, as cited in Reagan, 2005 p. 61). Thus education in a traditional African setting was not viewed as being separated from life itself, and all adults who came in contact with children in their community became their teachers (Reagan, 2005). In a sense, the village was allowed and expected to raise its children.

Similar examples from Asia will be provided throughout this book. No doubt valuable insights can be gained from examining educational traditions that are "non-Western" and in being so are nondominant and thus seemingly less credible (Reagan, 2005). This in itself is a strange contradiction when the very notion of "Westernness" itself is a construct, and Western forms of knowledge are directly indebted to older, non-European forms (Tikly, 1999).

Colonized Conditions

I first encountered the questions of whose knowledge and whose voice in the early 1990s during the beginning of my graduate work in the United States. Having had active bicultural teaching experiences in early childhood classrooms in India as well as in the United States, I would often be confronted by questions that highlighted pedagogical and childrearing differences between the two culturally different school systems. But much to my frustration I could not explain these differences. Awed by the seemingly unquestionable dominant discourse of the West, I could at first only criticize the non-Western approaches in Indian schools. I later began to feel the need not only to understand educational ideas in culturally different contexts but also to explain and articulate them in a language that would engage the research community at large. In my desire to make sense of the behaviors and attitudes encompassed within the classroom life I observed and experienced in some Indian schools, I began an exploration of ideas and practices that were Indian and Western, traditional and modern, not only within my own mind but as being representative of a wider Indian psyche as well. Further inspiration came from the words of Loomba (1998), who urged that the narratives of women, colonized people, and non-Europeans don't erase the issues of imbalance but in fact revise our understandings of them.

An exploration of the core ideas of various worldviews that shape people's thinking, behaviors, and attitudes frequently brings the Western academic face to face with the deeper differences between the "self" and the "other." In grappling with the differences we see in the similarities and the similarities we see in the differences, a two-way transaction or dialogue is initiated between the "self" and the "other" which lends itself to a postcolonial framework.

> I found myself in the challenging position of being the marginalized voice speaking from within the realms of Western academia, the voice of a female scholar of color questioning the discourse of mainstream early childhood education in the West, trying to find a space to make a statement with an opportunity to be heard, attempting to bring out into an open forum the realities of early childhood education in a non-white, non-Western culture through the voices of teachers in India. (Gupta, 2006/2013, p. 209)

The above manifestations of "self" and "other" are categories that can occur within any group where some are accorded privilege and exert their power over others. According to Donaldo Macedo, if colonialism is viewed as imposing an ideological yardstick against which others are measured and found wanting, then the colonized experience can be seen to be found everywhere—"in concentration camps without the barbed wires in the First World, in ghettos, in the rural mountains of Appalachian and Indian reservations, in the large scale exploitation produced by the policies of neo-liberalism" (Macedo, 1999, p. xii). Examples of political or economic power struggles between groups within the same society were very apparent during this research study, such as those between individuals of different levels of castes and classes within India; between the Tamil Tigers and the government within Sri Lanka; between "urban" Malè and the more remote islands of the Maldives. Along similar lines of power, the colonized condition can certainly be found in early childhood classrooms when schools in the non-West are evaluated by standards of pedagogy and curriculum that are based on an understanding of child development in the context of young children growing up in the West. Many in the developing world feel compelled to use Western curricular materials and approaches to ensure that their children develop "appropriate" social and intellectual behaviors. But what gets overlooked is that these appropriate behaviors are mostly those that are valued by the socially, racially, and linguistically privileged who most resemble the West.

Curricular reformers in Asia today are grappling with the hegemonical expectations of Western culture at the global level on one hand and the need for a more culturally relevant curriculum at the local level on the other hand. During the course of this research in Asia, it was observed that many educational centers/schools for young children were touting philosophies and mission statements that were couched heavily in the language of the Western discourse. Being seen as an "international school," a "world-class school," a school having "global standards," a school based on "international methods" and offering "English-medium instruction" seemed all of a sudden to afford the centers credibility and make them eligible for funding from a variety of local, national, and international sources. This is painfully reminiscent of the educational policies in colonial India that required schools to use English as the language of instruction if they were to be funded by the British Administration. Today, that language of pedagogy is taken from the progressive discourse of the West against whose standards schools are evaluated around the world. An example is seen in a poor evaluation of preschools in Sri Lanka issued by a Western early childhood consultant: "Pre-school education in Sri Lanka has developed a style of its own that is uniquely out of step with the more widely accepted Early Childhood Education theories and practice valued in most developed countries" (King, 2010).

Next, I will discuss the theoretical concepts that have framed the findings and discussions in this book, namely, comparative education, postcolonial theory, and globalization. Aspects of these ideas that are pertinent to this book will be discussed, and readers are encouraged to situate the findings presented in the ensuing chapters of the book within the constructs of these frameworks.

Theoretical Frameworks

Comparative Education

This book is based on data collected from educators and educational institutions located in five different countries in Asia—India, Singapore, China, Sri Lanka, and the Maldives. By virtue of being a multicountry study, it becomes situated naturally within the realm of comparative education. Therefore, it is relevant that

I present the comparative education framework within which I have described and discussed the research data. Comparative and international education research is essentially interdisciplinary as education has to be examined within larger cultural contexts. This study, too, draws on data not only from schools and other educational institutions but also from the overarching social, cultural, spiritual, and political ethos of these countries. Single-country studies do not technically fit the definition of comparative education in the same way as do studies located in two or more countries or regions that have an explicit focus on comparing issues. The Bray & Thomas Cube offers a good illustration of the various levels of analyses that are possible in the field of comparative education. The levels of analyses are described as occurring along three possible dimensions:

> The first dimension is the *geographic/locational* level that can include world regions/continents, countries, states/provinces, districts, schools, classrooms and individuals. The second dimension is the *nonlocational demographic* groups including ethnic, age, religious, gender groups or entire populations. The third dimension comprises of *aspects of education and of society* such as curriculum, teaching methods and strategies, finance, management structures, political change and labor markets. (Bray, Adamson, & Mason, 2007, p. 8)

Comparative education research can range from studies examining educational issues in two different locations to issues in multiple locations. The strength of a study conducted in fewer locations is naturally the depth of understanding that can be achieved. A study located in multiple countries that vary widely in size of population, economic strength, sociocultural beliefs, political values, and educational structures does not necessarily achieve depth but can succeed in achieving greater breadth and a wider vision of the larger, more overarching trends in a particular world region. Large-scale studies are often quantitative and are challenged by the wide range of differences with regard to structures of education, curriculum, pedagogy, and assessment techniques. There is, after all, an intimate relationship between education, literacy, and cultural context within each country (Bray, Adamson, & Mason, 2007). Qualitative studies, on the other hand, are usually located in fewer countries and are able to capture the local educational and cultural contexts in a more meaningful and accurate manner. A deeper contextual understanding and the building of bridges in the field of comparative education are further enabled by researchers who investigate countries in which they have had previous experience (Crossley, 2000).

As an example of a study located in multiple locales, Bray, Adamson, & Mason (2007) point to one that was conducted by Morris & Sweeting (1995) which included Hong Kong, Macao, Malaysia, China, Singapore, South Korea, and Taiwan. Each of these countries is discussed as a separate chapter, thus resulting in a more in-depth look at the issues within each. Other studies, rather than providing an in-depth focus on one single issue in a country, present a wider and larger picture of current shifts and structures across several countries. This book is based on a qualitative study on early childhood education policy and practice that includes data from five different countries. Each chapter is organized not around a specific country but around a particular theme, presenting findings that draw on observations, interviews, and policy documents from the included countries. The themes range from general sociocultural contexts and early childhood policy, pedagogy, curriculum, classroom resources, and materials to issues in teacher education. Although the data draws from five different countries, the aim of the book is less about comparing these countries than it is about highlighting overlapping themes and patterns that emerged in the context of the five countries.

An important issue that needs explanation is why comparative research in education is important and how it contributes to the field in general. According to Dimmock (2007), a comparative approach to educational issues in different cultures is helpful for a number of reasons: (1) the concept can be applied at different levels—organizational, local, regional, and national; (2) with increasing globalization, the need to increase awareness of the importance of cultures and dangers of underestimating them also grows; (3) the study of education-related issues ultimately centers on people and their behaviors; and (4) a cultural perspective holds the potential to break the dominant grip of Anglo-American beliefs, conceptualizations, and practices (Dimmock, 2007, p. 298). Stewart & Kagan (2005) further suggest that cross-national comparisons are helpful in (1) encouraging a spirit of self-examination and in urging teachers and teacher educators everywhere to reflect on their own practices; (2) initiating a dialogue between teachers of different countries; (3) establishing research partnerships across countries in the areas of early childhood education policy and pedagogy; (4) encouraging cross-country institutional partnerships between schools, teacher education colleges, and early childhood professional organizations; and most importantly (5) motivating the internationalization of teacher preparation content so that future teachers can integrate an international dimension into teaching their own students.

The advantages of comparative education research are reiterated by Bray, Adamson, & Mason (2007, p. 377) who underscore the importance of studying other systems of education to become better able to understand our own systems; of looking outward and in other places and learning what is unfamiliar; and of reflecting on the familiar and challenging taken-for-granted assumptions underlying educational aims, philosophies, structures, and policies. Bray et al. (2007) caution against using comparative education to identify models that are employed and are seemingly successful elsewhere and the shallow import of such selected educational models without considering the societal context of their functions and purposes and the complexities involved. An important question to address during comparative education research is "what is the cultural context that produces the educational institutions and practices under study?" (Mason, 2007, p. 180). After all, "the practice of teaching and learning … relates to the context of culture, structure, and policy in which it is embedded" (Alexander, 2000, p. 3). While academics can use findings from comparative education studies to deepen their own knowledge and understanding, practitioners can use the academics' insights to enhance or reconsider aspects of their own pedagogy and policy within a specific context.

This book attempts to translate the findings of the study to address both academics and practitioners in the field of comparative and international early childhood education and teacher education. The detailed descriptions of classroom environments, classroom materials, and classroom activities are particularly relevant to early childhood practitioners, while the theoretical discussions throughout the book are helpful to academics. In its explicit attempt to bridge the gap between practice and theory in early childhood education, the book as a whole is relevant to both researchers and practitioners.

Postcolonial Theory and Pedagogical Hybridity

Postcolonial theory, though a difficult concept to define, allows for a discussion on a wide range of experiences such as migration, slavery, race, gender, representations, colonial and neocolonial domination, and so forth (Ashcroft et al., 1995). It is a useful approach to employ when exploring different positions and perspectives, to examine how knowledge is produced, and to explain the imbalances in the relationships between the center/periphery; dominant/marginalized; colonizer/colonized; or superior/inferior. Postcolonial theory enables a deeper understanding of the colonized/colonizer relationship by drawing attention to transcultural mixing and exchange (Tikly, 1999). In an earlier study, Gupta (2006/2013, p. 212) demonstrated how early childhood teachers in urban India were observed to navigate between tradition and modernism, and between the Indian, colonial, and postcolonial elements of their practice: The early childhood teacher's voice as the old-fashioned and unscientific was in dialogue with the voice of the dominant discourse of the West that seemed appealingly rational, scientific, and modern. A hybrid classroom practice thus seemed to emerge that was the result of a mix of different discourses. This socially constructed hybrid approach, though unfamiliar to educators in the West, can certainly be understood by those who live within the locus of intersecting and evolving sociocultural ideas that profoundly influence daily life inside and outside the Indian classroom.

Postcolonial theory as a research framework nevertheless presents its own unique challenges. In my own experience, as I attempted to bring the marginalized voice speaking the language of a non-Western discourse into the realm of dominant early childhood published research in the West, I encountered a dilemma: Would the juxtaposition of the two discourses reinforce the disparity between "acceptable" and "nonacceptable" early childhood practice? And yet, as already mentioned, the knowledge that is heard most is that which is presented by "Western" research, and if the "marginalized" is not brought into the domain of formal research, it will tend to remain marginalized. If research focuses only on subjects, issues, and concepts in the "West," then only these will continue to be highlighted and valued as sources of universal truths (Gupta, 2006/2013, p. 216).

The Western discourse undoubtedly seems to provide credibility to schools in the developing world. This is because discourses refer not only to what is said and thought but also to who has the authority to speak and when. Because a power is thus lent to the speaker of the dominant discourse, it becomes even more critical to make mainstream educational discourse inclusive of multiple voices and reflective of educational traditions other than the dominant. This creates not only an awareness of the "other," but also a recognition that we ourselves are an "other" among "others." At that point the voice of Western academia may experience a change in the authority with which it wields the dominant discourse.

Early childhood education as a field, as opposed to higher levels of education, still retains somewhat of a luxury in allowing schools and teachers the space and opportunity for minimizing a top-down academic curriculum and maximizing the "hidden" curriculum. Early childhood teachers thus play an important role in highlighting local cultural values that may or may not be in conflict with the Western values that drive policy and pedagogy in a national discourse. By providing specific examples of early childhood teaching practice and policy from countries in Asia, the intersections between the global and the local will be highlighted in this book, and the discussions will underscore how diverse educational ideas are often interfaced, resulting in hybrid practices. In increasing numbers of multicultural societies and schools, this examination can provide valuable insights for educators everywhere into how to combine diverse perspectives within educational philosophies and pedagogies. This ability will lead to a transcultural mixing between the philosophies, ideas, language, ideologies, pedagogies, and curricular practices of the colonized and the colonizer. When these categories are viewed not as binaries opposing each other but as cultures with fluid boundaries interacting with each other, then we will essentially be able to view the exchange as a form of cultural translation as ideas from one culture are modified and embedded into those of another culture. This process of transformation may then lead to the creation of a hybrid third space, a gray area that holds infinite new possibilities (Bhabha, 1994, 2009). By drawing attention to the transcultural mixing and exchange that is the result of cultural hybridization (Tikly, 1999), a deeper understanding of the knowledge production that occurs within the context of this transaction is possible. This process can also enable one to examine the curriculum enacted in the *space of pedagogical hybridity* as ideas from one educational discourse get embedded into those of another. The teaching and learning processes that occur within this space of pedagogical hybridity may subsequently constitute a *pedagogy of third space.*

Globalization

The influence and assimilation of "foreign" ideas and practices is certainly not a new phenomenon, nor is it restricted to the historical past. But the speed with which globalization is occurring is something new. Globalization has been defined as the "intensification of worldwide social relations which link localities in such a way that local happenings are shaped by events happening many miles away and vice versa" (Giddens, 1991, as cited in Arnove, 2013, p. 1), with economic and cultural globalization being the most prominent aspects of this process. Accordingly, globalization acts as the current channel for bringing Western influence into countries of the "non-West." Globalization of education refers to the "worldwide discussions, processes, and institutions affecting local educational practices and policies" (Spring, 2009, p. 1). It is best to view the process of globalization as waves flowing between countries in both directions, and not necessarily just one way from the developed world toward the developing word. Globalization is a crucial topic in critical education because as Apple (2011) states, this process influences "what counts as responsive and effective education, what counts as appropriate teaching … all of these social and ideological dynamics are now fundamentally restructuring what education does … and who benefits from it throughout the world" (pp. 222–223).

Globalization is having a profound impact on educational policy. Rui (2007) notes that while on one hand policy is created in a highly contextualized manner and is implemented in a very context-driven way, on the other hand it also tends to travel globally, having a deep impact on places far away from its origins. This fact increases the relevance of and need for comparative research on educational policy. Rui (2007, pp. 242–243) highlights six changes in the field of international policy resulting from the impact of globalization: (1) economic changes that have led to countries opening up to privatization, neoliberalism, and market economy structures under new economic policies; (2) demographic changes in the composition and age of populations that have impacted social policies for retirement and health care; (3) ideological changes that have shifted from equality to excellence, accountability, and choice and that have impacted business and educational policies in a major way; (4) changes in the nation-state framework with nation-states having less control over the flow of people, information, and capital while transnational forces have gained in power; (5) increased individualism under the forces of global capitalism and neoliberalism, which has a debilitating effect on public policy with regard to public agencies and services, including public education; and (6) an increasing skepticism toward and lack of trust of technocrats and political decision makers, which damages the essence of the democratic process.

The effects of globalization vary from place to place. In particular, its impact on postcolonial societies of the global South has not yet received adequate attention, particularly in the field of early childhood education and teacher education pedagogy and policy.

Implications of a Global Focus on Early Childhood Education

In 2000, 164 nations agreed to UNESCO's Dakar Framework for Action, which mandated the coordination of the United Nations Educational, Scientific and Cultural Organization (UNESCO), Development Programme (UNDP), Population Fund (UNFPA), Children's Fund (UNICEF), and the World Bank to ensure Education for All by the year 2015. The first of its six goals is "expanding and improving comprehensive early childhood care and education, especially for the most vulnerable and disadvantaged children" (*www.unesco.org/new/en/education/ themes/leading-the-international-agenda/education-for-all/efa-goals/*). As part of this goal, world organizations have been working relentlessly along with national governments to ensure the development of quality early childhood education in the developing world.

International organizations that fund education in the developing world such as the World Bank, the International Monetary Fund (IMF), and the UN have approached the education and development of the young child as part of a larger policy discourse on building human capital. Investing in children is integral to their broader social and economic investment projects. The current approach of world organizations that sponsor early childhood care and education in emerging economies and countries of the developing world has been closely defined by a child development discourse rooted in American research on neuroscience, behavioral science, and developmentally appropriate practice (Mahon, 2010). The dominant discourse stresses a future-oriented rationality that views the child as human capital in the making (Dahlberg & Moss, 2008). For example, the World Bank (2011) referenced Nobel Laureate economist James Heckman whose work has demonstrated the economic returns of investing in early childhood education (ECE). Reports such as those published by Legal Momentum's Family Initiative and the MIT Workplace Center (Calman & Tarr-Whelan, 2005) and by the Institute for a Competitive Workforce (Why Business Should Support Early Childhood Education, 2010) emphasized that the first five years are the most critical in the child's brain development. Achievement gaps develop well before children begin kindergarten, and high-quality preschool programs significantly impact all children, but especially those from low-income families. The reports recommended that good early learning programs for younger children reduce costs later in life while enhancing the nation's economic growth. Thus high-quality early childhood education can help break the cycle of poverty. These ideas have been shaping the most recent ECE policy decisions in the developed world as well; for example, investing in quality ECE is currently a priority in the Obama Administration.

What This Means for Children's Learning Goals

As global efforts to achieve the Millennium Development Goals (MDG) and Education for All (EFA) have been put into place, findings have emerged indicating that although access to schools for all children has increased in the developing world, the quality of learning is still highly questionable. As the 2015 deadline for EFA approaches, it is apparent that the efforts of the past decade to ensure that all children will be in schools by 2015 were rather narrowly focused on access and not on quality of learning. At this point in time, there certainly are more children in schools, but there are also a greater number of in-school children who cannot read at grade level. According to the 2012 EFA Global Monitoring Report, at least 250 million primary-aged children around the world were not able to read, write, or count well enough to meet the minimum learning standards even after having spent four years in school (UNESCO, 2012).

To address this concern, UNESCO created the Learning Metrics Task Force (LMTF) through its Institute for Statistics and the Center for Universal Education at the Brookings Institution. In Phase 1 of the project, the task force has proposed a framework for seven domains of learning for all children to develop. For each domain the specific knowledge, behaviors, skills, and attitudes are delineated as specific subdomains for early childhood, primary, and postprimary levels of education. Some examples of the early childhood subdomains follow (Toward Universal Learning, Report No. 1, Learning Metrics Task Force, 2013, p. 19):

Domain 1 constitutes physical well-being, and the subdomains include physical health and gross–fine perceptual motor skills.

Domain 2 constitutes social and emotional states, and the subdomains include self-regulation, self-concept, emotional awareness, social relationships, and moral values.

Domain 3 constitutes culture and the arts, and the subdomains include creative expression, self–identity, and respect for cultural diversity.

Domain 4 constitutes literacy and communication, and the subdomains include receptive and expressive language, print awareness, and vocabulary.

Domain 5 constitutes learning approaches and cognition, and the subdomains include curiosity, autonomy, initiative, cooperation, symbolic activity, reasoning, problem solving, and other early critical thinking skills.

Domain 6 constitutes numeracy and mathematics, and the subdomains for early childhood include number sense, spatial sense, patterns, classification, and measurement.

Domain 7 constitutes science and technology, and its subdomains address the development of inquiry skills, knowledge of the natural and physical world, and the awareness of technology.

On the heels of these curriculum standards and learning objectives comes a flurry of activity across the world to design assessments and tools that will measure children's learning. This is fodder that feeds into the current climate of neoliberalism, which is the latest wave of globalization, and risks reducing the measure of quality to a set of numbers on a rating scale. This risk applies to the quality of children's learning experiences, as well as to the quality of teaching, the quality of school administration, and the overall quality of schools. By quantifying aspects of children's learning that can be quantified, such as reading and math skills, we risk pushing aside aspects of children's growth and learning that cannot be quantified, such as the development of their socioemotional soft skills, their sense of well-being, their joy quotient, and their cultural intelligence. It would help if policies were to recognize and clearly state the expectation that the goal of schools should be to prepare children for both the soft skills and the hard skills, to do well in reading and math, but also to be able to understand and empathize with those who are different from them. As educators, we need to learn how to teach within spaces that reflect different but coexisting realities, whether with regard to cultural worldviews or to pedagogical ideologies.

What This Means for Teacher Education

The debate between an academic and a child-centered pedagogy and curriculum has been ongoing for a long time and remains unresolved. The debate can only end when all educators stop feeling compelled to side with one particular approach and begin to acknowledge the fact that both experiences are equally important. This accommodation can occur if learner-centered and teacher-directed approaches are positioned not as mutually exclusive categories but instead as being on the same line of continuum. Teacher educators and teachers must begin to feel comfortable with pedagogical hybridity and the notion of a *pedagogy of third space*. Even in this age of globalization there can be no one "appropriate" and universal early childhood pedagogy for all children everywhere at all times. It would behoove policy makers at local levels to conceptualize an integrated curriculum as developing out of the expectations, aspirations, and struggles of those who are experiencing the curriculum most intimately and who now reflect a diverse range of sociocultural-economic backgrounds and worldviews.

As local cultures evolve under global influences, respective school systems also witness a simultaneous evolution. The emergence of a hybrid space in pedagogy will reflect established practices as well as newly borrowed ideas in educational philosophies, pedagogies, and curricula. If previously the educational discourse and the prescribed curriculum in formerly colonized nations such as India were predominantly reflective of European colonialism, then currently prescribed curricula may reflect a predominance of the child development discourse of progressive education. At the same time, embedded within a prescribed curriculum that is based on a developmental perspective, the sociocultural ideas of the local cultural philosophies would continue to be transmitted by way of the "hidden" curriculum and the sociocultural-spiritual leanings of local teachers. The tenets and ideals of this newly hybrid discourse will likely be rooted in cultural beliefs that are both local and global, and will lead to a complex interplay of ideologies and interpretations.

Debates on educational quality have consequently led to a flurry of activities worldwide to reexamine and reevaluate teacher preparation processes. Globalization has led to concerted efforts in several Third World countries to improve and expand teacher preparation approaches. In much the same way as with early childhood education, the discourse of early childhood teacher education, too, is shaped by Western research, and this often compels efforts at the local level to be closely aligned with global (meaning Western) trends in teacher education. Therefore, systems of teacher training are shaped by both Western and local discourses. The need for a professional, nationally organized field of early childhood teacher education is currently a high priority for the policy agendas of governments in the developing world. This is a definite shift away from earlier views of teachers of young children as primarily caregivers and as personnel who did not require a university degree in education.

In order to address the current challenges emanating from the forces of globalization and neoliberalism that are bearing down on schools and society in Asia, it seems even more critical to prepare teacher candidates in a theory and practice that are informed by diverse pedagogical ideas; engage teacher candidates with ideas of social justice; create an awareness in teacher candidates of the implications of neoliberalism; emphasize diversity training and multicultural education in teacher preparation; and prepare teacher candidates to recognize the space and moment when a dominant discourse of education begins to encroach upon a marginalized voice (Gupta, 2012). The resulting hybrid pedagogy may very well be the homegrown solution that Lim & Lum (2012) refer to when they imply that "practitioners with local problems need not be marginalized in the international academic discourse." As an alternative to current teacher education theories, this *pedagogy of third space* would actively acknowledge the coexisting realities of both Asian and Western educational ideas within the flows of global forces, leading to more empowered teaching at the local level.

Privatization and Neoliberalism

By financially supporting nongovernmental organizations (NGOs), community-based schools, vouchers, and public–private partnerships to benefit the very poor, international organizations such as the World Bank maintain a neoliberal discourse on social policy (Mahon, 2010). Through this influence, education and teacher education in general are becoming positioned as regulated markets governed by neoliberal policies where test scores are a measure of student performance and good teaching. Educators are measured by their students' performance on academic tests rather than by their professional knowledge of how children learn and develop (Brown, 2009). This follows trends in the United States where teacher education programs are being increasingly shaped by standards-based accountability reforms in which teacher candidates are taught how to deliver curricula specific to a local district and how to comply with specific assessment systems (Mayer et al., 2008). In rapidly globalizing world systems of schooling, economic considerations have led to a push to impose neoliberalism and conservative reforms in the form of both global and local standards (Apple, 2001; Green, 2005; Ross & Gibson, 2007).

This development has also led to a spike in the privatization of early educational institutions. The number of private early childhood preschools and teacher training institutes in many Asian countries is skyrocketing. Private schools are no longer seen as options for the elite only. There is a range of fee-charging private schools that are both affordable and not so affordable. Historically, ECE has typically not been a mandate of the central governments in these countries, and with the 2015

EFA deadline to ensure that every single child is in school now approaching the challenge is to find an adequate number of ECE schools and trained ECE teachers to accommodate all the children in each of these nations. The niche created by the paucity of both early childhood education and early childhood teacher education has been quickly filled by private preschools and private teacher training institutions, many of which may have questionable standards.

Methodology and Significance

This book highlights current issues in urban early childhood education and early childhood teacher education in five Asian countries: India, Singapore, China, Sri Lanka, and the Maldives. In no way is it suggested that there is just one "Asian" context. Asia is a vast and diverse continent and comprises cultures that are as diverse from and foreign to each other as to those on any other continent. The countries selected here themselves demonstrate the enormous range of sociocultural, economic, political, linguistic, racial, and ethnic diversity not only among each other but also within themselves. The discussions in this book are based on research findings from a series of interrelated qualitative inquiries conducted by the author and situated within the urban social-cultural-political context of these countries. The inquiries employed a comparative and interdisciplinary approach to examining current trends in policy and practice surrounding early childhood education and teacher education within specific sociocultural contexts and worldviews. A triangulated methodology allowed for: (1) a bibliographic investigation to provide the conceptual framework and to situate the study; (2) an investigation and review of institutional and policy documents to provide an overview of current and proposed teacher education in each country; and (3) an empirical investigation to include (a) interviews with policy makers, institution heads, department heads, teacher educators, and teachers, and (b) nonparticipatory classroom observations in teacher education colleges and primary schools for each of the countries.

Data was collected from a wide range of sources in urban centers within these countries, including major policy-making organizations, research institutions, colleges of education, universities, teacher-training institutions, NGOs, and pre-primary/primary schools. Specifically, the sites across all five countries included: nine government schools, eight private schools, two semigovernment schools, two NGO-run schools, one lab school attached to a college, two policy and research institutes, and ten teacher education institutions. Pseudonyms replace the actual names of individuals to protect their identities as well as the identities of specific departments within universities.

Scholarship has been an important dimension in the educational landscape in Asia but has recently shifted from largely originating in the West to now being a mix of cross-border regional exchanges (Hawkins, 2013). At the same time, significant theoretical streams of scholarship from Asia, Latin America, Africa, and the Middle East continue to be marginalized in mainstream comparative research studies in education (Rui, 2007). It is my hope that this book will further contribute to the movement of ideas that are emerging in and from the East and global South and moving toward the West, and vice versa. In this book we take a peek at some early childhood classrooms in both government and private schools in India, China, Singapore, Sri Lanka, and the Maldives. We will have the opportunity to hear the voices of teachers, teacher educators, and policy makers in all five countries articulate their perceptions of current policy and classroom practice. In the ensuing chapters I will examine early childhood education issues, such as classroom pedagogy, materials, curriculum, and teacher education, in some of those intersecting spaces where the local/global, traditional/modern, Eastern/Western, child-centered/teacher-centered ideas come together, sometimes in harmony and sometimes as contradictions.

I will begin in the next chapter with a brief contextual overview of the social, cultural, political, and demographic landscapes within which early childhood educational policy and practice are embedded in each of these countries. Cultural values represent socially constructed orientations in the society where they are played out (Masemann, 2013), and thus policy and pedagogy, which are deeply influenced by cultural values, become highly complex and layered phenomena that have ramifications at global, national, and local levels. Comparing pedagogy demands a level of expertise that is far beyond just the knowledge of the compared countries and their cultures and policies (Alexander, 2000). I do not claim to be an expert on issues in policy and pedagogy in the five countries included in this book, and I am fully cognizant of the fact that "researchers on countries and cultures other than their own commonly become acutely aware of how little they know and seem 'naïve, presumptuous or simply too tidy in the face of what even insiders find baffling or contrary'" Alexander (2000, p. 4) as cited in Mason (2007, p. 187). Nevertheless, as Dimmock notes, a comparative approach based on a cultural perspective holds the potential to break the dominant grip that Anglo-American beliefs, conceptualizations, and practices currently hold (Dimmock, 2007). Once again I remind readers not to generalize these classroom images as being representative of an entire country or region, but rather to view them as continua rather than as poles. Please take each individual vignette for what it is— a glimpse into a particular space within a given moment in time.

Note

1 Throughout I am using the terms *West* and *Western* not as geographical directions but to refer to white, English-speaking countries of the world located in the Western Hemisphere (the United States, Canada, and the UK) or the Eastern and Southern hemispheres (Australia and New Zealand).

2
COUNTRY CONTEXTS AND RECENT ECE POLICIES

> In November 2011, at the Asian Pacific Economic Cooperation (APEC) meeting in Honolulu President Barack Obama announced that the United States is an Asian-Pacific power and is in the region to stay. … He reminded the participants that Asia is the fastest growing region in the world, accounting for over half of the world's Gross Domestic Product (GDP). This represented a shift in both international and domestic policy, clearly outlining a future in which events in Asia will likely dominate political, economic, and quite possibly cultural directions for many nations including the United States in the near future. (Hawkins, 2013, p. 341)

Several Asian countries may be said to place a cultural value and importance on education and to be committed to a quality educational system. However, it is also necessary to recognize the vast range of diversity and complexity the Asian continent presents. If there are some Asian countries with well-developed educational systems and high rates of literacy, then there are also some Asian nations where children lack access to a basic education and with high rates of poverty and illiteracy. Countries like Singapore are in the forefront of the digital revolution with regard to technology in education, but at the same time countries like Bangladesh lag very far behind in technology. Hawkins (2013) conceptualizes and describes Asia as being characterized by three distinct development trajectories: the more historically developed countries of Japan, Korea, and Taiwan, which are rapidly aging; the massive economies of India and China, which are rapidly expanding and creating a labor force to meet their own and global markets, and where government policies have been set to aggressively develop and expand the educational sector; and the in-between third group of countries such as Indonesia, Malaysia, Thailand, Philippines, and Vietnam with moderate economic development and high birth rates, which are creating a need for the development and expansion for higher education. In addition, there is a great deal of regional and sociocultural diversity among and within Asian countries in general, including issues of ethnic, linguistic, religious, caste, and class diversities.

The goal of this chapter is to present the sociocultural contexts and recent revisions in national policies for early childhood education in the countries included in this book: India, China, Sri Lanka, Singapore, and the Maldives. I will begin with some demographic information and a brief overview of recent educational policies in each country. This will be followed by a short discussion on some values and beliefs that lie at the core of the spiritual philosophies that shape the cultural ethos in these countries. I wish to reiterate what Alexander (2000) underscores: "Life in schools and classrooms is an aspect of our wider society, not separate from it: a culture does not stop at the school gates. The character and dynamics of school life are shaped by the values that shape other aspects of … national life. … Culture … is all" (pp. 29–30). These words emphasize the critical importance of taking into consideration the larger cultural contexts within which educational decisions on policy and pedagogy are implemented and enacted.

Although it is not in the scope of this book to provide detailed descriptions of the complex and multilayered social-cultural-political-educational contexts of India, China, Sri Lanka, Singapore, and the Maldives, aspects of their larger cultural contexts will be addressed briefly. Even though the study is based on data collected from five different countries with very diverse cultural contexts, I will attempt to refrain from conveying the construction of culture as a simplistic and monolithic entity, or to conflate the concept of culture with country. Rui (2007) notes that "the impact of globalization on the poorer postcolonial societies of the 'South' has received much less attention despite the dramatic implications for development processes in such contexts" (p. 255). In this book I will highlight the impact of globalization on early childhood educational policies and classroom practices in some urban schools found in these five countries.

Demographic Profiles and Early Childhood Education Policies

In most Asian countries, the gatekeeper to higher education is some form of a national entrance examination; a large body of scholarship critiquing these systems may be found particularly with regard to Japan, Korea, Taiwan, China, Singapore, and India (Hawkins, 2013). The pressures of this national system have traditionally filtered down to the lower grades, resulting in a primary school curriculum that has been very textbook oriented, exam driven, and teacher directed. With the looming deadline for Education for All (EFA) in 2015, countries around the world have been buzzing with the task of developing, expanding, and qualitatively improving early childhood education in order to meet the third of the Millennium Development Goals. Major revisions to early childhood education and teacher education policies are being made and implemented in countries across Asia, and many of these changes can be linked to the effects of globalization and neoliberalism shaped by the capitalist values of the West. These influences are certainly very evident in Asia within the business and commercial sectors, and parallel changes are increasingly also being seen in the field of education, such as increased privatization of schools, standardization of curriculum, and regulation of institutions through stricter licensing procedures, hierarchical control over teachers with a corresponding decrease in teacher autonomy, and education policy narratives couched more prominently in the "Western" discourse of early childhood education.

The concept of policy borrowing has been a central issue in the context of globalization as is evident in the work of comparative education researchers (Phillips & Ochs, 2003 as cited in Rui, 2007). Governments in Asia have become increasingly global in their outlook as they engage in a give-and-take process in which global policies are modified to meet local ends for local educational institutions through a prolonged process of transformations. Policies are thus best understood by first understanding policy context, and how policies evolve and are transformed when global trends interact with local values (Rui, 2007).

A significant relationship exists between educational policies and the global agenda to shape socioeconomic development in countries. The process of policy making itself is rife with the struggles between conflicting interest groups and conflicting value groups, and most often policies reflect the values of the winning and more dominating groups.

It is also pertinent to underscore the idea that global policy trends should be engaged with from a critical perspective, such that an imposition of the "one-size-fits-all" model and inappropriate application of "world standards" are avoided. Certainly this is experienced as a challenge in developing countries when working with foreign consultants using a global rhetoric and foreign donors promoting their own agendas and educational values.

The size, demographics, political contexts, and dominant spiritual and linguistic influences in each of the countries in this study vary tremendously. Even so, recent waves of globalization have influenced changes to educational and economic policy in each of them, and the shifts in early educational policies will become apparent in the following discussions. The sequence of the countries discussed (following no particular order) is India, China, Sri Lanka, Singapore, and the Maldives.

India: Demographic Profile and Early Childhood Education Policies

India is the world's seventh largest country by area and its tenth largest economy. Other indications of its significance and presence in the global arena are that it has the second largest labor force in the world, it has the world's fastest growing telecommunications industry and holds the third largest smartphone market after China and the United States (Lomas, 2013), and it has the second fastest growing automotive industry in the world. India's middle class is projected to grow to 580 million by the year 2030 (Farrell & Beinhocker, 2007) to become the world's fifth largest consumer market. The Indian film industry also produces the world's most watched cinema (Dissanayake & Gokulsing, 2004). But there is a vast economic disparity in the country, which also holds the largest concentration of people living below the World Bank's international poverty line (World Bank, 2006). India is also known as the world's youth bulge because more than 50% of its population is under the age of 25 years, and about 65% of the population is under the age of 35 years. A resulting concern for the Indian government is that it needs to create 10 million jobs a year to ensure jobs for the 300 million people who will join India's workforce between 2010 and 2040 (Rajendram, 2013).

The expansive ruins of Mohenjo-Daro and Harappa are considered to be the first carefully designed urban cities that flourished in South Asia about 5000 years ago. India's history is a complex anthology of numerous monarchies under Hindu and Muslim kings and emperors, and later its colonization by the British. As a Federal Republic, India declared independence from British rule in 1947 and today has a population of almost 1.2 billion, with 84% of it being primarily Hindu, 12% Muslim, and the remainder comprising Christian, Sikh, Jain, Buddhist, Zoroastrian, and some tribal groups. While Hinduism, Buddhism, Sikhism, and Jainism originated in India, the religious traditions of Islam, Christianity, and Zoroastrianism arrived in India in about the first millennium CE and are an integral part of Indian culture. Thirty to 40% of the population speaks Hindi, which is the national language, and there are 22 official languages, including English.

This book is based on data collected from visits to and observations of classrooms in a range of schools and institutions, as well as interviews conducted with policy makers, teachers, and school principals in the Indian cities described below.

The capital city of New Delhi is located in northern India and is the hub of politics and the Indian government. Metropolitan Delhi has a population of approximately 21 million people, and the official languages spoken by the masses in this city are Hindi, Urdu, and Punjabi. Delhi is an ancient amalgam of cultures, languages, ethnicities, religions, and architecture, a multilayered urban hub thousands of years old. The sites visited for this research study in Delhi included: pre-primary and primary classrooms in a government school; pre-primary and primary classrooms in four independent or private schools; an NGO-run pre-primary and primary slum school; a pre-primary lab school attached to a college affiliated with Delhi University; early childhood faculty in a college department of childhood studies and human development, and early childhood faculty at a teacher education college, both affiliated with Delhi University; early childhood faculty at an open university of distance learning; the early childhood department at a national institution for educational policy and research; and a principals' meet at a Kendriya Vidyalaya (Central School).

In Goa, a former Portuguese colony on the western coast of central India, the sites visited for this study included a private preschool and a teacher education institution affiliated with Goa University. The coastal city-state of Goa has a population of about 1.5 million and is India's smallest state known for its beaches, lively music, and mouth-watering seafood curries. The official language of the state is Konkani, and the overall culture of Goa is permeated with the nuances of Portuguese culture.

In Pune, a university city in the central Indian state of Maharashtra, the sites included a private pre-primary and primary school catering to children from economically challenged families; a semiprivate government-aided school for girls; and a privately run teacher resource center that provided programs and workshops for the development and support school staff for private as well as government schools. The population of the metropolitan city of Pune is about 5 million, and its official language is Marathi. This ancient city was ruled for centuries by Hindu princes who fought the Mughal emperors prior to India's independence, and for a very long time has also been an intellectual hub of schools and colleges.

In Ahmedabad, an industrial town in the western Indian state of Gujarat, the site visited was a private innovative school. The population of the metropolitan city of Ahmedabad is about 6.2 million, and the official language of Gujarat is Gujarati. Ahmedabad is also the home of Sabarmati Ashram where Mahatma Gandhi, spiritual and political leader of India, spent several years of his life.

In Allahabad, an ancient and intellectual city in the north Indian state of Uttar Pradesh, the site visited was the Department of Education at Allahabad University. The population of Allahabad is about 5.9 million, and the official language is Hindi. Allahabad lies at the confluence of three rivers; it is considered to be one of the three holiest cities in India and is the location of the famed Kumbh Mela, the most important pilgrimage for Hindus. Interestingly, seven of the thirteen prime ministers of post-independent India belonged to Allahabad—a city that for centuries has juxtaposed intellect and religion, academic learning and spirituality.

In Puducherry, a former French colony on the eastern coast of the southern Indian state of Tamil Nadu, data was collected regarding an ashram school. Puducherry is a small city with a population of about 1 million, and the official language of the state of Tamil Nadu is Tamil, with Telugu and Malayalam also spoken extensively.

India has had a long history of education, schooling, policy, and reform going back thousands of years, and its most recent educational system had been shaped by the colonial British administrators since the early 19th century. After the country's independence from the British colonial rule, several changes were made in the nation's educational policy, but none as massive as the changes in policy and practice that are currently sweeping India's educational landscape. A more detailed overview of the historical evolution of education in India may be found in Gupta (2007).

A variety of early childhood settings are to be found in India, including the government-sponsored Integrated Child Development Services (ICDS)

Anganwadis (which combine health, nutrition, and education); private nursery schools; private day care; and mobile crèches (Gupta, 2007). Most pre-primary schools in India are found in the private sector since government (public) education starts at the age of 5 years in Class 1. Recently however, some government schools have started pre-primary classrooms for children as young as 4 years of age.

Since the early 1990s, major changes effected in India's economic-political agenda have impacted the nation's educational policy from pre-primary to higher education. These changes in educational policy include the restructuring of the National Curriculum Framework in 2005 (NCF, 2005), the National Council of Educational Research and Training (NCERT) Focus Group on Early Childhood Education in 2007, the policy revisions by the National Council for Teacher Education (NCTE) in 2009, revisions to Sarva Shiksha Abhyan (2011) (Universal Elementary Education), and the Right to Education Act (2010) to ensure that all children had access to quality schooling.

The most prominent feature of recent policy changes has been a dramatic shift from a teacher-directed to a child-centered approach. In 2005, India's *National Curriculum Framework* for schools was restructured to emphasize learner-centered education through more activity-based teaching, learner-friendly textbooks, and elimination of annual examinations and retention policies in favor of social promotion in primary/elementary schools (NCF, 2005). The *Position Paper of the National Focus Group on Early Childhood Education* (NCERT) lists the following markers to emphasize the shift from a traditional teacher-directed approach toward a child-centered approach in early childhood education: developmentally appropriate, activity-based programs, related to the child's needs, interests, and abilities; an integrated set of experiences to foster holistic growth in all developmental domains; sufficient flexibility to meet the diverse social, cultural, economic, and linguistic contexts of India as well as to cater to individual differences between children; and ability to help the child adjust to the routines and demands of formal teaching of primary school (NCERT, 2006).

Other recent policies that impacted early childhood education in India are the revised recommendations for Sarva Shiksha Abhyan (SSA) (2011) and the Right to Education Act (2010). SSA was set up by the Indian government during the first years of the millennium in its efforts to achieve universal elementary education by providing free and compulsory education to all children between the ages of 6 and 14 years. This program was implemented as a partnership between the central and state governments to cover the entire country. In brief, the original aims of SSA included (1) opening new schools in places with no schooling facilities; (2) strengthening the infrastructure of existing schools (additional classrooms, toilets, drinking water); (3) providing additional teachers to existing schools with inadequate teaching staff; (4) strengthening the capacity of currently employed teachers through extensive training and development; (5) emphasizing life skills education and computer education; and (6) emphasizing the education of girls and children with special needs.

The Right of Children to Free and Compulsory Education (RTE) Act of 2009 was the resulting legislation of the constitutional amendment to ensure that every child had the right to full-time quality elementary education that satisfied basic norms and standards. The RTE Act 2009 went into effect in April 2010, and thereafter changes were made to the existing SSA vision, norms, and strategies to more closely align SSA with RTE 2009. As per the government of India's document on the *SSA Framework for Implementation* (2011), the revised SSA emphasizes (1) a holistic view of education aligned with the recommendations of NCF 2005; (2) equity and opportunity to increase school enrollment, attendance, and retention of disadvantaged groups of Indian society; (3) better access to schools with a deeper understanding of the educational needs of excluded and disadvantaged groups of children; (4) emphasis on gender issues to address the status of girls and women in Indian society; (5) teacher accountability to create an inclusive classroom culture; (6) greater moral accountability imposed on teachers, parents, educational administrators, and other related stakeholders; and (7) a system of integrated educational management. These features are based not only on the recommendations of RTE 2009, but also on the earlier child-centric recommendations of NPE, 1986/1992 and NCF, 2005. The revised SSA guidelines provide a broad framework within which individual States may determine more detailed approaches and strategies that are contextualized within their own social, economic, and institutional contexts. However, the RTE Act 2009 did not include children below the age of 6 years, and advocates of early education continue to urge the Indian government to work on mandates that will extend the mission of the RTE Act to all preschool children between the ages of 3 and 6 years that will allow schooling to begin at the age of 3 years.

The Integrated Child Development Services (ICDS), a government-supported national-level service, was initiated in the nation's efforts to ensure its constitutional promise of free and compulsory education for all children up to the age of 14 years. The ICDS program has now completed three and a half decades of its existence. The main tenets of the program are a package of services comprising supplementary nutrition, immunization, health checkup, and referral services to children below 6 years of age and to expectant and nursing mothers. Nonformal preschool education is imparted to children 3 to 6 years old, and health and nutrition education to women in the 15–45 age group. The concept of providing a package of services is based primarily on a "whole-child" approach to facilitate the holistic development of all children, along with the consideration that the overall impact would be much larger if the different services are delivered in an integrated manner. The unique feature of the program is that it utilizes, integrates, and mobilizes all available governmental services at the project level. The ICDS runs the *Anganwadi* centers in India. The goal of ICDS centers is to empower underprivileged children younger than the age of 6 years, and ensure that they are physically healthy, mentally alert, emotionally secure, socially competent and intellectually ready to learn when they reach primary school age. The *Anganwadi* centers are cost free to parents, are policy driven, and have a hierarchical management style under the ICDS. The teachers undergo three months of job training, and the objective of these centers is the comprehensive and holistic development of children using an activity-based nonformal teaching approach, but many *Anganwadi* centers lack quality. International organizations such as the World Bank and UNICEF, national bodies, as well as the local NGOs have partnered in delivery, research, and evaluation. Undoubtedly, whatever success the ICDS program has been able to achieve so far has been because of strong community support and cooperation. However, much remains to be done in this direction to ensure community participation in ICDS programs at each level, as well as to improve the quality of the experiences provided to the children in every center.

In the practical application of RTE 2009, all schools including those that are private are now required to reserve 25% of admission slots to children who belong to economically weaker communities. With RTE and SSA there has been a push to provide free and compulsory primary education, and primary school enrollment in India has grown rapidly to include a majority of children from sections of Indian society that are low income and culturally marginalized. This has led to the creation of integrated classrooms that now have children from diverse backgrounds who have thus far remained segregated and separated with regard to schooling. Currently, practicing teachers have not been prepared appropriately to teach children from diverse socioeconomic backgrounds or with varying abilities. Prejudices against poor children and their families may be commonly found among teachers. There is a tremendous backlog in the availability of trained teachers. Increasing commercialization of the field has added to this crisis by increasing the number of private schools for children, while the acute shortage of qualified teachers remains. Commercialization and a shortage of teachers have also led to the emergence of private teacher training institutes that are often substandard in quality. Such classroom challenges that have emerged as a result of policy changes have created a dire need for teacher education programs that will prepare teachers more adequately and appropriately for the realities of classrooms in the 21st century.

In conclusion, three major challenges face education reform in India today: (1) neoliberal policies that are resulting in the creation of private schools, many of which are unregulated and are of substandard quality; (2) increasing enrollment of children in primary schools, which is leading to overcrowded classrooms, teacher shortages, and teachers inadequately prepared to handle the increasing socioeconomic diversity in their classrooms; and (3) cultural incursions occurring when a Western progressive early childhood discourse is viewed as the basis of "appropriate" pedagogy in all classrooms in India.

China: Demographic Profile and ECE Policies

China is officially known as the People's Republic of China and is the world's most populous country with a population of about 1.35 billion, as well as the second largest in terms of land area. It is a single-party state governed by the Communist Party. The ancient Chinese civilization was one of the earliest of the world, and its history was marked by the rule of several hereditary monarchies known as dynasties. The last of the dynasties was overthrown in 1911, and the People's Republic of China was established by the Communist Party in 1949. Today China is the second largest economy in the world and the world's largest trading power with regard to exports and imports. At the same time, it is also the world's highest consumer of energy. The main spiritual traditions represented in Chinese society are Confucianism, Taoism, and Buddhism, with smaller percentages of folk religions, Islam, and Christianity (www.travelchinaguide.com). The official language is Mandarin, with Cantonese and Shanghainese also spoken widely (CIA World Facts).

A current source of concern for China is its aging population. In 1978 a population control policy called the one-child policy was introduced in China whereby urban couples were restricted to having only one child while allowing additional children in several cases, including twins, rural couples, ethnic minorities, and couples who are both only children themselves (BBC News Report, 2000). The result of the one-child policy was the 4–2–1 phenomenon: "four doting grandparents, two over-indulgent parents, all investing their hopes and ambitions on an emerging generation of spoiled, lazy, selfish, self-centered and overweight children" (Zhu, 2009, p. 52) and creating a situation in which one adult child was often left to support and care for two parents and four grandparents (Li Wen, 2008). This policy has resulted in China's aging demographic profile and burgeoning elderly population who often have no one to care for them. The one-child policy also altered family roles and childrearing practices, raising concerns about the harmful effect of too much attention and pampering "little emperors and princesses" who were more egocentric, less cooperative, and less persistent as compared to children with siblings (Jiao, Guiping, & Quicheng as cited in Vaughan, 1993, p. 1). But the policy has also resulted in a heavier emphasis on education for young children, and a deeper commitment of families to school in terms of their involvement and investment in their only child; parents even criticize teachers when they feel the teachers have been harsh or unfair to their child.

Data for this book was collected during visits to a college of education and a government nursery school in Hangzhou, the capital city of Zhejiang Province in eastern China and about 100 miles southwest of Shanghai. The Hangzhou Metropolitan Area population comprises about 21 million people, and the city has been one of the most prosperous ones in China for the last 1000 years. The local dialect is Wu, but the official language spoken is Mandarin; local handicrafts include production of silk, umbrellas, and folding hand-held fans.

Elementary education in China begins at the age of 6 years. Programs for children under the age of 3 years are usually termed nurseries, and full-day programs serving children between the ages of 3 and 6 years are called kindergartens and serve the dual purpose of child care and educational preparation (Vaughn, 1993).

A point to note with early childhood education in China is the absence of the dichotomy between child care and educational preparation as can be seen in the United States, for example. Unlike the United States, however, the history of early childhood education in China did not follow a dual development of centers where full-day programs offered child care for children of working mothers, and half-day programs provided education for children of stay-at-home mothers (Vaughan, 1993).

Recent publications by the Chinese Ministry of Education (official statements, legal codes, plans for school reform, manuals for teachers, and parenting magazines) reflect a new discourse about children and their education in contemporary China. All these sources are urging parents to recognize that children need to experience a childhood that is defined by leisure and play rather than study and toil because this is crucial not only for their individual development but also for a stable, strong, and vital Chinese nation (Naftali, 2010). *Education for Quality* (1999) limited the number of school hours, examinations, and amount of homework assigned to young students (as cited in Naftali, 2010); Shanghai's *2004 Second Phase Curriculum Reform* emphasized a theme-based curriculum and decreased the duration of a school lesson to allow children more free time to play and relax (Hsueh et al., 2004, Zhu, 2003, Yang, 2004, cited in Naftali; Zhu, 2010); Shanghai's People's Congress Standing Committee (2004) emphasized paying attention to children's physical and emotional changes as per their developmental stages; and schools in Beijing and Shanghai have been required to include psychological training classes to the school curriculum to strengthen the mental health of students (Naftali, 2010).

In Hong Kong, the website for the Education Bureau provides a list of do's and don'ts for kindergarten teachers to follow, emphasizing as a "do" the use of diverse teaching approaches and child-centered learning activities (Hong Kong Education Bureau, 2012). The website includes the following quote:

> The *Guide to the Pre-primary Curriculum* emphasises that early childhood education lays the foundation for life-long learning and whole person development. The core value of early childhood education lies in "child-centredness". Pre-primary institutions should formulate their curriculum according to the basic principles of "children's development" and "children's learning". Children's interests, needs and abilities should be taken into consideration. They should also create a stimulating learning environment that facilitates children's development of multiple intelligences. Through life experiences, sensory encounters, exploration and interesting games, children's holistic development can be fostered. (http://www.edb.gov.hk/en/edu-system/preprimary-kindergarten/overview/index.html, accessed on 4/2/13)

At the end of the Cultural Revolution and during the 1980s China, the Reform and Open Up policies influenced the move from traditional education to child-initiated activities in schools (Zhu, 2009). This indicated a shift away from the traditional approaches that deeply influenced early childhood education as well. The ECE curriculum reform began as spontaneous experiments in various parts of the country and gradually expanded from experiments in single subjects to the whole curriculum, progressing from one village to the next (Zhu, 2003). The most important result of this reform was the document titled *Rules on Kindergarten Routines* issued by the National Education Committee in 1989 (cited in Zhu, 2009). Reform according to this document emphasized child-initiated activity, individual differences, the importance of play, an integrated curriculum, and the process of activities (Zhu, 2009). But there was a gap between the child-centered rationale promoted by this document and educational practice. Deep-rooted cultural traditions and ideas steeped in either Confucianism or socialism such as obedience and upholding unity contradict these new progressive ideas of equality which are rooted in Western democracy. Thus, implementation of the new pedagogy has, to a large extent, remained a reform in theory only (Zhu, 2009).

Another document, *Regulations for Kindergarten Work*, issued by the State Ministry of Education in 1996, was a landmark event in the development of kindergarten education, emphasizing child-initiated activity; individual differences in children; the importance of play; an integrated curriculum; and process versus product in children's work. The following quote is taken from this document to illustrate the centrality of play in China's new ECE policies: "Play is an important way to carry out all-round development education. Children's play shall be selected and guided in accordance with the age characteristics of children. Kindergarten shall create favorable play conditions (time, space, materials). ... Teachers shall respect children's desire to choose the forms of play. ... Teachers shall provide proper guidance for children in their play and keep them joyful" (as cited in Gu, 2006, p. 35). Another document the Ministry of Education issued was the *Guidance for Kindergarten Education* (2001), which sought to bridge the gap between practice and theory by offering compromise solutions by specifying the requirements and content in different domains (Zhu, 2009).

With time, however, the traditional image of classroom arrangement is fading away, and one visible change is that the seating arrangement in rows is giving way to a group arrangement as children seated around a table participate in collective activities. Multiple activity centers or learning centers have been created in the classroom, "such as reading area, doll play area, shop area, hospital area, constructive activity area, animal area, plant area, painting area, music area, and so on" (Gu, 2006, p. 36). According to Gu (2006), even a single change such as moving the teacher's desk from the center of the classroom to one side indicates that the centrality of the teacher is giving way to a more student-centered classroom space, with greater consideration to the individual and the free play of children—in essence a more democratic education. The *Regulations* also urge a shift from the traditional idea of respecting the teacher to respecting the child. According to Gu's study, this notion was understood by teachers as "loving children but not spoiling them; giving them more freedom but not abandoning discipline and order; being more democratic but not completely giving up centralism; meeting the needs and desires of individual children but not forsaking collectivism" (Gu, 2006, p. 38).

Zhou (2011) notes that the year 2010 represents a critically important milestone year in the history of early childhood education in China: It was in this year that the *Outline of China's National Plan for Medium and Long-term Educational Reform and Development* was announced. The Plan recognizes the importance of the early years in children's development. Chapter 3 of this Plan refers specifically to early childhood education and emphasizes better access to ECE programs for children aged 3–6 years by the year 2020, while urging programs to acknowledge children's developmental levels to ensure happy and healthy childhoods (Zhou, 2011). The Plan also highlights an increase in the government's investment into early childhood services, stricter standards and licensing requirements for programs, improved teaching standards through teacher education and professional development, and strengthened early childhood education services in rural areas.

Also in 2010, following close on the heels of the above announcement, the China State Council released a document titled *Issues Regarding Current Development of Early Childhood Education,* with 10 top issues to be addressed. These issues, according to Zhou (2011) are: (1) a more prominent position of early childhood education in the government's agenda, with the government working closely with other social and private stakeholders; (2) increased government funding for early education services; and (3) enhanced teacher capacity to ensure an adequate supply of qualified teachers prepared according to minimum professional standards. This issue also addresses better quality and innovative preservice teacher training systems targeting the training and development of 10,000 early childhood directors and teachers in the next three years; (4) special funding to be provided by the central government for the education of minority children in underdeveloped areas, and for bilingual language education; (5) each province to develop program standards according to central government regulations and diverse social needs; (6) strengthened security in early childhood programs to ensure children's safety and protection; (7) fee regulation in early childhood programs; (8) early education to follow children's development, pay attention to the whole group as well as individual children, and combine play with care and education; (9) local governments' more active role in coordinating the stakeholders in early childhood education to create a more cohesive and integrated system; and (10) development and implementation of a three-year action plan with clearly stated developmental goals for the children (Zhou, 2011, pp. 32–33).

Globalization and neoliberalism are without doubt impacting education in China. Privatization of early education institutes has rapidly skyrocketed. Between 2001 and 2007, the number of public early childhood services dropped from 60% to 40%, but there was a jump in the number of private early childhood services from 40% to 60% during the same period (Liu, 2010a, as cited in Zhou, 2011).

The welfare model of the kindergarten that has been regarded as an outcome of the socialist system is certainly under the influence of neoliberal market reform as more and more Chinese kindergartens have become self-managed small businesses (Gu, 2006).

Nevertheless, in the current Chinese educational landscape, the persistence of the whole-group, teacher-directed emphasis continues to linger despite the policy push for individualized choice time and creative self-expression. In essence, progressive pedagogies are being enacted alongside neoliberal economics in a society that has for centuries been shaped by Confucian and socialist values. As Wang & Spodek (2000) note, these forces collide and result in creating tensions between "traditional and modern cultures, Eastern and Western spirits, socialist and capitalist ideological elements … within which changes and continuities coexist" (as cited in Gu, 2006, p. 39).

Sri Lanka: Demographic Profile and ECE Policies

The island country of Sri Lanka is a republic with a population of about 20.33 million and has a documented history of more than 2500 years. Its strategic location along the ancient Silk Route has resulted in a population that is ethnically diverse, with Sinhalese, Sri Lankan Tamils, Indian Tamils, Moors, Burghers, Malays, Kaffirs, and the aboriginal Veddas. The country was colonized by the Portuguese, Dutch, and the British and finally was declared independent in 1948. The country has a rich Buddhist heritage; 71% of its population is predominantly Buddhist; and the three main languages spoken are Sinhala, Tamil, and English (CIA World Facts). The capital city of Colombo is located on the western coast of Sri Lanka. With a population of about 5.6 million, Colombo is the commercial, industrial, and cultural center of the country. Because of its large harbor, Colombo was known to ancient traders even 2000 years ago. Its name is believed to be derived from the Sinhalese name *Kola-amba-thota,* which means "harbor with the leafy mango trees" (Wikipedia).

Data for this study was collected during visits and interviews with individuals at the following sites: the faculty of education at Colombo University, the department of early childhood and primary education at the university for distance education, the pre-primary and primary classrooms at an established private school, a Montessori preschool, the government arm overseeing early education known as Children's Secretariat, and a national educational policy institute, all located in Colombo.

Education in Sri Lanka has been a significant part of the culture from ancient times, and with a literacy rate of 93%, Sri Lanka has one of the most literate populations in the developing world. An overview of the historical development of education in Sri Lanka can be found in Jayaweera (2007). Sri Lanka's recent history has been marred by a 30-year-long civil war which ended in a military victory in 2009. With the end of the civil war and the Tamil Tiger movement, the country has been at a cross-road to bring back stability and security to a society marked by years of violence and tension between the Tamil Tigers and the government.

Sneha, an early childhood teacher educator, described vividly some of the effects of the civil war in the north and how things are beginning to change now that the war has ended:

> Before the peace, especially in the North and East ... [things] badly affected education. We conducted a research in Ampara district that is situated in Eastern province. Just after the war I went there and the people there were very relaxed. They lived in the jungle. They did not stay in their homes because sometimes the terrorists would come and kill all the villagers. In one night they would destroy the entire village. They told that they (terrorists) would not use the gun but swords. So in the night they [the villagers] would go to the jungle and sleep there and would come back in the morning. Everything was disrupted. Their living patterns, earnings, everything. So now they are really relaxed. Now they have expectation of the future. The Ministry [of Education] ... was appointed and they were very happy. So, we have to build that area.

Manju, another research participant and an early childhood educator, shared her thoughts on the lingering effects of the civil war on people's minds and behaviors:

> Some 30 odd years. So, people have been living with it. Although, it got over overnight, it's hard to get it out of our system ... with all that people are pressurized. Could be survival tendencies. Even if you are not directly affected the whole system is moving. Even now it is hard to think that the war is over and that we are calm and okay. It's hard to digest. I would not be surprised if somebody says that the war has erupted again.

She also noted that although the war had been waged primarily in the northern provinces of Sri Lanka like Jaffna, the effects were still being felt in the southern regions of the country:

> Yes, but in Colombo it happened in a different way. I think damage to Colombo is so great. Although, there was no direct effect of facing face-to-face war, the effect was very high. Because of the trauma people went through. People were crushed wherever they were. Tension was there. People got trained to think only about themselves. Unconsciously, we all started to think only about ourselves. It reflected in all the other things.

Undoubtedly, educational reform along with teacher education is an important goal in Sri Lanka. Abhyadeva (2003) conducted a study on the status of early childhood education in Sri Lanka and proposed an exhaustive outline with regard to preschools and day care centers, preschool teachers and caregivers, and preschool teacher education that urged an integrated approach to early education in Sri Lanka. Policy recommendations included (1) setting up a national committee in the Ministry of Social Welfare to include representatives from other relevant ministries, nongovernmental organizations, and specialists; (2) formulating national policies and guidelines in relation to early childhood care and development; (3) overseeing the implementation of such programs islandwide and ensuring standards; and (4) allocating a special fund as an expression of national commitment to the welfare of children.

The National Policy on Social Cohesion and Peace Education is aimed at raising Sri Lankan citizens capable of living in a multicultural society with democratic principles and willing to respect and ensure others' rights, transform conflict, serve others without expectation of reward, participate in the development of the world, and protect Sri Lankan traditions, culture, and values (Ministry of Education, 2008). Recent policy changes place a heavy emphasis on early childhood education and a detailed discussion on the role of early childhood education to facilitate peace education may be found in Gallardo (2009). The Early Childhood Development sector of education in Sri Lanka caters to children between the ages of 3 and 5 years. This stage is mainly outside the formal government education system, with nearly all preschools including nursery schools, kindergartens, and Montessoris operated by the private sector. To meet the 2015 EFA deadline, Sri Lanka established an action plan that included the following goals: expanding and improving ECCE (early childhood care and education); providing free and compulsory education to all, particularly girls, children in difficult circumstances, and ethnic minorities; promoting life skills and lifelong learning to all young people and adults—the life skills approach should incorporate the Four Pillars of learning which are learning to know, learning to do, learning to live together and with others, and learning to be; achieving gender parity and equality; and enhancing educational quality (EFA National Action Plan, 2004). Recommendations have been made that all early childhood institutions in Sri Lanka "should not be places where something is taught to the child but centres with multiple activities for the overall development of personality including child's education." In addition, those conducting preschool programs should be appropriately trained in child development pedagogies of children between 3 and 5 years of age (EFA National Action Plan, 2004).

Sri Lanka's national goal is to ultimately transform all preschools into "child-friendly" institutions with prescribed minimum standards required for basic administrative and physical facilities, furniture/equipment, learning and psychosocial environment, and teachers' qualifications and their professional development (Starting Right, 2006). These standards were determined by the National Committee after several discussions and a careful study of curricula from different countries. The policy was finalized and consolidated with UNICEF support. These parameters have been shaped largely by the ECE standards in the West and are now being articulated in the most recent ECE policy handbook in Sri Lanka.

According to the Ministry of Education, "good early childcare is a process aiming at improving readiness to formal school and enabling children to make optimal use of the educational opportunities provided improving their life chances to be productive citizens" (MOE, 2008). Although Sri Lanka has not yet completed a formal document to identify or define "developmental readiness," the standards called the Early Childhood Development Standards are being finalized and projected to be implemented shortly.

The 2005–2009 primary school enrollment is at about 99%, and the national average of early childhood/preschool enrollment at about 90% (UNICEF, 2010; UNESCO, 2011). Preschool education is supported by Children's Secretariat (CS), which is under the umbrella of the Ministry for Child Development and Women's Affairs (previously known as Women's Empowerment), whereas primary education is overseen by the Ministry of Education. Sri Lanka's Thirteenth Amendment of the Constitution positioned preschool education as a devolved subject, placed within the jurisdiction of the Provinces (Ministry of Social Welfare, 2003). Although the provinces have authority over the functions of preschool education, careful coordination between the national, provincial, and local government authorities is provided by a National Co-ordination Committee on ECCD within the CS which brings together all coordination committees at the provincial, district, divisional, and village levels. This is not quite decentralization inasmuch as the provinces receive some funding from the CS as well as from other sources in general. Some provinces offer preschool teacher training programs, but there is no national curriculum for training or preschool education, and the authority to register preschools remains at the provincial level. The registration and management of these training programs are done by the provincial education ministry or department, or sometimes by an independent authority. Education policy formulation, including preschool education, falls within the jurisdiction of National Education Commission. Curriculum development lies in the hands of the National Institute of Education. The National Committee makes important decisions regarding early childhood development. So far preschool education curriculum has been provided to schools and teachers in the form of guidelines rather than a comprehensive curriculum.

The central government does not run preschools, but local government authorities such as Municipal Councils, Urban Councils and *Pradeshiya Sabhas* do offer and run preschool programs. Most of the preschools are in the private sector, and a considerable number of them are Montessori schools. Visits made by Maria Montessori to South Asia between the years 1939 and 1946 (she was in Sri Lanka in 1944) popularized her philosophy and pedagogy there, so that many Montessori schools have now been established in the region. Some of them follow the original Montessori model and belong to the Association Montessori International (AMI), whereas other preschools claim to be Montessori but in essence are not. The Montessori method is so popular in Sri Lanka that the term *Montessori* has become synonymous with nursery school and early childhood centers and schools are often referred to as Montessori schools. Unfortunately, as in many other countries, in Sri Lanka, too, a large number of private preschools function as merely money-making enterprises, and the quality of these programs may be quite poor. Further, many preschool administrators and teachers are not appropriately qualified and do not have the knowledge or experience to offer early childhood education. Even though many preschools may be currently staffed by qualified teachers, it does not necessarily always imply good practice, as the standards of many institutes that award ECE certificates are questionable. As is the case in India, here too there is a huge need for formal degree programs for quality early childhood teacher education.

In a recent policy shift, teacher training institutions in Sri Lanka are now required to be registered with the CS in order to be approved by the provinces. Preschools that employ teachers trained at unregistered institutions will not be recognized by the provinces. According to one research participant, at the time of this inquiry about 22 teacher-training programs had been registered with the CS and provinces to not recognize preschools that employ teachers who have been trained at nonregistered institutions. During this transition period, teachers will be given time to complete their credentials, but going forward new teachers will not be recruited unless they are appropriately qualified.

The definition of what is "appropriately qualified" raises another issue in the formal training of teachers. Currently, students can be admitted if they have completed their A-level. However, research participants noted that teaching requires certain dispositions in addition to a formal college degree; thus entry criteria to identify preferred dispositions in teacher candidates need to be used. This is a current concern in teacher preparation debates globally as well.

Another concern is that in Sri Lanka, as in many other Asian countries, quality assessment of early childhood programs and preschools still takes place using Western measures and standards, as indicated by the following judgments: "there is a prevalent tendency to follow the primary curriculum in preschools, rather than a curriculum appropriate for preprimary aged children; centres which follow the play way method advocated by ECCE experts and developmentally appropriate curricula are small in number" (The World Bank, 2005 as cited in Gallardo, 2009, p. 47); and "Pre-school education in Sri Lanka has developed a style of its own that is uniquely out of step with the more widely accepted Early Childhood Education theories and practice valued in most developed countries" (King, 2010).

As seen in the earlier discussions of policy reforms in India and China, the potential for cultural incursions poses barriers for the full implementation of democratic, child-centered education. To illustrate, Abhyadeva (2010), a prominent teacher–educator and curriculum specialist, publicly advocates for the incorporation of the core divine abidings that underlie Buddhist philosophy: *metta* (loving kindness), *karuna* (compassion), *mudita* (sympathetic joy), and *uppekkha* (equanimity). Some of these core values may seem contradictory to the preferred attitudes supported by progressive education, such as helping children to develop

into independent, autonomous, assertive, articulate individuals who can participate in democratic acts such as free choice, activism and advocacy while openly
expressing their opinions. There can be a middle path, but educational reformers
and policy makers need to carefully think through these issues and then identify
the specific skills and attitudes that can be realistically supported by early childhood curricular reforms in Sri Lanka.

Singapore: Demographic Profile and ECE Policies

Singapore was under British rule from 1879 to 1959, after which it was granted self-
governance, but independence came only in 1965 (Ho & Gopinathan, 1999). The
island of Singapore is a city-state and is one of the four Asian Tigers, all of which
are free and highly advanced economies: Singapore, Hong Kong, South Korea,
and Taiwan. Singapore is a parliamentary republic with a population of about 5.2
million, of which about 77% are Chinese, while Malays and Indians form significant
minorities, along with smaller groups of Jews, Eurasians, and Europeans. About 44%
of the population follows Confucianism and Taoism, and the four official languages
of Singapore are Mandarin, English, Malay, and Tamil (CIA World Facts). Today
Singapore is one of the world's leading financial centers, and considered by many
to be one of the most diverse and globalized cities. It has created a world-class educational system. From the beginning, three basic premises have shaped Singapore's
educational system: giving students a sense of identity; remaining a multilingual
society; and placing a strong emphasis on science and technology.

Data was collected in Singapore during visits to the institute of education at Nan-
yang University; four community preschools; and one government primary school
in this island city-state of Singapore. An overview of Singapore's educational policy
reforms may be found in Ho & Gopinathan (1999) and Lim & Lim (in press).

In Singapore, early childhood education is known as preschool education and
is provided in two types of settings: (1) kindergartens, which are 3- to 4-hour
education programs for children age 3 to 6, and (2) child-care centers, which
provide all-day care for children aged 18 months to 6 years of working families
who require this service. Many parents expect child-care centers to also provide
educational programs for their children, and the curriculum in most child-care
centers is seen to be academic in nature, similar to that in kindergartens.

Under the Education Act, kindergartens have to be registered with the Ministry of Education (MOE) and need to fulfill the following requirements: (1) the
premises should meet all health and safety requirements and be approved for use
as kindergartens; (2) the program should be assessed by the MOE to be appropriate for young children; (3) principals and teachers should meet the minimum
academic and professional qualifications stipulated by the MOE; and (4) a formal
management committee should be responsible for the efficient administration of
the kindergarten. The largest provider of kindergarten is the People's Action Party
Community Foundation (PCF).

In Singapore, all public housing apartment buildings have an unconstructed ground floor at the street level which is left open as a "Void Deck." The community can use this large space for a variety of purposes. Families can rent it out for ceremonies such as wakes and weddings. This is an efficient use of space that can be offered to the public on a tiny island country where space is a commodity. Often the void deck is enclosed and turned into a space for a public purpose such as preschools sponsored by the People's Action Party Community Foundation (PCFs) for the children of the community. The PCF mission has always been to enhance the well-being of communities through educational welfare and community services. Its vision is to provide quality early education at affordable cost for all Singaporeans. Most of the PCF kindergartens are located on the ground level "void decks" of public apartment buildings. Unlike public housing in the United States, close to 80% of Singaporeans own and live in public apartment housing built and subsidized by the Housing Development Board, a government statutory board. Hence, most public schools and preschools within public housing estates have a fairly representative ethnic mix: "To achieve a 'balanced' ethnic mix, Singapore has implemented an ethnic quota policy on public housing since 1 March 1989. With 86 per cent of the population living in public housing, this policy has immense repercussions on the configuration of the ethnic residential landscape" (Sin, 2002, Abstract).

The PCF headquarters oversees all the numerous preschool branches in Singapore, with each branch operating one to six kindergartens that are located within a few kilometers of each other. The branches are clustered into four large districts around the island; each district has several Members of Parliament (MP), some of whom take on the role of branch chairperson, overseeing the organization and activities of the PCF preschools. Branch chairpersons are served by branch administrators who work together with kindergarten principals to ensure the smooth operation of the kindergartens in each branch. As more principals obtain their diploma in early childhood leadership, they are increasingly given more autonomy to hire and develop teachers and to decide on the curricular emphasis of their kindergarten.

Traditionally, the PCF kindergartens have been known to prepare young children for the academic rigors of Primary One (first grade) through worksheets and rote-learning methods. This became the main critique of the PCF kindergarten programs in the last two decades when the first government policy document for early years, catalyzed change in classroom practices and public perception increasingly. There was a demand for teaching approaches to become more child-centered, and class sizes reduced from the 1970s to 1990s ratio of one teacher to 40 children to the more recent MOE guidelines of 1:20 for kindergarten and 1:15 for nursery.

Singapore's Kindergarten Curriculum Framework (KCF), drafted in 2003, listed the following markers to ensure a child-centered approach: holistic development and learning, integrated learning, active learning, synthesized learning, learning through interaction, and learning through play (Nurturing Early Learners: A Framework for a Kindergarten Curriculum in Singapore, MOE, 2003). In 2008, the MOE increased its expectations for teacher qualification by requiring that all existing preschool teachers teaching nursery and kindergarten levels obtain a diploma in preschool teaching and a pass in GCE O level English (or equivalent) by the year 2013. In addition, all newly hired preschool teachers from 2008 must have at least five GCE O level passes (including English) and a diploma in preschool teaching.

In a typical PCF kindergarten of the last decade, foundations are laid for mathematics and language learning (English and a mother tongue language such as Mandarin, Malay, or Tamil). There are also activities for arts and crafts, music and movement, and learning through play and exploration. Many PCF kindergartens have incorporated computer-aided education (CAE) into the curriculum. In some branches, the curriculum has been revised and standardized across all the centers, training hours have been added for teachers, and the centers have been redesigned and renovated to match a more active and holistic curriculum.

Grace, an early childhood teacher educator, explained that "because the PCF has hundreds of kindergartens and no standard curriculum, centre programmes/approaches cover a wide range in diversity; also, every constituency is headed by a Member of Parliament (MP) who decides on funding for the kindergartens within the constituency. Whether a constituency is 'progressive' is also dependent on the MP's level of support. Salaries in PCFs have thus far not been standardised island-wide" (Interview notes from my research). Thus, specific PCF kindergartens, as a result of political influences and the desire to be more child-centered, have been allowed mentoring by nonprofit organizations to provide, for example, a more Reggio Emelia-inspired program.

In February 2013 the revised Kindergarten Curriculum Framework (KCF) was presented. At the core of the KCF is the belief that children are curious, active, and competent learners. The revised Framework starts with the existing principles for teaching and learning, and then proceeds to more strongly emphasize the holistic development of children; the need to build confidence and social skills during the preschool years; and the need to develop learning dispositions to prepare the children for lifelong learning. The new policy document also provides more details on the role of the teacher in facilitating purposeful play. Six learning areas with learning goals within each area are defined: aesthetics and creative expression, discovery of the world, language and literacy, motor skills development, numeracy, and social and emotional development. The MOE plans to provide greater support for curriculum design and training to equip preschool teachers to put the recommended teaching and learning principles into practice (www.moe.gov.sg/media/press/2013/02/refreshed-kindergarten-curricu.php). Thereafter, many kindergarten teachers/principals have children in primary schools and have experienced at first hand the high academic expectations placed on young children in first grade or Primary One. Concerns have been raised about the high academic standards for Primary One, but MOE officers are unable to provide satisfactory answers for why this is so.

As of April 2013, in order to ensure the holistic development of children during the preschool years, the Singapore government launched the brand-new Early Childhood Development Agency (ECDA), which attempts to integrate the various governmental branches that contribute to early education. The ECDA is to be an autonomous body, with oversight provided jointly by the Ministry of Education (MOE) and the Ministry of Social and Family Development (MSF). The goal, according to the ECDA website, is to allow ECDA to integrate the Preschool Education Branch and the Child Care Division, and work to develop children holistically, nurture positive attitudes toward learning, facilitate the transition of preschoolers to formal education, as well as increase efforts to support and strengthen Singaporean families (www.ecda.gov.sg/Pages/Launch-Of-The-Early-Childhood-Development-Agency-%28ECDA%29.aspx). The MOE budget of 2013 also plans to strengthen preschool foundations to ensure the success of every child, and accordingly it includes new subsidies for infant and child care to make these services more affordable to families. The MOE plan also includes strengthening the curriculum in areas such as physical education, art, and music. The Ministry believes these courses are integral to a holistic approach to education and enable students to enhance their creative and expressive capacities, shaping their personal, cultural, and social identity. Additionally, there is a greater emphasis on participation in extracurricular activities to help students learn the value of excellence and teamwork (asiasociety.org/education/learning-world/how-high-performing-nations-teach-global-skills, accessed on October 1, 2013).

The Maldives: Demographic Profile and ECE Policies

The island nation of the Maldives is essentially an archipelago, and as a republic it is the smallest of the five countries discussed in this book, having a total population of only about 329,000. The earliest of its written history is marked by the arrival of the Sinhalese people in about 500 BC. For most of its history, the Maldives has been an independent polity except for three brief periods when it was ruled by foreign powers: In the mid-15th century it was dominated by the Portuguese for 15 years, then in the 17th century it was dominated by the Dutch for four months, and lastly it became a British protectorate from 1887 to 1965. Almost 100% of its population is Islamic, and the official language is Dhivehi, with English spoken widely (CIA World Facts). With the highest point on these islands being less than 10 feet above sea level, the Maldives is also the planet's lowest country. It is anticipated by the Maldivians that global warming and continued rising sea levels will almost certainly inundate their beautiful islands in the near future. Almost 90% of the country's economy is dependent on tourism, with the fishing industry a close second.

Data for this study was collected on the island of Malè, the capital city, and included the following sites: the faculty of education at the Maldives National University (formerly called the Maldives College of Higher Education), the institute for distance learning, two government primary schools, and one government pre-primary school. A blog entry captures the urban essence of Malè, a tiny island with a population of about 100,000:

> The beautiful country of Maldives is a tropical archipelago of about 1200 coral islands—the shades of blue in the seas are spectacular. The capital city is the island of Malè, a charming, small town—very urban with narrow streets that are cobbled or bricked, and lined with clothing stores, shoe stores, food stores, technology stores, bakeries, tiny restaurants, bookstores, offices, schools, residential homes and mosques. People are seen to be walking everywhere, some cars and lots of motorized bikes can also be seen on the streets. The narrowness of everything is remarkable—not only of streets but also of buildings, hallways, staircases, sidewalks. Most women seem to have their heads covered either with beautiful scarves called *buruga* or with the more complete black robe and veil. But at the same time a large number of women do not cover their heads. The local language is Dhivehi which is an Indo-Aryan language with a mix of Sinhala, Arabic, Hindi, and Bengali. The people are very friendly, helpful and conversant in English … some even in Hindi. (amitagupta.com)

The Maldivian archipelago of 1192 tiny coral islands in the Indian Ocean is not only a delicately balanced ecological system but is also experiencing the pains of a democracy struggling to emerge. With the threats of global warming and rising sea levels, Maldivians are undoubtedly concerned about appropriately educating a generation of children who will be faced with these environmental issues. A recent and important development in the Maldives is the new constitution written in 2008, and a president who came to power in 2008 after democratic elections were held for the first time in 30 years. However, within four years of having been elected, the president was ousted in a coup staged in February 2012 by supporters of the former president. These political changes have considerably influenced educational policies in the Maldives. Distance education takes on a whole new meaning and value in this country where access is a huge issue. With almost 1200 islands, some extremely remote, running educational institutions and training teachers becomes a massive challenge solely dependent on ocean conditions.

Maldivian society has historically attached a great deal of importance to early childhood care and development. Prior to the modern day preschools, the traditional *edhuruge* (gathering of children in a private home to learn to read the Quran) functioned as an early childhood educational setting. The *edhuruge* would usually be a free, home-based service provided by respectable members of the community. The concerns of this formal system of schooling included a heavy emphasis on rote learning, low qualifications of teachers, and limited equipment, classroom materials, and resources (UNESCO, 2007).

With regard to policy, early childhood education is not supported by a specific policy ruling but is provided for within a more encompassing Education Act (Fariq, Farhath, Mufeed, & Rauffiya, 2010). In 2004, an Early Childhood Development unit was created within the Education Development Center in order to strengthen preschool education in the Maldives, advocate and promote best practices in early childhood education, develop appropriate learning materials, and build the capacity of preschool teachers and managers.

UNICEF has been sponsoring the global development of child-friendly early childhood education models in the developing world since 1997 and has been working with the Maldivian Faculty of Education and the Center for Open Learning to develop an early childhood curriculum for the degree program. Efforts toward achieving the Millennium Development Goal of EFA were documented in the *EFA National Plan for the Maldives (2001)* outlining the four major goals for EFA in the Maldives: expanding and improving comprehensive early childhood care and development; ensuring that all children, regardless of gender, ability, and location, have access to good quality basic education; ensuring equitable access to basic and continuing education for all adults; and ensuring that young people's learning needs are met through equitable access to appropriate learning and life skills programs (EFA National Plan, 2001). This plan in turn facilitated the creation of the Maldives National Early Childhood Care and Development (ECCD) Strategy. One goal of the ECCD Strategy was to create five model community-based ECCD centers in the Maldives that would function as demonstration centers in the country for best practices in ECCD. These centers would be based on developmentally appropriate play-based learning (Fariq, Farhath, Mufeed, & Rauffiya, 2010). The government proclaimed an educational mandate to support early childhood education, with the aim of not only ensuring that every young child was enrolled in preschool by the end of 2010 but also having certified professionals teaching in preschools. These mandates have thus created a high need for ECE teacher training as well. Recommendations were to produce developmentally and culturally appropriate media for and about young children—songs, stories, books and rhymes; such "child-friendly" methods have more appeal and impact than conventional channels (Kolucki, 2006).

This report has influenced the identification of key competencies for young children and a draft of the *National Framework (2011)* has been positioned as a practical guide for teachers on how to turn these key competencies into reality. According to the National Curriculum, the key competencies for early childhood education have been identified as the following (2011 draft on *Turning the Key Competencies into Reality: A Practical Guide for Teachers*):

Relating to people
Thinking critically and creatively
Making meaning
Understanding and managing self

Living a healthy life
Practicing Islam
Using technology and media
Learning for sustainable development

Educational policies reflect a nation's preferences and values, and this list can be seen to incorporate goals for child-centered education based on children's developmental domains, along with educating students about 21st-century issues with reference to technology and the environment, while at the same time holding onto the teaching of the local traditional culture and religion of the Maldives. These feed into the larger goals that the Maldives have established for the next generation: to develop (1) successful individuals who are motivated to learn and explore, who are inquisitive and eager to seek, use, and create knowledge; (2) confident and competent individuals who have a firm belief in Islam, a strong sense of self and cultural identity, and who believe in their own capabilities; (3) responsible and productive contributors to their own family, their local community, and the global society (2011 draft of the *National Curriculum Framework*).

In Malè, the capital city of Maldives, most preschools are nongovernmental institutions (Latheef & Gupta, 2007). As in India and Sri Lanka, no pre-primary teacher training has been offered at the college level so far. The Faculty of Education at the Maldives National University (previously known as the Maldives College of Higher Education) offers teacher training programs for the primary and secondary levels only. A research participant who was the first grade supervisor at a local government school mentioned that most of the primary teachers at her school and other schools in Malè had been trained in either Sri Lanka or the Maldives. She also identified definite procedures that the school had put in place to facilitate the professional development and assessment of teachers within the school: "The teachers are offered staff development workshops—last year they had several workshops on technology-related approaches. … Teachers are evaluated by the supervisor by conducting at least 3 classroom observations, 1 window observation, and by checking their lesson plan books and also the children's notebooks" (from my interview notes).

Today the preschools in the Maldives cater to children 3 to 5 years of age: Baby Nursery for 2½-year-olds, Nursery for 3-year-olds, Lower Kindergarten for 4-year-olds, and Upper Kindergarten for 5-year-olds. A comparison of the *edhuruge* and a modern preschool uses the following language in highlighting the differences: home based versus school based, untrained teachers versus trained teachers, free versus fee based, lack of learning materials versus modern equipment, flexible attendance versus scheduled attendance, no curriculum versus set curriculum, rote learning emphasized versus play-based method learning (Fariq et al., 2010). International preschool models like the Kangaroo Kids Preschool have been recently established and have been described as using "action-based learning using innovative teaching methods" (Brochure for Kangaroo Kids Preschool,

2010). According to Laila, an early childhood teacher educator at the faculty of education, as per the new curriculum policies soon to be implemented, the Foundation Years that include Lower KG and Upper KG will use Dhivehi as the medium of instruction and English will be taught as a foreign language. This approach is the reverse of what is currently practiced. In primary and secondary education, English will continue to be used as the language of instruction, with Dhivehi taught as a content area to master the mother tongue.

Thus far, almost all preschools in the Maldives are private enterprises. The early childhood education four-year undergraduate degree program for preparing early childhood teachers was crafted for the first time at the Faculty of Education in 2009. According to the head of the Center for Open Learning, the main impetus for this college-level ECE program was the Maldivian government's recent focus on ECE aligned with UNICEF's strong thrust on ECE. With the government mandating that early childhood education be compulsory, as is primary and secondary education, it has made sustained efforts to offer pre-primary teacher training. Laila explained that an immediate requirement was to create widespread awareness for the need of a formal system of ECE before any of the related policies could be fully implemented. Until the time of this research, there was no available formal teacher education guiding policy or curriculum specifically for the early years. Since then, there have been sustained government efforts to offer early childhood teacher training. However, like all reforms, this too will be a slow process, and curriculum guidelines will need to be designed thoughtfully and in great detail before an effective and efficient program can be offered at the university.

Spiritual Philosophies, Human Development, and Traditional Education

In order to get a deeper understanding of the cultural contexts of each of the countries, I will next highlight the core principles underlying the dominant spiritual philosophies of Confucianism, Islam, Hinduism, and Buddhism encountered in the countries included in this book. I will also discuss the manner in which these ideas influenced and shaped traditions of education in these countries in the past. It is not within the scope of this book to describe and discuss these spiritual traditions in detail. Only a few selected ideas and concepts that have direct bearing on educational issues in the early years are provided as illustrations. It is also important to bear in mind that none of these spiritual or philosophical traditions are monolithic; instead they reflect great diversities within themselves in the form of several sects and subdivisions. Further, countries that share the same dominant spiritual philosophy may still differ from each other in every other aspect: ethnically, linguistically, socioeconomically, and politically. But since deeper cultural and spiritual ideas are often projected onto educational decisions with regard to pedagogy and philosophy, a little background information on these traditions is helpful to contextualize the discussions in this book.

Confucianism and Taoism and Their Influence on Education

Two countries included in this book, China and Singapore, are largely characterized as Chinese societies. Although Singapore also includes Indian and Malay ethnic groups, these groups represent a minority. Chinese societies have two dominant philosophical traditions that originated in ancient China—Confucianism and Taoism. The philosophy of Confucius and related theories that developed after his death are referred to as Confucianism, and the ideas and writings of Lao-Tzu are believed to comprise Taoism. Confucianism deals with social matters, whereas Taoism centers on the search for meaning. Both philosophies have influenced East Asia for over two thousand years.

According to Taoism, an underlying force called the Tao permeates the entire universe and everything in it. It is Tao that explains the universe and the wonder of human nature. The means to salvation is to follow the Tao, the goal of which is to be one with nature. The Tao teaches compassion, moderation, and humility (www.ushistory.org/civ/9e.asp).

The goals of Confucianism are to learn to be human and to have a structured society, with each person being expected to act with virtue in all social matters. This philosophy promotes faithful observation of *Li* (ritual, propriety, and etiquette); *Hsaio* (love between parents and children); *Yi* (righteousness); *Xin* (honesty); *Jen* (benevolence); and *Chung* (loyalty to one's state). Within this philosophical system the concept of *li* is an important one to understand and refers to propriety, a sensitivity that allows for a modification of behavior to fit the circumstance. It represents a kind of balance wheel of conduct to prevent either deficiency or excess, and it helps guide one toward the middle path of socially beneficial conduct (Creel, 1949 as cited in Reagan, 2005). This would have direct relevance to the teaching and learning of socioemotional skills in children in schools as well as at home. Reagan (2005) explains that education is the means through which an individual learns what type of *li* will be required in a particular situation. Therefore, the cultivation of character is an important component of education. According to Confucius, the *good man* seeks to develop five constant virtues: right attitude, right procedure, right knowledge, right moral courage, and right persistence, which collectively lead to a society based on justice and wisdom (Ozmon & Craver, 1995).

Another Confucian idea grounds moral thought in five basic human relationships: those between ruler and subject, father and son, husband and wife, older brother and younger brother, and between friends. Each of these relationships is hierarchical but of mutual responsibility. This notion would have direct impact on the relationship between adults and children and thus define the nature of interactions between teachers and students in a classroom. It was also believed that a good education would change the individual for the better and thus should be available to those capable of benefiting from it (Cleverly, 1986). It is interesting to note that preparation for the civil service examinations began prior to the birth of a child: Detailed advice was given to pregnant women on eating appropriate foods, sitting with an erect posture, and reading classical literature and poetry (Cleverly, 1986).

Traditionally, children in China were brought up to be affable, obedient, respectful, polite, and gentle, and they were taught how to be content with their lot. Formal schooling and expectation of other responsibilities started at the age of 7 or 8, while during the early childhood years children were happy, had a great deal of personal freedom, tended to be spoiled, and were rarely punished (Gernet, 1962 as cited in Reagan, 2005). However, even though schooling began later, a more formal part of a child's education began at the age of 3, when the child started to learn how to read characters. The Chinese language is a complex system of tones and thousands of characters, and so literacy acquisition is a much more time-consuming process than it is within other linguistic systems (Huntsinger et al., 2000). According to Gu (2006), "Chinese traditional pedagogical philosophy is that only by mastering the form one is able to come up to the level of creativity, the underlying idea of this is through the structure one can then finally achieve the freedom" (p. 36). Thus repetition and imitation were instructional strategies used by kindergarten teachers who expected the children to listen closely to their instructions, pay close attention to their demonstration, "and then copy the teacher's work stroke by stroke, detail by detail, as best as they could" (Gu, 2006, p. 36).

In summary, the concepts of filial piety, interdependence, maintenance of harmonious relationships, the priority given to the parent–child relationship which results in strong parenting, mastery of impulse control at a young age, discouragement of expressing aggression, a high value given to education, a view of failure as inadequate effort and not an indicator of intelligence, and a high degree of respect shown to teachers have traditionally characterized education in China and other Confucian societies (Huntsinger et al., 2000; Kristof, 2011; Gauld, 2010). Ideals such as cultivating the person, regulating the family, governing the state, creating peace in the world are core ideals in Confucius' teachings on morality, ethics and the right way of life (Lim & Lim, 2013).

Islam and Its Influence on Education

Islam is certainly not a simplistic and monolithic religion, and the Maldives may be very different from many other Islamic countries. But its society is nevertheless permeated with Islamic ideas, and it would be helpful to understand some aspects of this worldview specifically with regard to education, teaching, and learning. The word "Islam" means submission, as in submission to God, and the Prophet Mohammed's life story is perceived as a perfect example of how a Muslim should lead his life. In Islam, there is a close relationship between beliefs and practice, and though the core beliefs may remain the same, their application may be adjusted to suit circumstances, which may result in varying perceptions of practice in different Islamic societies. At its core, there are five pillars of Islam, or essential practices, which are accepted by all Muslims. Reagan (2005) lists them as: (1) profession of faith (*shahadah*) in which the believer accepts the monotheism of Islam, the oneness of God, and the obligation to inform others of the faith; (2) prayer (*salah*) in which Muslims pray five times a day at daybreak, noon, midafternoon, sunset, and evening; (3) almsgiving (*zakaha*), which is an act of worship or thanksgiving to God and of service to humanity—Muslims are required to donate 2.5% of their income to support the poor; (4) fasting (*sawhm*) in which all adult and able Muslims are required to fast for a whole month from sunrise to sunset during the month of Ramadan—the fasting signifies a time to thank God and to atone for one's sins; and (5) the pilgrimage to Mecca (*hajj*) in which all Muslims who are able to are expected to make this pilgrimage at least once in their lifetime. Thus, as Haneef (1995) notes, underlying all these beliefs and practices is the idea that Islam is not just a body of religious beliefs but a way of life.

The holy book of the Quran is considered to be the exact transliteration of the very words of God. Education is closely related to the religious beliefs. Thus the role of the Quran has been important in shaping educational beliefs, and mosques have traditionally been perceived as Islamic schools. The best known Islamic educational philosopher was the theologian and mystic Al-Ghazali, and his ideas provided the bedrock of Islamic education for generations (Tibawi, 1972). According to Tibawi (1972), Al-Ghazali (1) based his views on deep spirituality, common sense, and an affection and concern for children; (2) implied that knowledge could be acquired in two ways: through human reason and through the light from God, and both ways should be balanced in a good educational setting; (3) perceived that children had a basically good nature and that all children had the capacity to learn; and (4) showed that the purpose of education was not one of correction or remediation but one that guided children.

Traditionally then, the Islamic philosophy of education in emphasizing three kinds of development in children (physical, spiritual, and mental) required education to be both realistic and idealistic, draw out the unique characteristics of children, prepare children for this life and the hereafter, and ensure that educational aims and objectives were translated into observable behaviors (Abdullah, 1982). Memorization of the Quran and the ability to read Arabic were important parts of the school curriculum. Readers should note, however, that in many Islamic countries schooling today may be seen to be based on a system inspired and derived from "Western" systems of education (Reagan, 2005). The recent educational policies in the Maldives as per the National Curriculum seem to continue this emphasis of traditional education to ensure that children develop in a threefold manner—physically, spiritually, and mentally.

Hinduism and Its Influence on Education

More than 84% of India's 1.2 billion population is Hindu. Hinduism is an incredibly ancient but continuing spiritual philosophy. Some of its oldest scriptures are the Veda, which in their oral form date back to 6000 BCE but in their written form are believed to have originated in about 1500 BCE (Fisher, 1994). The Vedic texts and their underlying beliefs form the core of Hinduism and have intimately defined the Hindu cultural and spiritual philosophy, and even today shape the

Hindu worldview and way of life. A more detailed discussion of core Hindu values and beliefs, ancient systems of education, the Vedic educational curriculum and pedagogy, early childhood educational aims and purposes, and the nature of teacher–child relationships may be found in Gupta (2006/2013). For the purpose of this chapter, I will present a brief overview of this philosophy according to which the goals of life are fourfold: Dave (1991) describes the four main aims of life encompassed within the Hindu concept of *ashramadharma* as: (1) *artha* (the earning of money or sustenance); (2) *kama* (the enjoyment of sensory pleasures; love, and reproduction); (3) *dharma* (the leading of a moral life and holding on to moral codes of conduct); and (4) *moksha* (the seeking of liberation, or final union with the spirit after release from the cycle of birth and death). Thus, within the Hindu worldview there is an apparent juxtaposition of all dimensions of humanity as spiritualism and materialism, mind and body, morality and physical pleasure, which are all seen to coexist harmoniously in one's life.

Two concepts that are at the core of understanding the Hindu worldview are *dharma* and *karma.*

> *Dharma* is a hard-to-define concept but can be generally understood as that which maintains the order of the universe; a social cement that holds a society together. According to the *Mahabharat*, people secure mutual protection not through the state, the king, the mace, or the mace-bearer but only through *dharma*. *Dharma* is explained as being the principle and the vision of an organic society, with all the members who participate in this organic society being interdependent and their roles being complementary (Kakar, 1981). To *dharma* are ascribed such social concepts as duty, responsibility, and morality. ... *Karma* refers to the actions of the individual human being, and the consequences of these actions. *Karma* views human actions within a cause–effect paradigm. It emphasizes the careful selection of words and deeds by an individual. *Moksha*, or liberation from human suffering, cannot be attained if we do not live by our *dharma* while being mindful of our *karma*. (Gupta, 2006/2013, pp. 19–20).

The child within the Indian worldview is subsequently perceived simultaneously as a social being and as a unique individual, given that the concept of *karma* emphasizes the individual in terms of the choices one makes, one's actions, and the consequences of these actions. In contrast, the concept of *dharma* emphasizes the relationships the individual has with family and society. Underlying this approach is the view that a child's growth and development occurs as a complex, three-dimensional whole. Traditionally, the idea of the child being born twice was commonly accepted in India, and there are still ceremonies in many Indian communities that mark the two births. The first birth is the actual biological birth of the infant. The second, "social" birth, occurs any time between the ages of 5 and 10 years and symbolizes the child's separation from the adult–child unit and his birth into the larger community as an individual member of society. The principles of *Ayurveda*, the system of ancient Indian medicine, define five childhood periods: *garbha* (the fetal period); *ksheerda* (birth to 9 months) when the infant lives entirely on milk; *ksheerannada* (9 months to 2 years) during which weaning takes place and the child moves from milk to solids; *bala* (2 to 7 years); and *kumara* (7 to 16 years). These periods are defined by stages that mark the gradual physical separation between the infant and the mother rather than by milestones in the child's individual socioemotional development (Gupta, 2006/2013, p. 107). It might be reasonable to say that the young child in India is considered to be a gift from God: energetic, mischievous, charming, lovable, intelligent, competent, playful, and certainly not a blank slate. Until the age of 5 years, this infant–child may be suckled, carried around, crooned to, snuggled, fed, clothed, and cleaned, all of which would be widely acceptable in Indian society. The child is filled with the belief that elders love and protect her or him, and the schoolgoing child is also told that his or her teacher is a very important and respectable adult in one's life (Gupta, 2006/2013, p. 103).

According to the Hindu scriptures, education has been deeply concerned with knowledge and epistemology. Ancient Hindu philosophers identified six different methods of "knowing" something. Organ (1970) summarizes these methods as: (1) *pratyaksha*, or sense perception by which we learn through the use of our five external senses as well as our internal sense, the mind; (2) *anumana*, or inference, which refers to processes of logical argument such as inductive and deductive reasoning; (3) *shabda,* or authority, which refers to the study and analysis of the scriptures; (4) *upamana*, or analogical reasoning, which involves using comparisons between two things as a possible source of new knowledge; (5) *arthapatti*, or hypothetical supposition, which involves identifying a missing premise in a dilemma or argument; and (6) *abhava*, or negation, which refers to the idea that "non-existence … can be known by non-cognition" (Organ, 1970, p. 50).

Another critical concept that is central to the teaching and learning process is the relationship between the teacher and the pupil. Traditionally, schools, or *ashramas*, were run by individual teachers for a group of students. The school functioned as a home for the teacher and students who lived together as members of a family in a common home (Mookerji, 1969). Apart from *ashrams* there also existed more formal schools and universities of very high caliber. Traditionally, through ancient times, the practice of Hindu education broadly included three steps in the learning process: *shravana,* which refers to the process of listening to one's teacher and learning the oral tradition on which Hindu religion is based; *manana,* which is an intellectual process whereby one begins to think and reflect on the meaning of what one has learned; and *nididhyasana*, which is the process of meditation to realize truth and consciousness (Mookerji, 1969).

From this discussion it would be easy to paint a portrait of the kind of education that was traditionally imparted to young children in India before the Western educational policies were implemented under British Empire's colonial rule. More on this topic may be found in Gupta (2007, 2006/2013).

Buddhism and Its Influence on Education

Buddhism emerged in India during the 7th and 5th centuries BCE and spread across Asia. Today it is the dominant religious tradition in countries such as Tibet, Sri Lanka, and Thailand, but it has also significantly influenced other societies such as those of China, Korea, Japan, and Singapore. Thus Buddhist influences were certainly seen in many of the countries included in this book, though most overtly in Sri Lanka where 71% of its population is Buddhist. Buddhism as a religion developed in the context of classical Hinduism, and though it diverged from Hindu tradition in significant ways, it still shared many core ideas and themes with the older religion. Buddhism emphasizes compassion, tolerance, and moderation; provides a clear path for spiritual and personal development; encourages questions and investigations; urges the taking of full responsibility for one's actions; and is in harmony with modern science (Lee, 2007). Given these underlying themes, it would be relatively easy to visualize an educational program based on this philosophy.

Buddhist teachings are basically concerned with human suffering and how to achieve liberation from that suffering based on the following ideas: *dukkha* (human life inevitably experiences suffering); *samudaya* (our desires are the root cause of our sufferings); *nirodha* (this is the state of being where there is no suffering); and *marga* (this is the road to achieving this state of being). Buddha taught a systematic approach called the Eightfold Path of Liberation whereby one could be free from suffering. The eight factors can be broadly categorized in three groups: (1) *dana* (generosity) and *panna* (wisdom), which refer to right understanding and right intention; (2) *sila* (ethics or morality), which refers to conduct and the rules underlying appropriate conduct such as right speech, right actions, and right livelihood to ensure that one's conduct is not harmful to the self or others; and (3) *bhavana* or *samadhi* (meditation), which refers to right effort, mindfulness, and right meditation (Reagan, 2005, p. 178).

According to Lee (2007, inside front cover), the Five Precepts underlying the Path of Liberation are to abstain (1) from harming or killing any living being; (2) from taking what is not given; (3) from sexual misconduct; (4) from lying and false speech; and (5) from the abusive consumption of intoxicants and drugs. The goal of this Path is to become free of the life and death cycle and finally to achieve liberation or *nirvana*.

Traditional Buddhist education took place in monasteries, which were immersed in the surrounding communities. Education was based on an intimate and reciprocal relationship between teacher and student where each had responsibilities and obligations toward the other. All students had to observe the two basic rules of monastic life—celibacy and poverty. Instruction was primarily oral, but the focus of education was much more than the memorization of texts. Dialectic skill in argumentation was viewed as an important and intellectual component essential to leadership. The ancient scriptures provide detailed accounts on the subject of debate, the place where debate should take place, the means and rules governing a debate, the qualifications of the debaters, the points of defeat in a debate, the appropriateness of a debate, and the need for self-confidence in the debaters (Mookerji, 1969). Detailed discussions of schooling, content areas in the curriculum based on ancient Hindu and Buddhist texts, and instances of higher education in universities that were renowned all over the world can be found in Gupta (2007) and Jayaweera (2007).

In conclusion, I have attempted to provide in this chapter a basic idea of the social-cultural-political-spiritual context as the background against which current early childhood education policies and pedagogies have been shaped in India, China, Sri Lanka, Singapore, and the Maldives. My hope is that this discussion will allow readers to better contextualize the descriptive accounts of classroom curriculum, materials, and teaching strategies in some schools as they are presented in the following chapters.

3

PLAY-BASED AND CHILD-CENTERED PEDAGOGY

The previous chapter presented an overview of the sweeping changes that have been made recently to national policies in the areas of early childhood education in India, China, Singapore, Sri Lanka, and the Maldives. As is evident from the discussion in Chapter 2, these policy revisions reflect a shift away from an age-old teacher-directed approach toward a more child-centered pedagogy. In this chapter I will describe the urban early childhood classrooms I observed as examples of how and to what extent these shifts in national policies are being manifested in actual classroom practice. The examples will illustrate how play-based and child-centered intentions were evident in classroom materials and teaching methods as observed in some schools. It is important that these descriptions not be perceived as typical early childhood classrooms across all these countries. Rather, readers should view these images as being specific to the school described, but with the understanding that similar practices may be seen in other school settings as well. What was strikingly uniform across countries was the widespread mushrooming of private, "child-centered" early childhood settings variously named nursery schools, play schools, playway schools, or preschools. All of them claim to be built on "world-class" and "global" standards, and to implement a child-centered and play-based curriculum, using English as the language of instruction.

Before proceeding, I wish to define child-centered education in the context of the discussions in this book. Generally within the Western discourse of early childhood education, the concept of child-centered education is seen to be rooted in the tenets of progressive education. This philosophy of education is most closely linked to John Dewey's ideas of starting with the needs and interests of the child, permitting the child to participate in planning his or her own course of study, and promoting group learning and experiential learning as primary classroom strategies (Semel, 2006). In other words, in progressive education the locus of control shifts more toward the child and away from the adult, as opposed to the locus of control in test-oriented and academically rigorous educational systems, where it lies predominantly with the adult. In many American early childhood classrooms, a child-centered pedagogy in classroom practice appears in the form of constructs, strategies, and routines that include, for instance, circle time, multiple learning centers, small class sizes, individualized and differentiated instruction, a whole-language approach, thematic units based on children's interests, experiential and project-based learning, portfolio assessment, an emphasis on block building, and stress on social studies, with a particular focus on neighborhood and community.

In Asia, early childhood education has historically been offered mostly within the private sector. Thus most preschools in this region have been owned privately and have functioned independently. A brief description of one of the private preschools I visited in India will give readers a sense of the sort of environment one could expect to encounter in other similar private preschool settings. The Play School is located in Goa, a small state on the western coast of central India. Goa is a tropical seaside community along the beaches of the Arabian Sea; it was a Portuguese colony from 1510 to1961, and its culture is defined closely by both Hinduism and Catholicism. The two dominant regional languages spoken in this city-state are Konkani and Marathi, though a small percentage of the population still speaks Portuguese.

The Play School was an established and well-resourced preschool the likes of which are widely found in cities and large towns across metropolitan India. Situated in a picturesque section of the city, the school was specifically designed for the education of young children, with low walls and open archways that served as doors and led into each classroom. There was a sense of openness in the school as one space flowed into another. Other architectural features included narrow staircases, small-sized toilets, low furniture for children to use, shelves and hooks at eye level, and classrooms that were oval in shape with rounded walls replacing sharp corners.

The children enrolled in the school were between the ages of 2 and 5 years and were housed in four classrooms. The toddler classroom housed the 2-year-olds, the nursery classroom housed the 3-year-olds, the kindergarten classroom had the 4-year-olds, and the prep classroom the 5-year-olds. The school hours were 9 am to 4 pm, although the toddlers could go home at noon. School buses were used to transport children from the neighboring districts of Panjim, Mapusa, Baga, and Porvurim. Lunch was provided by school and offered a wide range of dishes, although some children opted to bring lunch from home.

The design and architecture of the Play School supported the playway method or play-based pedagogy that it claimed to use in classroom teaching. At the same time, the more structured approach of phonetics was also used to teach the older children in the 4's and 5's classrooms. Figure 3.1 presents a sample daily schedule for any classroom that include several periods, each of about 20 or 30 minutes duration except for the hour-long lunch period:

09:10 – 09:40	3R's
09:40 – 10:00	Writing
10:00 – 10:20	Games
10:20 – 10:40	Break
10:40 – 11:00	Poetry/Singing
11:00 – 11:20	Drawing/Writing
11:20 – 12:00	Puzzles/Construction/Imaginative Play/Indoor Games
12:00 – 01:00	Lunch
01:00 – 01:30	Story Time
01:30 – 02:30	Reading Time
02:30 – 03:00	Resting Time
03:00 – 03:10	Freshen Up
03:10 – 03:50	Clay/Film/Arts and Crafts/Outdoors
03:50 – 04:00	Tidy Up
04:00	Dismissal

FIGURE 3.1. Daily school schedule of a private preschool in India

This schedule could be broadly applicable to all classrooms throughout the week. The same curricular activities were offered every day but could be distributed at different times of the day depending on the day of the week. For younger children writing was replaced by drawing. Verbal activities called Orals were sometimes substituted for other activities and included conversation, questions and answers, poems, and stories. Indoor games included "Oranges and Lemons" and "A Tisket, A Tasket." Dramatic play was encouraged in the Doll's House, which was located in a separate room other than the classrooms. On Fridays children engaged in imaginative play in which they would enact a popular social custom such as an Indian wedding or some other traditional event familiar to them. The lunch room was located on an outdoor balcony, with an overhead awning for protection from rain, and contained an arrangement of benches and tables with the children's tiffin boxes (lunch boxes) neatly placed on the tables. For lunch, the children and teachers were not grouped together by class but were mixed up so that everyone got an opportunity to see new faces and make new friends, thus refining social skills such as the ability to initiate friendships and form new relationships.

Two teachers were assigned to every classroom: One was the class teacher and one was the assistant teacher. The total staff in the school included eight teachers in the classrooms, one remedial teacher who worked with children with learning difficulties or developmental delays, and one substitute teacher to fill in for absences. Teachers were hired on the basis not only of their qualifications but also on their willingness to learn and their creativity. Every year the school held a sports event or a concert, and teachers were expected to write their own script for an act that their class would then prepare for and perform. The teachers in the school were mentored according to the school's philosophy, which focused on play, creativity, and imagination.

The description of this private playschool serves as an appropriate example of how numerous preschool settings have moved away from the explicitly teacher-directed, workbook-based pedagogy that was traditionally delivered in classrooms where children were seated in rows of desks all day long. This shift clearly indicates a move toward a more progressive play-based and child-centered pedagogy.

The next section presents the perceptions of some early childhood teachers on classroom play and play-based pedagogy.

Teachers' Understanding of Play-based Classrooms

In an earlier but related study, a survey questionnaire was distributed to 20 early childhood teachers across four schools in urban New Delhi, India. The schools were all private but catered to a variety of socioeconomic backgrounds from very affluent to lower middle class to semirural. They were of different sizes ranging from a large comprehensive school with a student population of more than 3000 to a small neighborhood primary school with a student population of about 200 students. The teachers were asked about their definitions of play, as well as how they saw play happening in their classrooms. Their responses revealed a wide understanding of what play meant to them, but there seemed to be a general consensus that play was essentially an activity in which the child found joy, freedom, interest, enjoyment, and creativity but at the same time promoted development and the learning of various skills. Play, as the teachers variously responded on the survey, had the following qualities:

Joyful activity that involves motor, technical and intellectual skills

A range of self-chosen activities undertaken for the child's own interest, enjoyment and satisfaction

The gross development of a child where he had freedom to do whatever he likes

Something that assists learning and self-development

A spontaneous, creative and entertaining activity

A physical or mental leisure activity undertaken purely for enjoyment or amusement

Play was an essential element of the learning process of young children

Play is when a child enjoys and helps in her/his growth

Play provides children with the opportunity to actively explore, manipulate and interact with the environment

Play is the freedom of movement, taking part in games, jumping, skipping, running

Play can be free or guided/structured

Play may be a physical or mental activity undertaken for either enjoyment, amusement or learning, or for a combination of these

It is a process of learning and growing physically, mentally and emotionally that takes place with/without the assistance of adults ... play gives the children an opportunity to let loose their creativity and imagination

Any activity that children find enjoyable ... when children play they take initiative, choosing what to pay, where to play, coming up with ideas

Play is interactive—it might seem like a simple game, but it's actually a powerful behavior modification tool

Children must enjoy playing but also learn some sort of discipline and moral value

The years 2–5 are called the play years ... children spend nearly all their waking hours playing ... they chase each other, dare themselves to attempt new tasks, play games and dream fantasies and they learn social skills and moral rules

It is through play that much of children's early learning is achieved

A private nursery school teacher in India described a typical day in her classroom, specifically with regard to how she viewed play and work happening during the daily experiences children had:

> In our classroom children are playing and working with materials and other children ... have access to various activities throughout the day such as block building, pretend play, picture books, paints and other art materials, and table toys and puzzles ... the classroom is decorated with children's original art work, their own writing with invented spellings and dictated stories. Children learn numbers and alphabets in the context of their everyday experiences. Exploring the natural world of plants and animals, cooking, taking attendance, serving snack are all meaningful activities to children. Children work on projects and have long periods of time to play and explore. Children have an opportunity to play outside every day ... teachers read books to children throughout the day.

A second early childhood teacher from a private school in India shared her perception of how play occurred within the context of her classroom:

> Play activities in [my] classroom vary from time to time and according to the theme ... singing, movement of body parts, dancing, recitation of rhymes ... activities that foster concepts like that of numbers, shapes, sizes to enhance cognitive skills ... activities like tearing, pasting, clay modeling, painting, freehand expressions ... to help children explore and enhance their creativity ... playing pretend games like acting like different helpers, members of family to help children express their emotions and enhance their imagination.

Yet another teacher in India described more specifically how classroom instruction could be conducted in a manner that would be more interesting and enjoyable for the child:

> The act of learning how to write a letter of the alphabet, for example, may take place by the child trying to imitate an arbitrary set of lines/curves/shapes from the blackboard/textbook to his/her notebook. The same task, however, may be performed in a fun-filled manner with the child associating the letter and its shape to a simple story or poem about two children playing with matchsticks, pencils or clay.

Teachers expressed their ideas about children and teaching in child-centered ways in Singapore as well. One preschool teacher viewed each child as a "unique individual who has the right to learn and develop within a secure environment," and observed "that teachers are the role models for children and influence their development significantly." Another teacher in a child-care center in Singapore stated that she perceived play to be "like fun learning" and explained that in her view learning skills could come about as a result of play and not only through the use of worksheets. A third teacher believed in an inquiry-based learning approach, where the curriculum is shaped by children's interests. Her school has adapted some of the best practices from Reggio Emilia and utilizes an Inquire–Think–Learn process. For every investigative process, the teacher and children together drew a mind map about what they already knew and what they wanted to know, similar to a KWL chart. This teacher also saw herself as a facilitator and a co-learner who stepped in to help children just as they were ready to give up.

Most teachers agreed that adopting a play-based pedagogy was important for teaching young children, and there seemed to be some clarity on what constituted appropriate indoor play. For instance, one teacher explained that "In classroom life one should not allow play which creates noise or indiscipline. It should provide fine motor development, gross motor development, physical and mental development."

Based on other such responses to related questions obtained through this survey and from interviews, it appeared that play occurred within the school setting in the following three ways: (1) when children were engaged with activity-based learning in their own classrooms; (2) when children were engaged with play materials for about 30 minutes per day in a separate room that was designated the "playroom"; or (3) when children had outdoor time and they played freely with each other or engaged with the playground equipment such as slides, monkey gym, or swings. Examples for each of these instances will highlight those moments when and how children were presented with opportunities for play-based and child-centered experiences while they were in school in the different countries.

Child-Centered Classrooms to Promote Play

The PCFs I visited in Singapore presented child-centered classrooms with multiple learning centers, and in this aspect they more closely resembled Western progressive classrooms. Space is an important commodity on this island nation, and the classrooms were small with about 20 children and two to three teachers. But the classroom space had been clearly arranged so as to offer a variety of learning experiences. At the Jasmine PCF, for instance, the classrooms were set up with learning centers, and children were engaged in playing either individually or in groups of two or three on floor games, or sitting at the table in groups of two or three while working on art activities with a teacher. The walls displayed bright art work done by individual children as well as art collages done in small groups. The learning centers were equipped with materials that reflected the local Singaporean culture. The dramatic play area in the classroom contained three food stalls that reflected the diverse food courts found around Singapore, offering Chinese, Malay, Indian, and American cuisines. The print in the classroom reflected a trilingual approach, and labels for materials and spaces were printed in Chinese, English, and Malay.

At another preschool center, the Panda PCF, an early childhood consultant had worked with the staff to transform the environment of the preschool from a very structured and traditional one to one that was Reggio-inspired, with a stronger emphasis on parent involvement, art, and documentation of children's experiences on display everywhere. Children's work as well as teachers' efforts on each project had been painstakingly documented. The classrooms were bright, the children seemed happy, and the teachers seemed energized and excited by what they had been able to accomplish at their center. The demographics of the children at this center were very multicultural as was the curriculum, reflecting Chinese, Malay, Tamil, and English language and lifestyles.

The island of Malè, the capital city of the Maldives, has six primary government schools. Space is a huge commodity on the islands of the Maldives as well; the island is less than 2 square kilometers in area but is populated by about

100,000 people. In order to accommodate all the children on the island, schools must offer at least two to three shifts for children during the day. Some schools even have four shifts a day. Since classrooms are shared spaces for multiple groups of children on a daily basis, students cannot leave their books in their classroom and end up carrying heavy book bags every day.

The educational approach to curriculum at the Jay School in Malè appeared to be a combination of teacher-directed and child-centered approaches. At the time of my visit, the first grade classrooms at this school were buzzing with two teachers and 25 to 30 students in each room. The four first grade rooms were all following the same curriculum and appeared identical with regard to the current unit of study based on the theme of "Family"; children's work on display; the common slogan "Reading Is Fun" posted on the walls of all first grade classrooms; the exact timetables or daily schedules for morning and afternoon shifts; the same workbooks used in each classroom; and the same table arrangements. Students were expected to take their shoes off before entering their classroom, and all the shoes were kept neatly arranged on a shoe rack outside the classroom door. The students, both girls and boys, seemed engaged and busy. In keeping with the common first grade curricular theme of "Family" at the school, displays on the walls inside the classroom, on the doors of the classroom, and on the bulletin boards outside the classrooms included photographs of children's families, children's drawings of members of their families, and some commercially produced posters illustrating family activities. The children's artwork was accompanied by labels and/or narratives about their families in English or Dhivehi.

Similarly, the second grade classrooms in this school were also identical, and the slogan "Read to Lead" shaped the second grade curriculum and student work. The slogan for the third grade curriculum was "Dream Big, Learn More," and the doors to each third grade classroom displayed students' work in the form of creative writing and art. In one of the third grade classrooms, children were placed in small groups that were each named for a sea creature such as lobsters, seahorses, and jellyfish. Although the language of instruction in all the schools in the Maldives is English, there was also a strong emphasis on the teaching of Dhivehi. At the time of my visit, student elections for two school presidents or co-presidents (one boy and one girl) were going to be held, and a total of 239 candidates were in the running! Students as well as teachers were expected to vote in the elections, and the candidates were allowed to campaign only on the eve of the elections. The day of my visit was the day prior to the elections, and all the candidates had displayed their respective posters with photos all along the walls of the hallways in the school.

Another primary school I visited on Malè was the Alpha School. At the front entrance was a large wall with the name of the school, logo, and motto: "Excellence is taking the lead with strength of character." The preschool section of the building was colorful and painted in bright neon orange, pink, lime green, and blue. The preschool classes in this school catered to children 3–5 years of age.

The grade levels for preschool were known as Nursery, Baby Nursery, Lower KG, and Upper KG. As in the other schools in the Maldives, shoe racks were placed outside each classroom, and all the students placed their shoes on the racks before entering the classroom. Each shoe rack was neatly stacked with clean and polished black leather or white canvas shoes.

The preschool classroom that I observed at this school had 25 to 30 boys and girls 4 years of age. They were all dressed neatly in school uniforms that consisted of white buttondown shirts and navy skirts for the girls and navy shorts for the boys. The children sat around brown wooden tables on green, blue, and pink chairs in groups of eight. This particular group was working on worksheets that had a picture of a crescent moon framed within a window, and each child, with quiet focus, was coloring the window frame red. There was one teacher in the classroom who was wearing black trousers, a mid-thigh-length long-sleeved tunic, and a green *buruga* or scarf around her head and neck. The classroom walls were posted with sheets of students' work that reflected identical drill sheets in which they had colored the same object and some of their creative artwork. Also posted were some teacher-made materials that displayed letters of the alphabet and numbers in English and Dhivehi. In yet another classroom, a small group of children, both boys and girls, were seated on a straw mat on the floor and were playing with a handful of dolls and stuffed animals they shared. Although English has been the language of instruction in schools here, Dhivehi was being used more extensively by the teacher and the children. The physical environment in the classrooms was colorful, clean, and orderly, and received a fair amount of teacher-direction. New educational policies to be implemented shortly will require preschools to use Dhivehi as the primary language of instruction.

In China, my observations of a government kindergarten school in Hangzhou presented bright and welcoming classrooms. The physical classroom environment at the Dogwood Kindergarten was visually very different from traditional classrooms that usually held rows of individual desks and chairs for children, with no evidence of children's work displayed on walls and bulletin boards. Teacher-directed and knowledge-based teaching and learning was characteristic of Chinese education for decades, including at the kindergarten level. Most kindergartens commonly followed a curriculum comprising the direct teaching of knowledge and skills arranged around six subjects: language, math, general knowledge, which combined social and natural sciences, music, art, and physical education (Gu, 2006). But in recent times, "the greatest change in kindergarten pedagogical practice is a shift from subject-based instruction model to play/experience-based activity model in organizing the child's learning" (Gu, 2006, p. 34). The Dogwood Kindergarten followed a daily schedule that permitted more opportunities for children to engage in physical activities and play throughout the day and offered less time for teacher-directed whole-group instruction. Figure 3.2 shows the daily schedule for 5- and 6-year-olds at the Dogwood Kindergarten for 2009:

Time	Curriculum experience
07:40 – 08:00 am	Arrival/Free play as children enter classroom
08:00 – 08:40 am	Morning physical exercises Mondays: Flag-raising ceremony and speech
08:40 – 08:55 am	Cleanup after the physical exercises
08:55 – 09:25 am	Whole-group instruction in the classroom
09:25 – 09:40 am	Break time (use bathroom, change shoes, eat snack)
09:40 – 10:00 am	Morning physical exercises
10:00 – 10:50 am	Free activities and playing at the various learning centers in the classroom; special activities. On Fridays, this time is divided between 30 minutes of group instruction and 20 minutes of games
10:50 – 11:00 am	Break time, prepare for lunch, hand washing
11:00 – 11:30 am	Lunch time
11:30 – 12 noon	Outdoor walk, gardening, and planting
12:00 – 02:30 pm	Nap time
02:30 – 03:00 pm	Wake-up time, snack
03:00 – 03:30 pm	Sports and Games (on Fridays—free activities)
03:30 – 04:00 pm	Group instruction (on Fridays—free activities)
04:00 – 05:00 pm	Dismissal

FIGURE 3.2. Daily school schedule of a government kindergarten in China

Designated "Playrooms" to Promote Play

A distinct feature of a progressive child-centered classroom is the presence of multiple learning centers or play areas that children can choose from. This feature is very difficult to incorporate into each early childhood room in Asian schools due to limited space and large class sizes. With an average of 40 or more children in a room, maintaining order by keeping children restricted to their seating space becomes necessary. Consequently, with an adequate number of chairs and tables to seat 40 children, it is almost impossible to find space for additional clearly delineated areas in the classroom that can offer experiences such as circle time, block play, art, reading, dramatic play and dress-up, and also house a science table, a writing center, a math area, a listening center, table toys, and so forth. In New Delhi, one elite and trend-setting private school in 1994 shifted its early childhood education curriculum toward a more child-centered approach and resolved this dilemma by designating one room as an activity room that would offer multiple choices to children, with each class visiting the room on a regular schedule for 30 to 40 minutes every day (Gupta, 2001). Today several schools in New Delhi have adopted that model. At the Oxford School, this activity room, located in the basement of the building, was an enormous rectangular room lined with shelves along the walls that held a variety of materials: One wall was lined with shelves that held numerous stuffed animals, puppets, and dolls, with a rocking chair close by; against another wall was a table topped with small-sized baby dolls, and cabinets that held table toys, art materials, and scissors; and the fourth side of the room held a large playhouse in which children could enter and play. In the center of the room were rugs and a few tables, as well as some indoor play equipment such as a small slide and cars that the children could ride. Each classroom from nursery through grade 1 was scheduled for a visit to the activity room for 40 minutes on a daily basis. Even in this private school the materials available were limited in quality and diversity, reflecting the paucity of early childhood, reasonably priced learning materials that are locally manufactured and easily available to classrooms in Asian schools. Early childhood classrooms in government schools would have even fewer resources.

The concept of an activity room is a step away from the rigidity of a test-oriented, teacher-directed system based on academic rigor and rote memorization of textbook content. It is not the child-centered environment that can be seen in a progressive early childhood classroom in the West, it does offer young children a more enjoyable, hands-on school experience than is possible with the traditional teacher-directed classroom.

Outdoor Areas to Promote Play

Early childhood teachers in India who participated in a survey as part of this study perceived play outside of classrooms as comprising a variety of outdoor activities and forms of play, as is evident from the following responses:

> Playing with balls or simply running around, rolling, jumping, sliding, swinging was a favorite activity
> Swings, football, athletics, yoga
> Sliding, swinging, see-sawing, merry-go-round, sand play
> Hide and Seek, cycling, football, skating, cricket, racing with each other
> Outdoor games, football, aerobics, co-curricular activities

Most of the preschool settings observed in this study offered outdoor areas for children's play, although the nature of the outdoor space varied tremendously.

Lotus School, the private school in Sri Lanka, possessed an elaborate playground with metal equipment painted in bright greens, yellows, pinks, and blues. Situated in a large sandy area with tall mature leafy trees arching over the play area, the playground offered a variety of climbing equipment, including a slide, a tunnel, and a tree loft, as well as a large rubber tube that lay half hidden in the sand. The bright colors of the playground equipment matched the wooden furniture inside the preschool classrooms.

At the Rajanigandha child-care center, a lab school attached to a college of education and human development in India, the preschool classrooms led to an outdoor area with a brick-lined floor and were surrounded by a brick wall enclosure. In the center of this outdoor space was a large, square tree bed with a tall, leafy tree growing in the middle. The tree bed was filled with loose dirt and was large enough for half a dozen children to comfortably play and dig with spades, shovels, and pails. Some children were using the small metal climbing equipment and a very small merry-go-round, while others played among themselves on the brick floor of the courtyard. There was nothing artificial about this outdoor courtyard that served as the early childhood play area; it offered a refreshingly natural environment comprising bricks, trees, potted plants, and fresh-smelling earth.

The islands of the Maldives are made of delicate coral, and any kind of vertical construction on these islands is limited as the islands cannot support much weight. That is one of the major challenges for further construction and development on the Maldives, and limits the space available for schools and playgrounds. The outdoor playgrounds in the government and private schools observed in Malè contained large, open-air spaces within the school buildings and were lined with the same white coral sand that the Maldivian islands are made of. The periphery of some of the play areas was fringed with palm trees, and a few swings and metallic climbing equipment were available for the children to use. Since the school playgrounds are open to the sky, the children are exposed year round to the scorching tropical Maldivian sun, which can be damaging to health. Many of these play areas are thus covered by long lengths of insulated netting that hang between the roofs of the buildings surrounding the open space, sheltering the courtyard below from the sun's fierce rays, yet allowing light and air to filter down on the children playing below in the courtyard. This novel contraption protects the play areas from unwanted radiation and makes it a safer space for children to play. Being a coral island, the Maldives have no dearth of powdery white sand. Sand is plentiful and is often the ground cover in several public spaces. With so much sand readily available in the playground and outside of the school, one wonders if there is indeed a need for a sandbox within classrooms. It would seem that the sandbox that is usually a staple learning center in most Western preschool classrooms would be a redundancy in the Maldivian classroom.

At the Oxford School in India, each of the nursery classrooms opened up into the outdoor play yard—a large grassy area with swings and open spaces in which young children could run around. This space was reserved exclusively for the youngest children in the school who had outdoor time as part of their daily schedule. The school had a separate sports field for the older children. While referring to outdoor play and the influence of technology on children's play, one kindergarten teacher at Oxford School, a private school in New Delhi, noted the change that had occurred over time:

> Lifestyles of children have changed over the last 10 years—at home it used to be that young children would play with toys, dolls, with each other, make believe, housekeeping, cars and trucks, out in the streets on bikes, with balls. These days children are engaged with computers, TV's and video games. They are not getting the play they used to get at home—neighborhoods have become crowded and dangerous and unsafe. ... But this is seen in wealthier families. Very poor families who cannot afford computers and video games, their children one still finds playing outdoors on the streets and lanes. So the disappearance of play is primarily a plight of the affluent.

The digital age has brewed many debates on how technology has minimized outdoor play as well as imaginative play, and school curricula around the world continue to separate play-based learning from the learning outcomes achieved through the use of technology. But perhaps here, too, one has to move away from the classic definitions and perceptions of play that we have been familiar with and begin to reconceptualize the meaning of play to include new forms such as digital play. One also needs to begin to understand that children's experiences with digital technology and digital media provide a platform for their consumption of popular media (Edwards, 2013). This consumption of popular media may be a form of "new" play, as it is an activity that brings children pleasure and one that they look forward to.

Discussion

The belief that play is important and beneficial for young children is not new. In the Western world, past educators and philosophers including Rousseau, Froebel, Montessori, and Isaacs have urged play-based pedagogies (Dockett & Fleer, 1999). In Asia, too, Asian educators and philosophers have embraced this belief for centuries, and recommendations for holistic child-centered approaches based on a particular view of the child can be found in ancient texts on not only education but also philosophy, health, and socialization. Some mention of this matter is made in Chapter 2 in the discussion on various cultural and spiritual philosophies, but I will provide illustrations from ancient Indian texts as an additional example. Accounts of children and childhood can be obtained from Indian texts such as ancient law books (*The Laws of Manu*); from the traditional medical texts of India (*Ayurveda, Charaka Samhita, Sushruta Samhita*); from the two epics (*Ramayana* and *Mahabharata*); and from folktales and historical narratives in ancient, medieval, as well as modern Indian literature. Included in all these texts is detailed information on child development, the relationship between childrearing and personality development, intense parental longing for children, and children's upbringing that has often been marked by affectionate indulgence and divine protection (Gupta, 2013). In the approximately 1000-year-old literary tradition in northern India, *Bhakti* literature, the child is described as an exalted being who grows up surrounded by a circle of admiring adults; the child is completely absorbed in interplay with his mother and is loved for the childlike qualities of freedom, spontaneity, simplicity, and delight in the self, all of which are considered divine attributes (Kakar, 1981 as cited in Gupta, 2013).

Until recently, however, such local cultural worldviews in Asian countries were not successfully translated into child-centered approaches in national educational philosophies and mainstream systems of education. This failure was particularly evident in formerly colonized nations where education and schooling were shaped by European colonial influences that held a different view of the child. Although the recent global emphasis on play-based pedagogies is not a novel approach, it has gained prominence and a sense of urgency in both local and global debates on early childhood education. This new prominence is partly a reaction to current policies of academic teaching and high-stakes testing. As discussed in earlier chapters, the current forces of globalization and the efforts of world organizations in early childhood development in Asian countries support an early childhood narrative that promotes a child-centered and play-based pedagogical approach. This promotion of a developmentally appropriate early childhood discourse by prominent world organizations such as the UN and the World Bank seems to have sanctioned the value to be placed on play in the early childhood education narrative in India and other countries. Recent policy changes in Asian education reflect this new attitude. Nevertheless, complete implementation of this pedagogy as defined within the context of Western progressive education remains elusive.

Also problematic in Asia and elsewhere is the lack of a clear definition of exactly what a pedagogy of play looks like (Dockett, 2011). In fact, there is no clear definition of play in the first place. This is largely due to the diverse nature of play and the different forms that acceptable and appropriate play take on in diverse cultural contexts. For instance, the word for play in Hindi is *khel*. The word *khel* encompasses a range of activities, including fun and frolic; games and sports; gambling; participation in fairs and celebrations; dramatization of stories; dance, music, and rhythm; fierce competition of skills and abilities; and so forth—activities that are structured or unstructured, player centered or externally controlled (Gupta, 2011). Play in its various benevolent and malevolent forms appears to encompass not only preferred skills such as cooperation, sharing, taking turns, and following rules but also survival skills such as harassment, deception, teasing, and trickery, which are not encouraged in any classroom context but which are inherent in successfully navigating the world of human relationships. Therefore, attempts to define an activity as play are challenged because of the wide range of features that characterize activities viewed as play.

One of the most basic features of play is "pleasure," but even that argument fails when it is used with respect to an activity such as piano playing, which is often hard work and not always pleasurable (Wittgenstein as cited in van Oers, 2013). On the other hand, Vygotsky noted that sucking a pacifier is a pleasurable activity for babies but is not an activity that is acknowledged as play (Vygotsky as cited in van Oers, 2013). Within the Western discourse of play in early childhood education, however, some consensus has developed on very fundamental characteristics of play such as the following: Play is incompletely functional, and the actions involved do not contribute to a goal; play is spontaneous, rewarding, or voluntary; it has a repetitive quality; it can be fragmented and exaggerated; it is initiated in the absence of acute stress; and there is a preference for performance over outcomes (Burghardt, 2011; Smith, 2010). But with national debates focusing so intently on play-based pedagogies, there is no doubt that early childhood educators the world over feel the intense pressure to justify the notion that play is learning and that activities performed in the classroom are characterized and labeled as learning through play.

The above ideas involved in the conceptualization of a child-centered and play-based pedagogy are nevertheless still challenged in their actual implementation in most schools in the developing world. The practical application of child-centered approaches is consistently hindered by the difficult ground realities of classrooms, such as a paucity of classroom resources, including physical space and materials; teachers trained inadequately in child-centered pedagogy; lack of tools to document children's learning and developmental progress; and a lack of basics such as water and electricity in schools (Gupta, 2011, 2013).

To sum up, the serious challenges confronting the implementation of play-based pedagogies include:

- cultural incursions that occur due to conflicting worldviews
- political contexts that do not support the democratic essence of learner-centered education
- inadequate space available in schools and classrooms
- inadequate basic health care and nutrition available to all children
- scarcity of basic supplies in schools and classrooms such as furniture, running water, electricity, and sanitation facilities
- inadequate classroom resources, including learning materials, time, and space
- teachers who have inadequately, or never, been trained in the pedagogy of play and child-centered approaches, and who are unable to make classroom decisions on a regular basis with regard to the use of classroom materials and of classroom time
- teachers who have been inadequately trained and equipped with the tools and time to document children's voices/experiences to create assessment portfolios that are key to assess individual children in a learner-centered

classroom. Assessment techniques recommended in the "Western" discourse of child-centered education include capturing moments of children's play and work using tools such as cameras, camcorders, anecdotal reports, and observations of children in centers like the block area, book corner, writing center, dramatic play, and art center

- large class sizes that do not support the one-on-one teacher–child instruction that is central to learner-centered pedagogy, children in classrooms of 40 to 60 cannot voluntarily engage with activities related to their interests
- children who do not start school equipped with decision-making skills that are essential to successfully navigating a child-centered and choice-based classroom, and are unfamiliar with making choices with regard to their engagement with classroom life

The last two items on this list are perhaps the most challenging in terms of cultural differences and reflect the fundamental nature of the Asian worldview regarding the child–adult relationship: First, there is generally a longer dependency period and a more extended child–adult continuity within Asian families; and second, the right to choose according to one's own interest is based on an individual-orientation worldview, whereas general childrearing practices in Asia are based on a group-orientation worldview.

Tobin et al. (2009) demonstrate that schools in urban China have embraced the concept of dramatic and imaginative play in the early childhood curriculum because imagination and creativity are now viewed in China as prerequisite skills for later success in entrepreneurship. But here too, as is to be expected, the full implementation of this pedagogy is challenged by factors such as teachers' own inexperience in play and play methods, and parents' expectations for quick mastery in playing musical instruments, writing Chinese characters, and using the abacus to solve math problems (Vong, 2012).

Thus, although in most of the pre-primary classrooms I visited there had been a noticeable shift toward child-centeredness with regard to the physical environment of the space, the teaching strategies, adult–child interactions, roles and responsibility of teacher versus student, the curriculum content still reflected a distinct teacher-centeredness. The locus of control still seemed to lie within the adult. Priya, a teacher educator at an all-girls' college of education in New Delhi, summed up the debate by noting why the new learner-centered policies were still not being seen in practice:

[W]ith the NCF, the learner centered approach, the idea that children are active constructors of learning and that they construct the world around them and this idea of seeing the child as a constructor of knowledge. ...The only problem with so many ideas is that [of] how to translate them into classrooms, how to bring them into classrooms and how to make that a part of teaching practices. Because unfortunately what happens is that in spite of training, in spite of years of professional program, we end up teaching in the way we were being taught. So bringing about not just minor changes but major changes in the classroom is still a struggle … unfortunately, teacher training in India has always been a top-down kind of thing. Teacher trainers also talk down to the teachers. Any teacher training that happens, or any in-service teacher training that happens for teachers who are in job, are also based on modules that constantly talk down to the teacher, constantly telling her that she is not doing things right. She is not managing the classroom well, she needs to do this and she needs to do that without giving any form of credit to her for any kind of experience that she might have gathered or even empowering her to do any research on classroom.

Despite these challenges, commendable efforts by teachers and practitioners to engage in a differently defined "learner-friendly" early childhood approach could be observed in many schools across Asia.

The Gardenia School, an urban pre-primary/primary in Pune, Central India, had a student population of about 600 from a range of very-low-income families to middle-class families. The language of instruction was English, even though the majority of the children came from Marathi-speaking homes. The school's mission was to provide low-cost quality education in English to those who didn't have access to it. On the day of my visit, the pre-primary children were expected to participate in a Fancy Dress competition for the Christmas pageant. No doubt, the more financially strapped parents felt challenged in spending money for buying or renting costumes for their children. This may not be in keeping with the ideals of egalitarianism and democracy of progressive child-centered experiences as defined in the West. Yet one could not ignore the high degree of excitement, pride, and participation among not only the children but also their parents as the pageant proceeded and children paraded in their costumes. The question here would be whether this experience could be considered *family-centered* and could accordingly also be viewed as *child-centered* from the perspective of a worldview based on a group orientation in which the individual's interests are viewed within the social context of the group.

In the Dogwood Kindergarten in China, despite the colorful classroom environments and the activity-based curriculum that was dominated by arts and crafts projects, the ethos in the classroom was decidedly teacher directed and teacher created. Whole-group instruction was typical, and children seemed to work on the same activity at the same time and were expected to proceed at the same pace, respect the teacher, and obey school rules. However, during free play children were allowed noisy interactions and could choose their own play materials. The socialist ideology was not so much evident in teamwork and group projects with respect to the curriculum, but, as Vaughn (1993) describes in her study on early childhood education in China, the encouragement of group lay in the emphasis on teaching children altruistic and nurturing behaviors such as helping others, solving disagreements constructively, or giving up a toy to another child without prodding from the teacher. During my visit to the Dogwood Kindergarten, in every classroom I was honored as a visitor and was presented with a piece of craftwork done by the children, with the teacher helping one of the children in walking up to me and presenting the gift to me. This indication of acknowledging and valuing the "other" is characteristic of group-oriented societies. At the same time, the school possessed distinct child-centered features. During the school day, which began at 7:40 am and ended at 5:00 pm, the daily schedule included morning sports and exercise, a hot nutritious lunch, a long nap time, two snacks, taking a walk, and caring for plants, in addition to teaching activities (see Figure 3.2). Again, one cannot argue that this was not a child-centered curriculum and a school in which children were loved and valued by the adults, as well as considered to be family and national resources.

In Maldivian society, Islamic spirituality permeates the way of life and thinking of its citizens, and children are expected to sit at length and memorize the Quran. This approach to learning would not be considered child-centered in the Western understanding of the term. But an example of inclusion and child-centeredness may be provided in the context of the Jay School in Malè. This primary school had a special needs program to accommodate students who were hearing impaired. Due to a lack of resources and the unavailability of teachers trained in special education or sign language, an inclusion or mainstreaming model was not possible in this school. So the hearing-impaired students were educated in classrooms separate from the mainstream classrooms, but they had the opportunity to mingle with the other students during sports, recess, and concerts. The school had also implemented a system of co-teaching between a content area teacher and a sign language teacher. The Math and English classes were taught in English, but the class on religion was taught in Dhivehi. The Maldivian government had just recently compiled and published a bilingual English–Dhivehi dictionary for sign language. One dictionary had been given to each hearing-impaired student and one to his or her family so that they could learn how to communicate with their children. At the school assembly every morning, all the students in the school were taught five new words in sign language every week so that they in turn could learn how to communicate with the hearing-impaired students. In this manner, the most marginalized voice of the child with special needs had been deeply incorporated into the school's ethos. This philosophy can be viewed as an inclusive child-centered one that strives to meet the needs of a small but vulnerable group of students in the school.

In Sri Lanka, some schools available to the child victims of war and violence in Jaffna, or the child survivors of the tsunami in Galle and Matara seemed to reflect traditional academic environments contradictory to the open explorer-friendly environments urged by Western progressive child-centered pedagogy. But these students were hungry for structure, predictability, security, and learning. The traditional forms of teaching and learning they were experiencing were important to them and could not be disregarded. Again, within this context, the school experience could be viewed as child-centered as in meeting the needs of the children in that group. As van Oers (2013, p. 196) asserts, "when children's goal-directed activities that early childhood educators tend to call 'work' are actually carried out with high involvement, respecting the rule-governed nature of the activity and the freedom of children with regard to the organization of this activity, there is no need to distinguish between play and work." And yet, the current policies for child-centered education result in establishing more child-centered schools even in the northern provinces such as Jaffna. The words of Yamini, the head of a policy-making institution in Sri Lanka responsible for the care and education of the very young children, will illustrate this trend: "On 19th I am going to open in Jaffna three play areas and two innovative preschools. We identified 50 preschools in northern areas. On the 20th we have discussion with the northern provincial authorities and our development partners on how we renovate preschools ... all this in resettlement areas."

Although child-centered pedagogy is couched according to a Western definition of developmentally appropriate and progressive discourse, what gets implemented around the world is an iteration of a child-centered pedagogy that is more aligned to the local context. As seen in the examples provided in this chapter, on the one hand programs in which the classroom environment was child-centered in being colorful and expressive may not necessarily have been really child-centered with respect to the locus of control that still lies within the teacher. On the other hand, classroom environments that may not have visually appeared to resemble the Western progressive child-centered classrooms may, in fact, have offered more authentic child-centered experiences to meet the needs of the students. But does it matter if the pedagogy does not fully fit into the Western definitions that drive the dominant discourse? The problem arises when programs at the local level are evaluated and assessed by early childhood educators who have been trained in the Western discourse and who apply the standards of the Western definition to the local version of the pedagogy and find it lacking. This is the danger of using labels such as child-centered and teacher-directed, as perceptions of these approaches fall within very specific practices considered to be either appropriate or inappropriate in the Western world.

The dichotomy between teacher-centered and child-centered pedagogy is a false one, as early childhood teaching usually combines elements from both a play-based/child-centered approach and a teacher-directed approach. It's not the pedagogy that is problematic but the naming of it. The important thing is to rename the pedagogy in such a way that it forces us to move away from labels that can encourage educators to perceive them as being mutually exclusive. There is a need for an approach that will permit practitioners to combine both child-centered and teacher-directed teaching approaches in a guilt-free manner, acknowledging that both are required in order to prepare children with skills to succeed in the highly globalized and connected world of the 21st century. Cultural and pedagogical hybridity is a natural outcome of the forces of globalization. The pervasiveness of global forces creates postcolonial hybrid third space within the early childhood classroom in urban Asia within which a hybrid pedagogy is often seen. An example of such a hybrid pedagogy in practice is described in Gupta (2006/2013), in which early childhood teachers were seen to implement the teaching of values and academic proficiency in classrooms, with 40 children each using activity-based and interactive, hands-on teaching strategies. This is a pedagogy that sometimes comprises teacher-led experiences and sometimes child-centered experiences, sustaining children's interests and enthusiasm. Most of the teachers who were interviewed or surveyed for this study did believe that there was a need to help prepare children for primary or elementary school education since the primary school syllabus was so academically rigorous. So while they believed in a child-centered approach, they had not abandoned the task of preparing children for primary school and the use of structured learning materials altogether.

One preschool teacher in India believed that the "coupling of play and pedagogy may or may not be problematic. It is not problematic if we balance the use of playway activities in the method of teaching. It can be problematic if we include more of free play and less of learning through play." This statement indicates that the learning of skills and academic content was also important but could be better achieved through use of a play pedagogy. The words of another early childhood teacher from India sum up the juggling act that teachers must perform in balancing play and work in their classrooms:

> Children in schools today are increasingly over burdened with academics. Most parents make all efforts to get them [to] excel at studies. But all work & no play is not necessarily the best strategy to improve a child's performance. For children to grow & develop as healthy individuals there needs to be a reasonable balance between work & play. As play helps a child in maintaining good health, cultivates team spirit, becoming confident, coping with failure, surpassing limitations. It is very much evident that a blend of two "Play & Work" is the need of [the] hour.

This kind of pedagogical hybridity that can occur in the third space—where two diverse pedagogical discourses intersect—should be used as the starting point in the creation of a new and specific early childhood education discourse that may be used to empower rather than colonize. And it is this kind of pedagogical hybridity that can help children develop a broader range of skills and flexibility and give them the ability to draw on appropriate set of skills whether in individual or group settings, or whether in local or global contexts as is needed.

4

TEACHING CHARACTER, CITIZENSHIP, AND CULTURAL VALUES

The term *culture* has been variously defined and conceptualized, with the earliest and most encompassing definitions emerging within the field of anthropology. One of the definitions I employ in this book was inspired by Masemann's conceptual understanding of culture as referring to all aspects of life, including the mental, social, linguistic, and physical forms, and to the beliefs and ideas that people have; the diverse ways in which people interact with each other; their relationships with their families, larger institutions, and physical environment; the languages they speak; and the symbolic systems they engage with, such as written language and art forms. In other words, culture expresses the value system of a particular society or group (Masemann, 2013). Preferred traits for citizenship and human character, as well as qualities for appropriate conduct for its citizens, are subsequently rooted in the society's cultural values.

Based on the findings of my study, the explicit teaching of character, citizenship, and cultural values seemed to be widely prevalent in schools across Asia. The interesting observation was that in Asia citizenship education seemed to be characterized more by moral virtues and personal values rather than by civic and public values (Kennedy & Fairbrother, 2004). Several pre-primary and primary schools demonstrated the importance given to the teaching of good character and family values, which were reflective of a deeper and more overarching national, cultural, and spiritual ethos. The teaching of citizenship values was additionally influenced by the post–World War II attempts of some countries in Asia to build relationships between the state and civil society as they struggled to shed colonial rule and establish independent nation-states (Hirata et al., 2005). Moreover, under the influence of the current waves of globalization and demands for democratization, Asian countries have been attempting educational reform strategies to enhance the international competitiveness of their educational systems. The emphasis of global education here on citizenship, human rights, and peace education has further influenced the teaching of values, virtues, and preferred attitudes in many schools in Asia.

Toward this end, world organizations such as the UN have proposed specific strategies to support teaching and learning for a sustainable future, with a special emphasis on values education. The UNESCO website presents a module on values education according to which "The values and attitudes we live by affect how we relate to other people and to all our activities in the environment, and so are a major influence—on our prospects for achieving a sustainable future. ... This module provides an opportunity to consider the importance of human values and attitudes in shaping the future. It also provides ideas and examples for two categories of strategies for exploring values in the classroom—values clarification and values analysis" (www.unesco.org/education/tlsf/mods/theme_d/mod22.html, accessed 4/15/2013). This global emphasis on values/virtues/character development also seemed to support the emphasis on values inherent within the cultural ethos of Asian worldviews.

Thus, under the influences of some or all of the above factors, widespread attempts have been made in schools across Asia to instill in children values that variously reflect their national cultures, values that support a democratic way of life, and values and virtues that promote civic sense and citizenship. A clear example of such a phenomenon was seen to occur within the context of urban Indian private school, early childhood classroom practice where the prescribed and explicit school curriculum led to the teaching of academic skills, and the more implicit "hidden curriculum" drew upon the sociocultural influences on teachers' beliefs and ideas leading to the teaching of socially preferred values and attitudes (Gupta, 2006/2013). In China, there seemed to be a wider expectation from schools as parents "turn[ed] to kindergartens as the proper place for providing the children with the opportunity to develop their cooperative consciousness and behavior. ... the primary function of the kindergarten is regarded as not only to give children a good start academically but also to offer good citizenship training" (Gu, 2006, p. 39).

In this chapter I will highlight the more overt and explicit emphases on the teaching of values and virtues as promoted by, and observed in, many schools. I begin by describing ways in which the promotion of values and virtues was apparent in the overall environment of schools and classrooms.

Values and Virtues Reflected in School Settings

Jay School is a government primary school (Grades 1–8) on the island capital of Malè in the Maldives. The first thing that struck me about the school was its clean and neat environment. The large, three-storied school building had colorful and spacious classrooms, as well as open hallways, and displayed numerous motivational and inspirational posters and slogans. There was a heavy emphasis on being mindful of one's character and behavior. Posters on hallway walls and in stairwells boldly proclaimed virtues such as *Fairness, Trustworthiness, Respect, Citizenship, Caring, Responsibility,* and *Cleanliness,* to name a few. Each poster not only displayed the name of the virtue in bold colorful lettering, but also provided the meaning of the word as illustrated by the following examples:

> **Caring**: Be kind, helpful, giving, and value the feelings of others
> **Citizenship**: Work to make your school and community a better place to live
> **Responsibility**: Make good choices, do what is right and be accountable for your behavior
> **Trustworthiness**: Tell the truth, keep your promises, and do the right thing

On the school playground were wooden plaques that listed these same values so that students would be reminded of them even during outdoor play. At the main school entrance near the front gates was a large wooden board on which were painted the following words:

> Watch your thoughts; they become words.
> Watch your words; they become actions.
> Watch your actions; they become habits.
> Watch your habits; they become your character.
> Watch your character; it becomes your destiny.

On a bulletin board outside one of the primary grade classrooms at the Jay School were posted drawings and essays of children on a variety of topics such as *My Teacher, Two Cats, My Grandmother, Flowers, Skin,* and *My Best Friend.* One girl had written an essay on *Morals* which included the following list:

1. Respect and obey your elders.
2. Do not lie, steal or cheat others.
3. Always speak the truth.
4. Be kind and gentle towards all.
5. Be honest and sincere.
6. Use sweet and polite language.
7. Rejoice in others' happiness.
8. Accept defeat gracefully.
9. Be generous and kind.
10. Do not feel proud when you win.
11. Love animals.
12. Love all.
13. Be cheerful always.
14. Greet your teacher whenever you meet her. Help her when she needs your help.

In Iris School, another government primary school in Malè, stickers with inspirational sayings were posted on the walls in the staff room and teachers' lounge. Some of the stickers read:

> To teach is to learn twice.
> Being entirely honest with oneself is a good exercise.
> Where there is an open mind there will always be a frontier.
> Success is the ability to go from failure to failure without losing your enthusiasm.
> Goals determine what you are going to be.

In Lotus School, a private school in Colombo, Sri Lanka, the following posters were observed on the hallway walls of the principal's office:

> Respect is not a gift, you have to earn it.
> People may doubt what you say but they will always believe what you do.
> 30 years from now it won't matter what shoes you wore, how your hair looked, or the jeans you bought. What will matter is what you learned and how you used it.

On a bulletin board at the same school were displayed two charts to indicate the schedule for Prayer Assembly during the January to April term in the 2010 academic year. One chart announced the schedule for the Kindergarten Buddhist Prayers, and the second chart announced the schedule for the Kindergarten Christian Prayers. For every Monday, Wednesday, and Thursday of each month, a particular teacher had been designated to lead the Prayer Assembly.

Values and inspirational sayings were also seen in the Neon Primary School in Singapore. The school was housed in a large building appearing very much like public schools in New York City. A security guard at the gate ensured that visitors signed in and were given visitor stickers. The school's name was displayed in large, bold signs everywhere, along with the school motto for social, cognitive, moral, and physical development. A beautiful water fountain at the front entrance contained a large smooth stone that had been engraved with the Chinese characters that read *I love my school, Neon.* A banner over the front gate declared "*Every Neon Pupil, a responsible and useful citizen.*" Interestingly, its placement implied that it would be read by those leaving the school compound more easily than those entering the school. Yet another slogan, *Sincerity and Perseverance,* was written in large letters across the face of the exterior wall of the school building. The instilling of institutional pride was a reflection of Singapore's larger goal of instilling national pride and developing national identity in its citizens. Clear attempts were made to foster religious and racial harmony not only socially but also institutionally, along with the national focus on the notion of "all together as Singaporeans." This concept was variously reinforced in daily newspapers in the form of advertisements and policy articles.

The importance given in Singapore to developing national pride and national identity in its students was evident in the curriculum of the Salvia Kindergarten. This school's enrollment was made up of about 505 children between the ages of 3 and 6 years in classes called Nursery, K1, and K2. Instruction was provided in English and Tamil, or English and Chinese (depending on what the families desired), thereby ensuring that all children learned at least two languages. Most striking about the school was the diverse and colorful children's artwork that had been displayed everywhere. Children appeared to have one classroom as a home room, and then they would move for auxiliary subjects to the Art Room, Dramatic Play Room, Music Room, Science Room, Computer Room, Indoor Gym, and the outdoor playground. The Water Table was located in a common area rather than within each of the classrooms because, according to the school director, Ms. Padma, no "messy" activities were offered in the classrooms. The academic subjects of Math and Language were taught in the home room through the use of flash cards, word games, counting games, and drill sheets. A strong emphasis was placed on print and numbers, as was clearly evident in every room. Each time visitors entered a classroom, the children would greet us. The children would say "Good morning Ms. Padma and may God bless you," and Ms. Padma would respond by saying "May God bless you" in return. The art room had a group of children working on drawing with charcoal. They were drawing images of the sports day events that had recently taken place. On the wall were displayed children's work done using a variety of art media such as water colors, markers, and charcoal. The dramatic play room was being used as a language immersion room where play would be encouraged in the children's second language—Tamil or Chinese. At the time of this observation, the room was occupied by a group of children with their teacher, all speaking in Tamil.

The school curriculum was driven by thematic teaching. At the time of the visit, the whole school was studying the theme of *My Singapore* since the National Day of Singapore had just recently been celebrated. Each classroom had a web or flowchart starting with the central theme of Singapore and then moving out toward the exploration of a variety of topics related to the city of Singapore such as Hospitals, Museums, Restaurants, Cable Cars, Sentosa (amusement park), Temples, Schools, Parks, Beach, Supermarkets, MRT (mass transit), and so forth. Each of these was further detailed with specific examples. Children's projects focused on the exploration of topics such as *What We Want to Know about Cable Cars, Local Newspapers,* and *Singapore's People,* which included photographs of Malays, Indians, Chinese, and Eurasians. Children's artwork was based on topics that included *My Singapore, My Home, Where Do You Live in Singapore,* and representations of children's visits to local sites in Singapore. A large bulletin board in one of the older classrooms was titled *Our Singapore Army,* on which was displayed children's drawings depicting scenes associated with the armed forces: planes, parachutes, and people dressed in uniforms either standing in groups or marching in squads. This topic is important in the context of Singaporean society where every male citizen who has reached the age of 18 years is required to serve a two-year term as full-time National Servicemen and enroll in Singapore's armed forces, police force, or civil defense force.

Prominently displayed in the Jasmine PCF in Singapore was a large poster that read *PCF Core Values,* which was meant to remind parents and teachers, and inform visitors of the following values that the PCF school system intended to uphold and promote:

Professionalism: We aspire to ensure quality and high standards in our services through continual learning and development

Commitment: We commit to delivering quality care and services through building competence and excellence

Fortitude: We meet challenges together with perseverance and courage

Integrity: We value and respect people by being honest and open

Compassion: We value, care, and nurture every individual to realize his or her potential through our programmes

Accountability: We take pride in personal excellence and responsibility in all our endeavors

Nimbleness: We promote creativity and innovation in response to change

Evidence to support the teaching of values was also clearly observed at the Maitreyi School, a government school in urban New Delhi, India, where numerous inspirational sayings were prominently displayed in the principal's office, along the school hallways, and elsewhere on the school grounds. In the principal's office was a wall-length bulletin board with a poster in English that read "*Education is not the filling of a pail but the lighting of a fire.*" Another wall displayed a handmade poster that read: "*Thinking together is just a beginning, Working together leads to progress, Marching together ensures success.*" Along a hallway was a dilapidated board with the words painted in Hindi "*sacche bharatiya baniye, bharati maal kharidiye*" (be Indian, buy Indian, which had been a popular slogan during the time Gandhi led the Civil Disobedience movement for India's freedom from British colonization). On another wall in the school was a wooden board painted with the words: *samay mulyavaan hai, ise na khoiye* (Time is valuable, do not lose or waste it). Directly below this board was another poster that displayed two sets of prayers—one for the morning and one for the evening. In Eastern philosophies such as Hinduism and Islam, spirituality is closely related to the diurnal cycle, and prayers have been specified for different times of the day. In the same school, above the doorway to what must have been a music room, were the words *Welcome* accompanied by a large picture poster of the Hindu goddess Saraswati playing the *veena*, which is a string instrument with a recorded history that dates back to at least 1500 BCE. Saraswati is revered as the goddess of wisdom, learning, and the arts and is worshiped by students to gain her blessings in their quest for knowledge and academic excellence. On the school grounds was a marble bust of Gargi, one of the most learned women in Ancient Indian scriptures, a well-known philosopher, Vedic scholar, and a formidable debater, born into the family of Garga around 800 BC in ancient India. Under the bust of Gargi were engraved the words *param vidushi, brahmavadini Gargi* (most learned and composer of hymns in the Veda, Gargi).

A similar emphasis on values and inspirational sayings and mottos was seen in the environment of the Delphinium School, a private primary school in New Delhi, India. At the school gates, the outer courtyard displayed several posters with statements such as:

If I take care of my character, my reputation will take care of itself.
To give happiness to others is a great act of charity.
Failure is success if we learn from it.

Along one wall were portraits of the Indian spiritual philosophers Mother Teresa, Mahatma Gandhi, Rabindranath Tagore, & Swami Vivekananda. Directly under these portraits was a poster which at one end showed printed pages from a book with the word *KNOWLEDGE* written across it, and a picture of the globe painted on the other end. A string of butterflies connected the globe and the book. Under the artwork appeared the following words: "With knowledge as our biggest asset, we will fly like colorful and cheerful butterflies to conquer this world." On another wall in the school was a large poster with the following words:

Five important lessons to learn from a humble pencil

1st, it tells you that everything you do will always leave a mark
2nd, you can always correct the mistakes you make
3rd, what is important is inside you and not outside you
4th, in life you will undergo painful sharpenings which will make you better in whatever you do
Lastly, to be the best you have to allow yourself to be held and guided by the hand that holds you.

Another poster framed in glass was meant to specifically inspire teachers. It was titled Teacher's Prayer, and it read as follows: "*Let me be more mother than the mother herself in love and defense of my child who is not flesh of my flesh. Help me to make one of my children my most perfect poem and leave within him or her my most melodious melody*" – *With this same spirit let us care for and nurture young children.*

In Kamalika School, a school in the heart of an urban slum in New Delhi, was a pillar in the inner courtyard which was painted from top to bottom with the following words: *The C's have been a part of our classrooms forever: Curiosity, Creativity, Competence, Confidence, Concern, Cooperation, Citizenship, Concern, Critical Thinking.* In a creative and playful manner, the values emphasized by the school mission were thus shared and declared to everyone visiting the school.

At Sonakshi School, yet another private school in New Delhi, value education was part of a schoolwide curriculum. According to the school's principal, a *Value of the Month* was selected and emphasized throughout the school from class nursery to grade 12. Classroom teachers were expected to monitor the program, but the content area teachers were also required to include the month's highlighted value in teaching their respective content areas. Schoolwide activities and competitions during each month were also required to incorporate the value of the month.

All these examples show that the teaching of values was widespread in many countries in Asia, and that this teaching was given an explicit position within the schoolwide curriculum. The next section will illustrate how specific cultural values were seen to be emphasized in the classroom curriculum and in the overall ethos of a school.

Classroom Rules

The values prioritized in a nation's overarching sociocultural ethos are reflected in the overall school culture and in its curricular objectives, as discussed in Chapters 1 and 2. Therefore, it was not surprising to see the national emphasis on rules in Singapore so clearly mirrored in the preschool curriculum at the Jasmine PCF. Children were active participants in creating and enforcing rules in their classroom community. This was a good illustration of how hygiene and orderliness could be supported and maintained in a classroom, as well as how the classroom environment could be designed to facilitate effective transitions and routines. The rules were printed on posters, each poster highlighting a specific classroom rule. The posters were created by a group of children who then printed their names on them. The posters were visible at strategic points in the room: in the bathroom, under the light switches, and near the door to the classroom. Each poster had a rule written on a white sheet of paper and accompanied by a drawing to provide a visual representation. On one corner of the sheet of paper were listed the names of the children in the group who had worked on that particular poster. The white sheet of paper was then glued onto a larger sheet of red paper in order to provide a frame. The completed poster was then taped up on a wall in the area of the classroom where the rule was most relevant. For instance, the poster taped near the light switch in the classroom read *Switch off the lights* and the words were accompanied by a drawing of a reading lamp with a switch. Near the door was a poster that read *Please put the slippers properly* accompanied by a drawing of a neat row of slippers. Near the sink was the poster reminding everyone to *Wash your hands,* and the drawing on it showed a faucet dripping water. In the bathroom was a poster with a drawing of a toilet bowl and a reminder that said *Please flush after use.*

Cleanliness and hygiene were important aspects of the preschools in Singapore and in the Maldives, as is apparent in the custom of taking shoes off before entering a classroom. In all the PCFs I visited in Singapore, children's shoes were stacked neatly on shoe racks that were available either outside or just inside every class-room. The same was true of classrooms in the Maldives. This indicated a deeper awareness of one's environment, and the need to keep the classroom environment clean and tidy. In Eastern philosophies cleansing practices and diets have been traditionally used to clean out the mind and body, and it is believed that a clean and tidy external space of human beings is often reflective of a clean and orderly internal space. This could explain the importance given to a clean environment.

Classroom rules were also prominently posted on the wall of a first grade class-room in Jay School in the Maldives, including:

> Say words like Thank you, May I, Sorry
> Be a good friend
> Raise your hand before speaking
> Always use your best handwriting (Dhivehi, the national language has an
> incredibly neat, artistic and carefully formed script)

More than one classroom in Jay School had the following list of rules posted on classroom walls:

> Helping Hands
> Listening Ears
> Quiet Voices
> Looking Eyes
> Walking Feet

In the children's library of the Lotus School in Sri Lanka was the following list of rules and "Library Manners" that students were expected to follow when visiting the library:

> Quiet
> Listen
> Silent for silent reading
> Be kind to books
> Use your bookmarks
> Put away your chairs

In the Computer Room of the Salvia Kindergarten school in Singapore was a poster created by the children with the following reminders:

> We shall speak softly in class
> We shall walk quietly to our computer class
> We shall handle the computer carefully
> If we follow these rules we will be a wonderful class!!!!

Making Guests Feel Welcome

A cultural value that is central to the Asian worldview and that appears to be emphasized in schools, homes, and in general society is the "importance given to guests and strangers–people who represent the 'other.'The notion of hospitality is pervasive and made a strong appearance during my meetings with the participants" (Gupta, 2006/2013, p. 73).Within the sociocultural context of India, for instance, a deeper explanation for this phenomenon "may possibly be found in the ancient scriptures where it is clearly written '*atitih devo bhavah,*' which implies that your guest is like your God. Thus across the various socioeconomic classes and castes in Indian society, it is believed that a guest should be welcomed with the utmost respect and hospitality, and this belief is practiced actively and widely ... extending hospitality toward a guest or a stranger is accorded high priority in the scheme of duty" (Gupta, 2006/2013, pp. 73–74). I want to quote one of my blog posts here which refers to this phenomenon during the course of my research in India.

> [The city of] Allahabad has its own nuanced culture—that of extreme polite-ness, graciousness, hospitality, welcoming, taking care of, putting the other before the self, putting relationships before the product. ... I went to Allahabad University to visit the Education Department.The campus of this very old university appeared dilapidated, worn out, even falling apart in some places. The Department of Education was a small single-storied run-down building with a broken metal signboard outside. Asking for the office I was shown a room and inside it were a couple of gentlemen conversing around a desk.The one behind the desk looked up and asked me to come in. Apparently he was none other than the head of the department. After I introduced myself he welcomed me and said that I was a real *Atithi* (guest). He explained to every-one present in the office that those who visit unexpectedly and unannounced are *Atithi* in the true sense and were to be welcomed and honored. Funny how the concept of *Atithi* has come up twice in two very different contexts but within the same week—once in a seafood restaurant in Goa, and now in a room deep within an academic institution in Allahabad (amitagupta.com/ india-allahabad-ancient-sacred-and-gracious, October 15, 2013).

The value given to hospitality was found in schools and institutions across other Asian cultures as well. At the end of a school tour at the Jasmine PCF in Sin-gapore, I was treated to a sit-down chat with the school administrators over hot coffee or tea and cookies in the office. It had been a friendly and warm visit, and both the staff and administration had been very welcoming and forthcoming with information.This Singapore experience was not unique to this school and, in fact, mirrored other school visits I made throughout Asia. Warmly welcoming guests and feeding them is a sign of good hospitality and was a cultural value that spilled over from homes into work environments. In schools, teacher education colleges, policy making institutes, or in non-government organizations I was always welcomed warmly, offered a beverage and a snack, and given the time I needed to complete my conversation with my host.

At the Singapore Neon Primary School I was met by the principal and two teachers who welcomed me into a large meeting room with a long conference table set up for a PowerPoint presentation. Along one wall of the room was a table with refreshments: coffee, tea, mini fruit tarts, and Chinese carrot cake, which is not at all the carrot cake I was familiar with. This version is a rectangular piece made by steaming rice flour with shredded turnip in it, and then deep frying the steamed cake after coating with a light batter. I have to say the carrot cake and the fruit tarts were just delicious, and our hosts were extremely receptive and attentive to us—welcoming and hospitable.

At the end of a school visit to the Panda PCF preschool in Singapore, after I had seen all the classrooms, met all the teachers, and taken lots of photographs, we gathered in the school office for refreshments and a conversation. Over cold Chrysanthemum tea served in cardboard containers and locally made sweet delicacies we were presented with a PowerPoint slide show of the center prepared by one of the teachers. My host at the National Institute of Education in Singapore also invited me to lunch at her mother's home, who had cooked up a storm, including the following dishes: stingray, garupa fish, fried chicken wings, vegetarian chicken fingers, stuffed tofu with bright green Chinese broccoli, and rice! For dessert there was fruit salad with dragonfruit and honeydew, and chocolate pudding. The lunch hour was warm, fun, and filled with a deep sense of generosity and hospitality.

I had a similar experience in the Maldives. My host at the Maldives National University treated me several times to delectable local snacks. Once we went around the corner from the Faculty of Education to a place called Cocktail House—a nifty little coffee place by the shore, with a sand floor and white plastic tables and chairs under a wooden canopy. I ordered some delicious cold coffee and tried a local dish called disc or *roshi* and *mashuni*. A disc or *roshi* is a round flatbread made from coconut husk and flour and coconut, lightly spiced and salted. It's a bit like an Indian *parantha* but made without the oil. This was served with *mashuni*—a dish of dry shredded tuna mixed with grated coconut, onions, green chillies and salt, and lime juice. This was a typical local breakfast and was incredibly delicious. The meal ended with a plate of finely sliced areca nut, betel leaves called *bileh*, cloves, and limestone paste.

When I visited Dogwood Kindergarten in China, I was greeted warmly and effusively by the school principal and assistant principal. They spent two hours taking me around the school and introducing me to the teachers in each classroom, allowing me to carefully observe the classrooms, interact with the children, and take pictures. In each classroom, the teachers encouraged one of the children to greet me and present me with a gift: a piece of art or craftwork that the children had made during their classroom activities. In the 4's classroom I was presented with a paper hat that children had made, which was a part of the costumes they used for enacting stories from Peking Opera. In the 5's classroom, one little boy presented me with blue and white design artwork done on paper plates, which reflected the traditional Chinese blue and white pottery style. The teachers and administrators were patient and tried to answer every question I had. They did not speak English and I did not know Chinese, so all conversations took place with the help of an interpreter who was a young PhD student at the local university. At the end of the visit, the school principal invited me into her office to chat some more over a hot cup of green tea, and then presented me with a beautiful finely woven muslin scarf that reflected the local handicrafts of Hangzhou.

One of the most memorable moments was in Sri Lanka. I was scheduled to meet with a group of early childhood educators—five women who were mostly retired or close to retiring from active service, but all of whom had been pioneers in the field of early education in Sri Lanka, having been deans, founding chairs, and professors in universities. They could be credited for laying down the foundations for the field of pre-primary and primary education by initiating and leading national projects for the Sri Lankan government in the 1960s and 1970s. After an enthusiastic and very informative conversation with the group, my host invited us all to her home for lunch in my honor. That she had organized a feast is a complete understatement as the lunch included at least 10 local Sri Lankan dishes—sear fish curry, prawn curry, fish cutlets, potatoes, jackfruit curry, ash plantain curry, a dry green leafy vegetable lightly tossed with grated coconut, a fresh salad with tomatoes, cucumbers and onions, papadam, and rice. For dessert there was wood apple, a new fruit to me where the pulp is strained from the seeds and then blended with jaggery and some coconut milk. We ended the meal with a round of coffee. The food was of course delicious, but it was highlighted by the rich conversation over the meal as everyone spoke comfortably and candidly shared their opinions and experiences in the field of primary and pre-primary education and teacher education in Sri Lanka, and of life in general.

Family Values and Filial Piety

Filial piety and age veneration is also a characteristic feature of Asian cultures and is generally reflected in schools, homes, and the larger society. Respect for elders who are parents, extended family members, friends, teachers, public leaders, or even strangers is an important value that is practiced actively and widely within Asian cultures. Taking the context of India as an illustration: "respect towards adults could take many forms such as exhibiting good manners, not being rude to them, being polite, volunteering to help with errands, carrying heavy things when accompanying someone older, not sitting down until everyone older has sat down first, not eating until the elders have eaten first, and so forth. In general, it implied that age was venerated and that each individual whether adult or child should demonstrate extra care, affection, concern and assistance to anyone older than themselves" (Gupta, 2006/2013, p. 71).

This value is important and widely upheld in other Asian countries as well. According to Lim & Lim (in press) "In the Confucian way of self-cultivation, an individual should learn first to show respect and filial piety to one's parents, and to love one's fellow beings towards becoming a benevolent person. It is when a nation has an educated and benevolent common people coupled with good governance that there should be peace under the heavens." While in Singapore I was able to participate in the seventh month of the Chinese lunar year, which, according to one research participant, brings with it the festival of the Hungry Ghosts and is taken very seriously in Chinese societies. It is believed that the Gates of Hell are opened and all the spirits are released from the ethereal world into the real world. Filial piety and the duty to look after one's parents and ancestors are observed. The spirits of deceased family members and ancestors are honored by the living descendants through food offerings and the burning of incense. Sometimes paper lanterns are floated into the water to light the path home for souls that might be lost. When meals are served at home, families ensure place settings at the table marked by empty chairs that are reserved for the deceased ancestors if they wish to dine along with the living descendants in each family. This is the time to pay one's respects and to honor the elders and the departed. This was another instance of how a cultural value—that of age veneration—got enacted in policy as well as education.

As an interesting aside, there was an ongoing national discussion in Singapore at that time about a government policy that would protect the elderly. According to the policy, adult children of senior citizens would be fined and penalized if they did not care for their aging and/or sick parents. The parliament in India passed a similar law in 2007 whereby adult Indians who neglect ageing parents over 60 years of age can be jailed for three months. This new law was passed in response to the growing elderly mistreatment in a country long known for revering the old. The legislation states "that old age has become a major social challenge and there is need to give more attention to care and protection of older persons" (AFP (Agence France-Presse): "India passes law to punish children who abandon elderly parents," December 6, 2007. Available at http://www.google.com/hostednews/afp/article/ALeqM5h-D8QxY-J5wpaNMshKiS2ouvHKLg).

In Sonakshi School, a private school in India, Grandparents Day was celebrated across grade levels. On the day of my visit, it so happened that Grandparents Day was being celebrated by all five sections of the Prep (kindergarten) class with a total of approximately 130 children. A complete performance with songs, dance, poetry, and skits had been planned. Each classroom had a specific act, and every single one of the 25 to 30 children in each classroom participated in it. The concert was held in the school's outdoor amphitheater, and the kindergarten parents and grandparents were seated on the stone steps. Above the stage was a large poster that read *We love you, grandparents*, and illustrated with generic portraits of *dadaji* and *dadiji* (father's parents) and *nanaji* and *naniji* (mother's parents). As everyone eagerly waited for the performances to start, the school orchestra started to play the Overture, which included old favorite melodies that would be familiar to the older generation in the audience: "Never on a Sunday," "Brown Girl in the Ring," "Five Hundred Miles," "Jamaican Farewell," "Che Sara Sara," and so forth. There was then a welcoming address by the school principal, who thanked the grandparents and asked for their blessings. She introduced the kindergarten staff made up of 10 classroom teachers and 2 auxiliary teachers. The classroom teachers then took turns to introduce their classes and begin the concert. All around the school, hand-drawn and painted posters declared the importance and love showered on grandparents. Some of the posters read: *Thank you for your unconditional love; Hearing stories from you is wonderful; We love spending time with you; Your hugs are the best;* and so on. A wall-length bulletin board was covered with "voices" of children that told about their experiences with and love for their grandparents. In the center of this bulletin board were the following words: *Grandparents are special people, with wisdom and pride they are always offering their love and kindness, and are always there to guide.* The children's quotes about their grandparents included expressions such as:

> They always understand me and care for me;
> They are always smiling at me;
> My grandparents buy me lots of things;
> My grand-dad loves me so much, I love him too;
> They always listen to me;
> I love my grandmother, she cooks yummy food for me;
> I love my grandparents, they give me pocket money.

A string of similar artwork was hung along the hallways in which kindergartners had painted their stories about their grandparents.

Community Values

A prominent education policy maker in Sri Lanka told me about a rural school on a remote tea estate for the children of the villagers that he had been involved in and had highlighted it as a case study on leadership for school reform. The fathers and mothers of the children at this school usually worked on the tea plantations. When the school first started several years ago, many men were in the habit of drinking excessively after work, and small-scale hunting was common. With widespread poverty and ignorance, many parents were failing in their duty toward their children. Lack of parental love and care made children antisocial. In response to these concerns, one school principal decided to carry out programs for parents to create better homes for children and a better community. These programs sought to inculcate positive values among the parents. Today, family bonds have been restored, hunting has totally ceased, and forest fires have stopped. The whole community has become vegetarian. All children go to school, resulting in 100% enrollment and literacy. The school takes special care of students who are orphans or with single parents (Perera, 2009). These efforts tie in seamlessly with the overall Buddhist values of nonviolence and compassion.

At the Salvia Kindergarten in Singapore, which had some of the most elaborate and outstanding children's artwork, a poster had been posted on the staff bulletin board in the school which declared the school's mission statement: *To prepare our children intellectually to meet the challenges ahead; to instill in them a sense of pride in their socio-cultural heritage and their identity as Singaporeans; to provide them with a moral framework to guide them in their daily living; to nurture them with the confidence to always achieve their best.* Another poster in the staff room served as a reminder of weekly expectations for teachers:

> Lesson Plan by Thursday 5 pm;
> Lesson Plan File on Friday;
> Instructional Reflection on Monday;
> 5 children's portfolios on Tuesday.

These and similar instances provided evidence for the underlying recognition and acknowledgment within the Asian worldview that values such as respect and individual responsibility are critical for the smooth and harmonious functioning of a community whether the word refers to a classroom, a school, or the larger society.

Discussion

To reiterate what was emphasized earlier: The culture of a society is usually an expression of the deeper value system of that group. According to Kluckhohn, value systems are patterns of responses to five basic questions that are common to all human groups: the character of innate human nature; the relationship of human beings to nature and supernature; the temporal focus of human life (past, present, or future); the valued modality of human activity (doing, being, etc.); and the valued modality of people's relationships to other people (Kluckhohn, 1961, as cited in Masemann, 2013, p. 115). Values thus should not be perceived as "individual psychological attitudes of an individual but socially structured orientations patterned in relation to the strictures of the society in which people played out their roles" (Masemann, 2013, p. 116).

Further, the philosophical and cultural values of a society subsequently become the basis for teachers' and educators' specific decisions about schooling and the curriculum. According to Gupta (2007, p. 7),

> Curriculum is not value-free or produced in a vacuum, and decisions regarding curriculum such as what to teach and how to teach are determined ultimately by a culture's beliefs and values which prioritizes that

set of knowledge, skills and attitudes which are to be learnt by its children in order to live a good life in a just society. Additionally, this body of knowledge, skills and behaviors are taught formally as well as informally to children through educational and social agencies such as schools, colleges, museums, religious institutions, media and entertainment, and at home from parents, grandparents, extended families, and friends. Further, the underlying values of a society also determine the "hidden curriculum" by which attitudes, beliefs and norms are communicated implicitly but powerfully to inform children of which specific sets of knowledge, values and skills are and will be positively reinforced and rewarded and which will not.

Therefore, underlying a school system's formal curriculum, policy documents, and the school's "hidden" curriculum can be found indications of the society's cultural values. This can be illustrated by the example of the daily school schedule for the Iris School in the Maldives, which includes the daily teaching of the country's official language, Dhivehi, religion, Islam, and the Islamic holy text, the Quran, over a school week that runs from Sunday to Thursday since the weekend in Islamic countries includes Fridays and Saturdays. The schedule as presented in Figure 4.1 refers to the afternoon shift of a first grade classroom (where ES stands for Environmental Studies, PE stands for Physical Education, and PA stands for Practical Arts):

	Sunday	**Monday**	**Tuesday**	**Wednesday**	**Thursday**
01:30 – 01:40	Assembly	Assembly	Assembly	Assembly	Assembly
01:40 – 02:15	English	Math	English	English	English
02:15 – 02:50	Math	Islam	Quran	English	Quran
02:50 – 03:25	ES	Library	Computer	Dhivehi	PE
03:25 – 04:00	Dhivehi	English	Math	ES	Dhivehi
04:00 – 04:15	Break	Break	Break	Break	Break
04:15 – 04:50	ES	English	Dhivehi	Music	Islam
04:50 – 05:25	Islam	Dhivehi	PE	Math	PA
05:25 – 06:00	Math	ES	ES	Math	PA

FIGURE 4.1. Daily schedule for a first grade in a government primary school in the Maldives

Welcoming guests and bestowing respect and honor upon them through gift giving and/or offering food and beverages is a deeply rooted cultural value in many Eastern cultures. Each of these instances, whether it was the explicit reinforcing of preferred virtues and citizenship values throughout the school environment, or whether it was offering food and beverages and gifts to visitors to the school, reaffirmed this cultural value. It also offered schoolchildren various opportunities to learn this value through the behaviors of the adults in the school, as well as through the display of inspirational sayings and mottos. It seems important to provide such opportunities for children to make a shift from the *self* to the *other* on the individual–group or self-other line of continuum. Many child-centered classrooms in the West encourage children to put the *self* first without allowing for sufficient opportunities for them to put aside the *self* in order to acknowledge and honor the *other*.

It becomes necessary to problematize culture as it is experienced in reality. The impact of globalization on traditional cultures may often lead to complex and sometimes conflicted relationships between the global and the local in issues such as the universal and the particular, or between developmental appropriateness and cultural appropriateness. Snarey (2007) provides two examples of value-oriented historic cultural themes typical of Asian cultures: holism and harmony. According to Snarey, moral education in the West focuses mostly on moral judgment or behavior. But the concept of holism supports the ability to view moral education as a simultaneous development of moral reasoning, emotions, and behavior. This allows the individual to take a global perspective on moral dilemmas. With regard to harmony, Snarey reminds us that globalization asks us to live in harmony in an increasingly interconnected world—"it calls for a directly experienced oneness with the larger social and natural environments ... harmony is essential to live well within networks of social care and by principles of social justice" (Snarey, 2007, p. vi).

The goal of teaching citizenship and moral values to children is a noble one. After all, when we talk about educating the whole child and nurturing all aspects of the child's development, the domain of ethical and moral development certainly cannot be overlooked or excluded. But how can children learn to practice the virtues deemed important by their societies? Being "good" or "moral" is not a skill to be learned through a lecture or a textbook or through posters in their school environment. Moral education has always been a part of both formal and informal education, and adults have traditionally imparted values to children through fables and stories from the epics and classic literature, folk tales, and popular culture during their childhood years. Chong (2007) reminds us that moral education is a continuous process of living a life. While the lessons may not sink in immediately, he states, it is hoped that students will come to appreciate the significance of these stories in the context of their own lives at some point. Chong invokes the teachings of the Confucian philosopher Mencius who contrasts human dignity with consumerist tendencies. Chong emphasizes that in a world marked by globalization and consumerism, it is all the more important for children to grow up knowing the difference between making a choice as a consumer and the choice involved in wanting to do one's duty (Chong, 2007). It is also important to be reminded that the posters seen in all the schools highlighting the values prioritized within the local contexts are not the only way that children are taught about values. In most children's lives, their teachers and families are reiterating the same principles through stories and fables and real-life examples that are particularly prominent and easily available in cultures with strong oral traditions.

In connecting the goals of teaching values to its actual application in educational settings, Hirata et al. (2005) suggest an outline for citizenship education and the specific characteristics of citizenship at local, national, global, and universal levels that may be taught to students. For each level they list the *knowledge and understanding, skills and abilities*, and *values and attitudes* that may be taught and encouraged by schools as part of citizenship education. Taking first *knowledge and understanding*: Knowledge at the local level would focus on local history, culture, traditions; knowledge at the national level would focus on national history and culture; knowledge at the global level would emphasize peace and conflict, social justice, equity, cultural diversity, world history, environment, and globalization; and knowledge at the universal level would focus on the understanding of human rights, peace, environment, cultural diversity, and democracy. For *skills and abilities*: At the local level students would be nurtured to learn the skills of cooperation and participation in local politics; at the national level the focus would be on politics at the national level; at the global level the emphasis would be on the peaceful resolution of politics; at the international level, the stress would be on the ability to speak a foreign language and to coexist with those from a different cultural background; and finally at the universal level the focus would be on students learning how to judge, reason, express themselves, work with others, and protect human rights. With regard to *values and attitudes*: at the local level the children would be encouraged to love and be proud of their immediate community; at the national level the focus would be on taking pride in one's national identity, and be mindful of national tradition and culture; at the global level the focus of citizenship education would be on democratic ways of life, respecting the diversity of cultures, developing a scientific mind, self-reliance, awareness of global issues, and identity as a global citizen; and finally at the universal level the goals would emphasize respect for law, moral values, self-discipline, rights and duties, democratic attitudes, self-actualization, tolerance, a search for truth, and similar values (Hirata et al., 2005).

These goals can easily be translated to the early childhood classroom as notions of democracy, and participation in politics at the local level may rightly refer to having pre-K children participate in the creation of classroom rules, voting to determine which book the teacher will use for Read-Aloud on a particular morning, discussing notions of respect and fairness when another child's block building gets knocked down, making decisions on how to share when there is a scarcity of resources in the classroom, and so forth.

Kennedy and Fairbrother (2004, as cited in Goh, 2012) refer to an additional eight characteristics that successful 21st-century citizens will need to demonstrate. These characteristics have been determined and compiled by several scholars of character and citizenship education and include:

- The ability to look at and approach problems as a member of a global society
- The ability to work with others in a cooperative way and to take responsibility for one's roles and duties within society
- The ability to understand, accept, appreciate, and tolerate cultural differences
- The capacity to think in a critical and systematic way
- The willingness to resolve conflict in a nonviolent manner
- The willingness to change one's lifestyle and consumption habits to protect the environment
- The ability to be sensitive toward and to defend human rights
- The willingness and ability to participate in politics at local, national, and international levels (Kennedy & Fairbrother, 2004, p. 293)

Once the goals of citizenship and character education have been identified, the next question naturally is that of preparing teachers so that they will be able to incorporate the teaching of values in their classroom practice. Although the teaching of values is indeed occurring in schools in Asia, it still needs to be systematically incorporated into the school curriculum. Even more importantly, it needs to be made an overt part of the teacher education curriculum. Some might agree that there is an important need for teaching values in the United States as well since there currently does not seem to be a systematic or explicit approach for the teaching of character, citizenship, and cultural values in most American schools. It is relevant to highlight here what Apple (2011) and Wang et al. (2011) have recently noted: that teacher education programs around the world are rethinking and redesigning their curriculum to meet these global citizenship demands. But the reform of teacher education curriculum to meet the needs of the 21st century is a topic for another discussion.

5
CURRICULUM AND LOCAL FUNDS OF KNOWLEDGE

In this chapter I highlight classroom practices that demonstrate how some schools in Asia have approached the issue of diversity and the impact of globalization on this issue. The multilinguistic, multiethnic, and multireligious nature of the student population in many of the classrooms was very apparent. The diverse backgrounds of children were clearly reflected in classroom environments and materials through the display of children's dictated stories in various languages, science tables that display locally found material, books written in the scripts of different languages, lunch menus that offer a diverse range of cuisines, and school celebrations that encompass diverse ethnic and religious traditions.

The following descriptions of and discussions on aspects of some early childhood classrooms in India, China, Singapore, Sri Lanka, and the Maldives will provide a more detailed look into the environment, activities, and materials used in the classroom, and how local and global issues are reflected in the curriculum. Limited financial resources were available to most schools included in this study, except for the elite private schools which are usually well funded and adequately resourced. Limited funding naturally constrains the schools' ability to purchase and use expensive commercially made learning materials and toys in order to equip and stock the early childhood classrooms. In many schools across the five countries, many of the learning materials in the rooms were made by the class teachers themselves, thus encouraging them to draw on their own imagination, creativity, and intimate knowledge of the local cultures to reflect local traditions in the arts.

The chapter begins with a description of the language policies and the use of multiple languages in the early childhood classrooms of three countries that reflected the widest ethnic diversity in their urban school settings: Singapore, India, and Sri Lanka. This discussion is followed by a description of the learning materials made by the classroom teachers in many of the schools and thereby provides a mirror into local cultures. The chapter concludes with a discussion of the current impact of globalization on many of the above issues.

Multilingualism in Schools and Classrooms

Singapore

According to Lim & Lim (in press) "The language policy for the nation recognises four official languages: Malay, Mandarin Chinese, Tamil and English and the bilingual policy in education ensures that all children attending primary and secondary schools become fairly proficient in English, the de facto working language in the public and business sectors, and one other official language (or another language that is offered in the school system)." Although the use of all four is encouraged in the classroom. In all schools, including preschools, teachers use either English or Mandarin/Malay/Tamil, depending on what subject area they teach (Ho & Gopinathan, 1999). In almost every kindergarten site I visited in Singapore, the use of all these languages was clearly evident in classroom and school environments, especially with regard to children's work. As explained in Chapter 2, most preschools are located in the "void decks" of public housing where the government has tried to ensure a balanced ethnic mix. This ethnic mix and the resulting multilingualism are reflected in the classrooms as well. Arts and crafts work done by the children was accompanied by their narratives dictated to the teachers in the child's home language. The classroom teachers themselves spoke these diverse languages so that every child was able to walk up to one of the teachers and dictate his or her story in English, Malay, Mandarin, or Tamil. Children's artwork accompanied by their narratives written in English, Malay, and Mandarin was displayed on the classrooms walls of several preschools.

One such PCF preschool I visited was the Panda PCF, a small center with two classrooms. An early childhood consultant had worked with the staff in helping to transform the environment of this preschool from a structured and traditional one to one that was more Reggio-inspired. This transformation was apparent in the aesthetic windows created to bring more light into the classroom, to emphasize parent involvement, and to exhibit the profuse amount of children's artwork accompanied by documentation that was displayed everywhere in the classrooms. The demographics at the center were multicultural, as was the curriculum. All the children's work along with their dictated messages and all the labels in the classroom were in Chinese, Malay, Tamil, and English. Art created on small and large sheets of paper using crayons, pencils, markers, paint, or various collaging techniques was strung across the classrooms and displayed prominently. Children's artwork was accompanied by their narratives in one of Singapore's four official languages, depending on the artist's linguistic background. The narratives told the children's stories and articulated their thoughts, filling the classroom environment with a rich display of ideas in contrasting scripts of different languages.

The center had a large bulletin board in the classroom dedicated to the Malay language. The topic on this board read *Mari Belajar Bahasa Melayu* (Let's learn Bahasa Melayu), and under this title were posted children's drawings and artwork with their dictated stories in Malay. One piece of artwork showed some drawings of worms with the child's narrative that read "*Aalisya melukis seput—seput ini hendak pergi menkari ibunya. Selepas itu, seput itu ingin menkari ayahnya*" [Aalisya draws snail—this snail wants to go to mother. After this, the snail goes to father]. Displayed on the same bulletin board were letters of the alphabet with photographs of objects, starting with the corresponding letter accompanied with the name of the object printed in Malay:

> Aa: *Api* (picture of flames in a fire), *Awan* (picture of a blue sky with white clouds)
> Bb: *Bola* (picture of a soccer ball)
> Cc: *Cacing* (picture of a caterpillar on a leaf), *Cawan* (picture of a cup of tea or coffee)

Similarly, there was another large bulletin board that was dedicated to Chinese numerals. It displayed children's math worksheets on which they had glued a specific number of circles cut from colored paper and had written a Chinese numeral to indicate the number of dots on each line. There were several pieces of artwork—drawings, collages, paintings—with Chinese narratives exhibited around the classrooms.

The use of English dominated children's work. One project had the children use different shapes of colored paper to create animals and dictate a story about their creations:

> The Rectangle Lion: This is a male lion. The lion is sleeping.
> The Rectangle Dragon: This is a dragon. The witch will become a dragon. The dragon will blow a fire.
> The Rectangle Horse. …
> The Rectangle Dinosaur. …

In another art project, the children seemed to have responded to a story about elephants. They had drawn their favorite part of the story and illustrated it:

> The elephants are sitting on one side of the sea saw together. They are playing with the sea saw. The baby elephant wants to sit with her sister.
> The baby elephant is afraid of sitting on the sea saw alone because the sea saw is so high.
> The baby elephant is sleeping with her sister. They went out cycling and the baby is afraid of riding the bicycle alone. The sister elephant is painting a picture of a flower for the baby elephant.

For yet another project children had made collages with paint and shaving cream and told the following stories:

> This is snake. It is gliding on the ground.
> This is at the seaside. There are people at the seaside.

The English language certainly seemed to be dominant in schools as most of the print seen in classrooms reflected the widespread use of English in Singapore.

India

Language is a source of enormous diversity in India. The official and administrative languages in the central government are Hindi (spoken by about 40% of Indians) and English (which had been the official language in India during the British Raj). Although 227 mother tongues and approximately 1600 dialects are recognized in India, none of them are spoken by any more than 10% of the population. Even Hindi itself has several dialects, including Awadhi, Bagheli, Bhojpuri, Brij, Bundeli, Chhattisgarhi, Hadoti, Magahi, Malwi, Nimari, Pahari, and Rajasthani (Dube, 1990/2000). The Indian Constitution lists 22 languages that the Indian government has the responsibility to develop.

The existing policy on language of instruction in all schools in India follows the three-language formula adopted by the Education Commission in 1964. The three languages that students are required to learn during their school careers are (1) their mother tongue or the regional language of the state in which they reside; (2) English, the official language of India, and/or Hindi, the national language of India, which is spoken by about 40 % of the Indian population according to the Census of 2001; and (3) a modern Indian language, which may be one of the 22 dominant regional languages recognized as official from the 845 spoken in India. In theory, this strategy aims to teach students English and/or Hindi, and two other Indian languages (NCERT, 2006). In support of this multilingual system, the Constitution requires all states to publish books in up to a dozen or more languages (Saini, 2000). Most children in school are exposed to multiple languages as a result of this policy, and they grow up speaking more than one language. Research on language development has amply established that exposure to more than one language is beneficial to children's linguistic and cognitive development. But whether or not the existing mode of language instruction in schools in India is helpful is another topic that remains to be researched and debated.

In schools in New Delhi, the languages learned are English, Hindi, and another language of the student's choosing. Hindi is significant because it is the local and regional language there. At the Snowdrop School, a private school in New Delhi, a bilingual word wall in English and Hindi was prominently displayed in the hallway near the kindergarten and first grade classrooms. The curriculum at this school was literacy-based, and many of the literacy activities on display demonstrated a bilingual phonics approach. An early childhood teacher explained that building vocabulary and learning the sounds of the letters of the alphabet in both English and Hindi exemplified this approach. For instance, for purposes of reinforcing the sound of the letter T, the outline of a large turtle was cut out from green paper and taped to the wall. On that outline of the turtle were written several words that started with the letter T accompanied by drawings of each item done by the children. Some of the words included were: table, TV, tub, traffic light, teacher, tiger, train, temple, telephone, tie, turtle, tiffin, tree, and torch. Another sheet of white paper showed the outline of a white cloud. In Hindi cloud is called *baadal*, and this sheet was filled with Hindi words that started with the sound "b": *baadal* (cloud), *barsaat* (rain), *billi* (cat), *battakh* (duck), *bandar* (monkey), *baingan* (eggplant), *bagicha* (garden), *baccha* (child), *bistar* (bed), and so on. Other posters were similarly created for other letters of both the Hindi and English alphabets. On another bulletin board was a sheet of paper titled *Our Trip to Nehru Park* under which were 23 responses from the 23 children in the class that had visited the park. The responses were in either English or Hindi. For example:

> Tanisha: I enjoyed sharing food with everyone.
> Udit: I loved the bus ride and to eat my food in the picnic.
> Arnav: I fed the bark of the tree to the *chidiya* (sparrow) and the *tota* (parrot).
> Sara: *bahut mazaa aya aur* birds *ko khana khilaya* (I had a lot of fun and fed
> some food to the birds).

In a first grade classroom there was a poster with sight words listed on one of the bulletin boards. The list included both Hindi and English words: tomorrow, because, together, their, friends, *paudha* (plant), *kyonki* (because), *chahiye* (want), *accha* (good), *tumhara* (yours), and so on.

In another instance a preschool classroom in Maitreyi School, an urban government school in India, presented quite a different picture. This school was a K–12 school participating in Sarva Shiksha Abhyan, or universal elementary education, and had just added the kindergarten class in 2009. The school campus was open, spacious, and sun-filled. The school hallways were covered with inspirational sayings and pictures. The students at the school came primarily from low-income communities in the neighborhood. Interestingly, almost all the displays and posters in the hallways were in English and made by the teachers, whereas the students all came from Hindi-speaking backgrounds.

The primary grades K–4 at this school were housed in a separate building. The classrooms all appeared in one row along a hallway that was open to the outdoors. The walls of the hallway were brightly painted with scenes of celebrations of the Indian holidays of Id, an Islamic holiday, and Diwali, a Hindu festival; prints of the solar system; and a large map of India marked with the outlines of each state, with each state name written into the outline in Hindi. The kindergarten classroom was an almost bare room approximately 15 feet by 15 feet, with no windows and only one door. There were a few charts on the walls that displayed numbers and alphabets in both Hindi and English. The classroom had no furniture except for a desk and chair for the teacher. All the 36 children sat on a *dhurrie* (rug) on the floor, and the class teacher, Seema, was assisted by one *ayah*, or maid. Seema explained that the curriculum of the kindergarten classroom consisted of letters of the English and Hindi alphabets, and numbers in both Hindi and English. She stated that they had already completed the teaching of the Hindi vowels and were now working on the Hindi consonants. A chart on one wall of the classroom showed pictures of a variety of fruit with names in English. During their conversations with me, both the classroom teacher and the vice principal of the school emphasized more than once that the curriculum in the primary school was mostly verbal, with very little written work expected of the children. But the vice principal also mentioned that the parents wanted to see written work since that was the only way they could gauge whether their children were learning. The school hours for the kindergarten classroom were from 7:30 am to 11:30 am. At the time of my visit, many children had already gone home, and about 10 children remained in the classroom waiting to be picked up. The daily classroom schedule consisted of morning prayers and devotional songs upon arrival, such as *he maalik tere bandhe hum, humko man ki shakti dena* (these are two widely familiar prayer songs made popular in two Hindi films produced in 1957 and 1971 respectively) and some patriotic and nationalistic songs. These devotionals were followed first by outdoor play or physical exercise, and then by periods of English, Hindi, and Numbers. The kindergarten classroom teacher, Seema, explained that the written and verbal work, music, and movement were related to what the students were doing academically.

Sri Lanka

In Sri Lanka, the education reform policies established during the 1940s replaced English with either Tamil or Sinhala as the instructional language in primary education. On one hand, this reform policy facilitated educational access at many levels by allowing rural children to attend schools, expanding student enrollment in schools, increasing the number of students who appeared for public examinations, and increasing the total number of universities in the country. On the other hand, it led to a decrease in English-language speakers among the Sri Lankan public. In the current sociopolitical-economic climate marked by globalization and neoliberalism, many Sri Lankans have perceived this to be a disadvantage in the global playing field. Thus, efforts are being made to reintroduce English as the language of instruction in schools and for teacher training. One consequence of globalization is widespread parental desire among both affluent and poor families to send their children abroad. To this end, numerous families in Sri Lanka and across South Asia in general want their children to have an English education starting at the pre-primary level, even if the teaching of English is limited to rote memorization of English nursery rhymes. Knowledge of the English language is viewed by poor families as a way out of poverty for their children, and so a popular demand is placed on preschools to teach English. Currently in Sri Lanka, at the preschool level, which involves mostly the private sector, the medium of instruction is commonly English, but there is also an extensive use of Tamil and Sinhala as teachers try to communicate with children from different linguistic backgrounds. At the kindergarten or primary level (Grades 1–5), the medium of instruction is Tamil or Sinhala, whereas English is taught as a subject or content area in these grades. At the secondary school level (Grades 6–12), the medium of instruction is mostly Tamil and Sinhala, but schools have the option of using English to teach three subjects or content areas, specifically Science, Math, and English. In schools I visited within the Colombo region, the languages commonly displayed were Sinhala and English, as was evident in the print in the school environment: posters, alphabet charts in the nursery classrooms, library books, school announcements, classroom instruction and curricular work, and in the general conversations among teachers and children.

Teaching Using Local Funds of Knowledge

Chicken Rice, Roti Prata, and Satay: A Housekeeping Corner with Multiple Cuisines

At the Jasmine PCF preschool in Singapore, I met with the district administrator and the center principal. The center had about 150 students between the ages of 4 and 6 who lived in the neighborhood and attended the school between 8 am and 2 pm. The grade levels were called Nursery (4's), K1 (5's), and K2 (6's).

The racial breakdown of the students reflected the national demographics of Singapore: 75% Chinese, 14% Malay, 9% Indian, and about 2% Eurasians. Despite a smaller Malay population, the national language is Malay, and even the national anthem is sung in Malay. Malay is dominant because the Malays were the indigenous people of Singapore, whereas the other population groups were immigrants who arrived into Singapore in subsequent years. There are four official languages in Singapore—Malay, Mandarin, Tamil, and English. As a national priority, the Singapore government promotes racial harmony, multilingualism, and national pride, as was clearly evident in the curriculum of the Jasmine kindergarten. Singapore had just finished celebrating its National Day and 44th birthday that week, and posted on one wall in the hallway was a large collage the children had created that depicted a lion (the emblem of Singapore which itself means City of Lion), followed by several smiling and celebrating children, surrounded by fireworks in the background in honor of what is akin to Independence Day in many other countries. The pictures of the children had been drawn, colored, and cut out by the children in the school and clearly reflected different racial groups. The body of the lion had been filled in with lentils and grains in four distinct colors—yellow, white, brown, and green—to represent the diversity of the four racial and ethnic groups in Singapore.

The classrooms in this school were set up as progressive early childhood education (ECE) rooms with learning centers, much like any Western ECE classroom. The children were engaged in small groups in various areas of the classroom. The walls were bright and covered with artwork done by the children individually as well as in groups such as collages and murals. Many of the learning centers were equipped with local materials that reflected the Singaporean culture. The dramatic play area held three food stalls offering Chinese, Malay, Indian, and American foods, just as is seen in the hundreds of food courts associated with Singapore. Each stall featured cutouts of foods from local cuisines that teachers had made by painting pieces of styrofoam to resemble chicken, eggs, and so forth. The local staple in Singapore is the famed chicken rice, and the stall offering Chinese cuisine was labeled the Chicken Rice Stall, displaying a large styrofoam chicken leg along with grains of styrofoam rice. In this stall was also placed a rice cooker, which is widely used to cook rice in Asia. The stall for Indian cuisine was labeled the *Roti Prata Stall* (a pancake-like flatbread served with a vegetable or meat-based curry), and a picture of the dish was on display. Pratas can be made with or without eggs, and so this food stall also had available styrofoam eggs made by the teachers and painted a light brown. A price list outside the stall indicated that a roti prata without egg cost SIN$1 and one with egg cost SIN$2. The third food stall in the classroom reflected Malay cuisine and was labeled the *Satay Stall*; it displayed Malay staples such as chicken satay (grilled chicken pieces on a skewer) and ketupat (a rice dumpling that is a traditional accompaniment to satay). The teachers had created chicken pieces out of styrofoam that were skewered and placed on a tray ready to be sold at this stall. A price list under the name of the stall informed customers that Set A (five skewers of satay and one ketupat) cost SIN$3, and Set B (ten skewers of satay and two ketupat) cost SIN$5. There was a small table covered with tin foil, with the table top replaced by a metal grid to make it look like a grilling station. It was placed next to the Malay stall where the "cooks" could skewer and grill or barbecue the chicken. Children were playing at each stall, some pretending to cook and serve while others took the role of customers and placed their orders. All the print in the classroom reflected a trilingual approach, and the labeling was done in Chinese, English, and Malay.

Apart from the classrooms, two special rooms at this preschool were of particular interest: the Chinese Room and the Phonics Room. The Chinese Room was used for teaching Chinese, and it was set up as a regular classroom except that all the centers were labeled in Chinese script. The Writing Corner in this room was used to teach children calligraphy and how to write in Chinese. Chinese is a complex system of reading and writing based on characters rather than letters, where each character stands for a symbol, an idea, or a concept. According to Huntsinger et al. (2000), all Chinese dialects have a common system of writing that consists of thousands of characters or ideographs, each representing an idea or an object; basic literacy requires the memorization of 1500 to 3000 characters (Chan as cited in Huntsinger et al., 2000), and the writing of these characters is done in calligraphy. Thus, in order to learn how to write, children not only have to learn and memorize thousands of characters but they also have to master the technique for the specific strokes used for that character using a calligraphy writing tool. (For comparison there are 26 letters in the English alphabet; 52 letters in the Hindi alphabet; 54 letters in the Sinhalese alphabet; and 23 letters in the Dhivehi alphabet.) This certainly highlights the challenges encountered by early childhood teachers when they help young children become proficient in reading and writing but in child-centered ways. The Chinese Room also had a game corner that offered traditional local games for the children to play: a Malay game called Congkak and the Singaporean game of Five Stones, a variation of which is played as Jacks or Knucklebones in many other countries. The Chinese Room supported a range of other learning skills: telling time in Chinese, learning to write by tracing sandpaper characters posted on one wall, and artwork accompanied by children's narratives in Chinese. The block area held unit blocks accompanied by pictures of the individual photos of the students pasted on a cardboard outline. Each picture could be stood up and used on their block buildings as block accessories.

The Phonics Room was arranged with brightly painted furniture, including rows of bright yellow tables and blue chairs all of which faced the front of the classroom. Large teacher-made charts were displayed as Word Walls in English; one chart with three-letter words and one chart with four-letter words. There was also one large poster with the letters of the English alphabet in both upper case and lower case. Clearly, this room was used for direct and large group instruction for the teaching of English. Each class in the school was scheduled to work in the Phonics Room for 40 minutes every day to teach children English reading and English writing using workbooks. The administrators explained that most children in the school read and wrote in English with more ease and fluency after attending the Phonics classes, as opposed to earlier times when there was less of an emphasis on "correct" reading and writing. This approach, they observed, was better in preparing the children for academic work in primary school. They noted that although the children found the process of learning by phonics difficult in the beginning, once they were past the initial difficulties and higher learning curve, students developed a higher level of comfort, confidence, and expertise in speaking, reading, and writing using the English language.

At the Panda PCF, preschool arts and crafts projects were displayed abundantly all over the classrooms observed. One project made use of empty boxes and cartons of varying dimensions. Each child had colorfully painted the outside of the box after deciding what he or she wanted the contents to be, and then named the item they had created. For instance, a label for one box read *Elephant in the box: Zoo*; a label for another box read *Flowers in the box: Garden*; a third, *Shows in the box: Television*; and a fourth, *Money in the box: Handbag*. The various learning centers included a Science Corner; a corner to explore and experiment with mirrors, colored stones and gems; an area that held a light box; a small corner that said Kiddy Garden; a shelf that contained an array of storage containers filled with recycled materials for art such as cardboard rolls, scrap papers, wooden clothes pegs, styro-foam pieces and pellets, empty food and grocery cartons, shredded packing paper, pieces of yarn and colored string, container lids of varying sizes, and so forth.

The use and development of information and communication technology (ICT) in the primary and secondary school grades has been an important goal in Singapore's Five-Year Plans. Although these formal plans do not specifically apply to preschools, the importance given to technology in general does filter down to early childhood education. At one of the PCFs I visited was a poster outlining how ICT was used in that preschool: *At our kindergarten, we use ICT as a tool to learn, investigate, represent our ideas, and communicate with others—using videos to capture children's learning journey; documenting children's learning such as taking pictures of children at work: exploring the properties of light and shadow using the OHP/Light Box* (OHP stands for overhead projector). At the end of the school tour, the supervisor–teacher enthusiastically presented a PowerPoint slideshow that showcased this preschool. The teacher had prepared this presentation herself and had earlier been a recipient of an Excellence in Teaching Award from Singapore's Ministry of Education (MOE); the certificate was prominently displayed on the school bulletin board. The teachers and staff exhibited a clear feeling of owner-ship, pride, and accomplishment with regard to the hard work they had put in to bring about change in their school.

Yet another kindergarten school in Singapore, the Salvia School, boasted of an outstanding art program that reflected children's lives, experiences, and ideas. Core issues at the heart of children's day-to-day lives emerged in the topics and themes of the curriculum that were evident in the artwork, narratives, and the KWL charts displayed throughout the school. On one wall were several pictures painted by children depicting events in their daily lives:

> I am going to the bird-park in the bus.
> Me and my family went to Indonesia.
> I am going in a yellow taxi to NTUC Fair Price.
> I went to Tampines Mall to watch the movie *Hanna Montana*.
> The flats in Singapore look beautiful.
> The park and waterfall in the Chinese Garden.
> This is how Sentosa's cable car station will look like; and so forth.

Traditional Arts and Crafts: Peking Opera Masks, Yuan Dynasty Pottery Styles, and Jianzhi

Materials made by teachers and children were a striking feature of the Dog-wood Kindergarten in China, which specialized in the teaching of drama. The school was housed in a beautiful two-storey building in a residential neighbor-hood just off a busy and heavily trafficked thoroughfare in the heart of the large city of Hangzhou. The front yard of the school held brightly painted outdoor play equipment, and the school hallways and stairwells were lined with colorful and intricate artwork done by the children. I was welcomed enthusiastically by the administrative staff, which included the principal, assistant principal, and the secretary. They spoke Mandarin, and the conversations between us were facilitated with the help of a university doctoral student who had accompanied me and who acted as the interpreter. The enthusiastic welcome and eagerness to show me each and every classroom were heartwarming, and teachers cheerfully invited me into each of their classrooms. In every room one of the children, assisted by his or her teacher, gifted me with a piece of craftwork the children had made as part of the curriculum.

As discussed in Chapter 2, in China schools for children between the ages of 3 and 6 are called kindergartens. The mission of the Dogwood Kindergarten is to teach the basics of Beijing (Peking) Opera throughout the kindergarten years. The curriculum according to the school's handbook included the following goals specific to teaching opera: (1) the First Year Kindergarten Class (the 3-year-olds) engaged in activities on getting to know the basics of the Beijing Opera, look-ing at pictures of it, observing details such as makeup and costumes, listening to the music of the Opera, and imitating actors in the Opera; (2) the Second Year Kindergarten Class (the 4-year-olds) engaged in finding and collecting pictures of the Opera from their homes, and from newspapers and magazines to do show and tell, drew pictures of characters from the Opera, created face masks of the characters, and engaged in other similar activities; and (3) the Third Year Kinder-garten Class (the 5-year-olds) watched Beijing Opera performances, learned to enact some of the performances by imitating the gestures and body movements of the performers; familiarized themselves with the music, and actually performed certain chapters of the Opera. The school encouraged parent involvement, and parents could volunteer to help and provide suggestions and opinions for the school's curriculum.

The classrooms at the Dogwood Kindergarten were filled with materials made by teachers and children that could be used to support the develop-ment of cognitive, social, and physical skills. Few commercially made materials were to be seen in the classrooms. Since the school's curriculum was driven by the performing arts, there was an emphasis on the use of masks, musical instruments, costumes, and other theatrical props, and there were numerous examples of these and other materials made by teachers and children. In the 3's room, scallopped sea shells had been collected, and children had painted faces on the surface of the shells, creating masklike materials. The children used handmade paper and papier maché created in the classroom to make the masks, with each child designing his or her own mask. A variety of musical instruments using colored paper, cardboard, tins, cans, sticks, and so forth had been made by teachers and children together, and were used by the children to play and make music. One of the 4-year-old classrooms had a corner desig-nated for opera play, with a collage of a stage with fabric curtains posted on the wall, a small piano placed under the "stage," and a bin filled with props, such as weapons created by the children using cardboard tubes, and gold and silver foil. There was a basket full of handmade balls made out of recycled newspaper in one of the classrooms for 3-year-olds. Wads of newspapers had been rolled and scrunched up into small balls and kept in place by wrapping them tightly with wide and clear scotch tape. The children used these newspaper balls in their play. Another example of homemade toys was the "pogo-can" observed in one of the classrooms for 5-year-olds. Holes had been made in the tops of empty Coca-Cola cans, and sturdy string had been looped through the holes to make a variation of pogo sticks. One 5-year-old boy showed me how it was used: He placed one foot onto the top of one can, held onto the strings with his hand, placed his other foot onto another can and proceeded to walk on the cans along the hallway. There were also examples of learning materials such as mazes made by teachers for the children to use. Teachers had glued narrow cardboard strips or plastic drinking straws onto lids of cardboard boxes to create several different kinds of mazes. Children worked on these mazes to practice their cognitive, spatial, fine motor, and sensory motor skills.

At the end of the visit, the principal of the school invited me into her office where over a cup of hot green tea we discussed the school curriculum. She explained that the curriculum at this school was shaped by Chinese traditional culture and that this government kindergarten school served as a model early childhood school that focused on child-centered pedagogy. She herself as the school's director along with some of the school's teachers routinely visited other kindergartens in the city for staff development workshops to guide and train other teachers in child-centered pedagogy. She asked me to share with her other ways and ideas with which traditional culture could be taught to young children in child-centered ways, and we started the discussion by considering how parents might be more involved in enriching the school curriculum. That the curriculum was based on aspects of traditional Chinese culture was evident in the activities observed in the classroom at the time of my visit: The 5-year-olds were working on an art project to create intricate and detailed geometric patterns and designs on round paper plates painted in blue and white similar to the cobalt blue and white style of pottery made popular in China during the 14th-century Yuan Dynasty; the 4-year-olds were working on designing their own umbrellas, which are used extensively in China for protection against sun and rain, by creating their own intricate and detailed drawings on paper; the 3-year-olds were learning to fold and cut paper to create symmetrical designs using the traditional Chinese paper-cutting technique known as Jianzhi. Integrated throughout the school was an emphasis on introducing children to elements of Beijing Opera: A body movement class in one classroom consisted of the 30 children sitting around on chairs in a semicircle and the teacher leading them through a series of opera-inspired gestures, facial expressions, and body movements; in another classroom, children had been making paper hats and paper masks resembling those worn by popular characters in the stories from operas; and in one instance, the dramatic play area in the classroom was a stage where children could act out stories from the operas using the materials they had made.

Other Instances of Local Funds of Knowledge

At The Play School in Goa, India, which was also described in Chapter 3, the preschool provided lunch to all its 3- to 5-year-olds, although some children opted to bring lunch from home. Demographically, the schoolchildren belonged to families who were predominantly of Christian, Muslim, and Hindu backgrounds, and who represented local Goans as well as foreigners and expatriates. This was a private school, and even though many of the families were affluent there were several middle-class families too. The children came from diverse linguistic backgrounds, with the most commonly spoken languages in that region being Konkani, Marathi, Hindi, and English. Although most of the teachers and staff in the school were native Konkani speakers, this private preschool used English as the language of instruction. Konkani was taught as one of the subjects or content areas, as is the case in many private schools across Asia. Elements of Goa's Portuguese Catholic history and heritage featured prominently in the school environment. The class lists of children's names posted on classroom bulletin boards reflected a majority of Goan names such as D'souza, Vaz, Fernandes, D'costa, D'counha, and Verghese. Diversity also emerged in the school lunches that served a mix of cuisines, encouraging everyone to try everything (duly considering allergies and religious practices of course). A sample weekly menu posted in the lunch area presented the following menus:

> Monday: spaghetti, sweet and sour vegetables, banana
> Tuesday: puri, potato *bhaji*, fruit salad
> Wednesday: rice, chicken Manchurian, *boondi ladoo*
> Thursday: noodles, mixed vegetables, papaya
> Friday: rice, cauliflower curry, cake and custard

Another school tradition that addressed diversity at the playschool, like many other schools in India, was the celebration of India's diverse festivals such as Ganesh Chaturthi (to celebrate the Hindu God Ganesh), Christmas (to celebrate the birth of Jesus Christ), and Carnival (which is celebrated before Lent). With regard to holidays, schools in India acknowledge all the holidays from all the major religious traditions found in the country, and most of these are national holidays: Hindu holidays such as Diwali, Dusshera, Holi, Durga Puja, Ganesh Chaturthi, and Janamashtami; Muslim holidays, such as Id; the Christian holidays of Christmas and Good Friday; the Jain holidays of Mahaveer Jayanti; the Sikh holiday of Gurpurab; and so forth. My visit to the school coincided with the recent celebrations of Gandhi Jayanti on October 2, which marks the birth anniversary of Mahatma Gandhi, widely revered in India as the Father of the Nation. The day also is a national holiday, and like all holidays it is is celebrated in schools all over India. A bulletin board near the front entrance of the school displayed a poster with photographs of Gandhi and one of his messages that read *Live simply that others may simply live.*

Concern about issues of local diversities within the early childhood classrooms was also visible in preschools in Singapore. At the Panda PCF the following lunch menu was posted in the lunch room:

Monday: Biscuits and barley
Tuesday: Soup—noodles, mee hoon, macaroni
Wednesday: Bread and Milo—kaya/jam/peanut butter/butter
Thursday: Cornflakes, noodles, mee hoon, dessert
Friday: Oats, green bean soup, red bean soup

Parental involvement was encouraged in this school, and a large bulletin board served to document some of the activities parents had conducted in the classrooms to share with the children. Several photographs of families demonstrating celebrations, cooking a dish, or making a project were displayed, and the following captions could be read on the photos:

Malay child Ilhan telling the story of "Nian"
Lee Meng's mother and Adrina's grandma explaining to the children the process
   of frying nian gao
"Come and get the ang bao"!
Parental involvement in card making
"Dong chiang, dong chiang"!

To explain some of these terms, *Nian gao* is a sticky rice cake, and the Chinese believe it is good luck to eat it during the Chinese New Year. *Ang bao* refers to the auspicious red envelope that is given to children as a monetary gift during Chinese New Year.

In the Maldives, students in one of the first grade classrooms at the Jay School seemed to have been working on tasks in small groups named Jellyfish, Octopus, Seahorse, Lobster, and Dolphin. These names are not at all out of place in the Maldivian classroom, as the Maldivian seas are known for their amazing coral reefs and feature some of the richest biodiversities in the world. Children growing up in the Maldives are intimately familiar with a diverse range of sea creatures that they may encounter frequently in their daily lives.

Locally found material was used extensively in the curriculum at Lotus School in Sri Lanka. A first grade classroom I visited contained wooden tables and chairs all painted a pinkish-red. The color coding was interesting, perhaps reflecting the universal gender color stereotype as this was a private girls' school. The tables were arranged in groups to facilitate group work, and six girls sat around each table. One teacher was leading the lesson, and all the girls had their notebooks out on the table in front of them. The girls appeared to be at ease as they did their work. On one bulletin board was a display of artwork done by the students. They had collected leaves from several varieties of locally growing flora and used them to make beautiful and creative collages of animals. The shape of each leaf was taken to be the base of their portraits as they used each leaf to represent the head, belly, ears, wings, or tails of some kind of animal or bird or insect. It was a creative project, and each was labeled with the name of the artist. A Nature Table for the younger children of the nursery class held a variety of objects that are typically found on tropical islands like Sri Lanka, such as coral pieces, a variety of shells, local flora, and a tree branch with intact weaver bird nests.

Other instances of project work as well as teacher-made and commercial posters in the classrooms reflected the use of both languages—English and Sinhala. In a kindergarten classroom at the Lotus School, an entire wall had been covered with colorful teacher-made alphabet charts depicting the letters of the Sinhala alphabet. Approximately 12 chart papers in green, blue, red, and yellow, each measuring about 2 feet by 3 feet, served as the background on which one letter of the alphabet was written boldly in the center. In each of the four corners of the chart paper was pasted another colorful sheet of paper on which the teacher had drawn and colored an object that started with that letter. Spread across the wall therefore were pictures and colorful drawings of items such as an earthenware water pot, a crow, a pair of scissors, a child's face, a mortar and pestle, water flowing out of a tap and into a bucket, a pumpkin-like orange squash, a pear, an earthworm, an open door, a trumpet, a green leaf attached to a green mango, a half moon, a girl dancing, a mushroom, a white swan on blue water, a tree, a comb, a Buddhist stupa, and many other images.

The Element of Design

The theme of design emerged during my observations in many of the early childhood settings I visited: Not only "design" as in artwork was in evidence but also there was an emphasis on "designing" an effective classroom environment. With respect to designing artwork, design and creativity in arts and craftwork were seen in the detailed and intricate drawings and patterns and the unusual projects that young children produced in various classrooms; in the narratives that accompanied children's artwork; and in the ideas that they voiced regarding a range of topics such as family, their country, their grandparents, or their environment. Several teacher-made and children-made classroom materials and activities enhanced mathematical thinking using the element of design such as activities like origami, calligraphy, and paper cutting as seen in Singaporean and Chinese classrooms, or drawing *rangoli* (patterns drawn on the floor and colored in with flower petals or colored powder) in some schools in India, especially during Diwali.

Design with regard to efficient classroom and school environments to facilitate transitions could be seen in several instances. The explicit classroom rules and routines at the Jasmine PCF in Singapore as teachers helped children create and illustrate classroom rules and displayed these rules on the walls appeared to streamline the daily flow of routines and help maintain hygiene in the classroom. The emphasis on design also surfaced in Kamalika School, the slum school in India. This school was constructed in the midst of an impoverished and densely populated urban neighborhood in India. But once inside its building, the filth of the outside gave way to colorful folk art painted on the walls along the school's staircases and hallways, and on the pillars of the verandah.

Design also appeared in the multiple shifts in all the schools in the Maldives. Due to a lack of space on the island of Malè, schools offer three to four shifts per day to ensure that all children can attend school. The school day had thus been designed to accommodate many more children than the space allowed for. Architectural design was a factor in the way first grade classrooms in the private Lotus School in Sri Lanka were placed: The classrooms were conceptualized as three-walled alcoves off of a hallway that was open to the outdoors. Each classroom was thus enclosed on three sides, but lacking a fourth wall, they were totally open to the outdoor light and temperatures. Sri Lanka is a tropical island and since it never gets too cold it made sense for classrooms to be open and to be ventilated by fresh air. The architectural design in The Play School in India was another case in point. The architecture of the school in this tropical coastal town supported an open plan, with no doors between classrooms and hallways. Rounded archways served as open doorways, and the lunch room was located on an open patio-like terrace.

Discussion

Pedagogy That Is Culturally Responsive

The emphasis placed on the creative arts and on teacher-made materials using local funds of knowledge was quite impressive, as was the absence of "commercial clutter" in the classrooms. The classroom environment in the Singapore classrooms certainly resembled the physical layout of most progressive classrooms seen in the United States. The space in the classrooms was taken up by learning centers such as a science center, a book area, an art center, a housekeeping center, and tables where children could work on manipulatives and other table toys. The Singapore classrooms also reflected multilingual work in the children's narratives and therefore stood in marked contrast to the mostly English narratives usually seen in early childhood classrooms in the United States. In the classroom observed in China, locally found materials dominated the environment, as did toys and games made by teachers and children. There were very few commercial charts and toys.

A Singapore kindergarten teacher emphasized teacher-made learning aids that were used extensively in her school:

We strongly believe in reusing materials and recycling. Initially the idea got started by our principal. She keeps things. She stores away boxes, bottles, paper and packaging materials. She would think about how she can use them in a different ways … more and more teachers experimented with reusing materials … we started to share with each other how to create teaching materials for our classrooms. Now most of our teaching resources are made from reusable materials such as Yakult bottles and potato chip canisters. When we invent new resources, we ask children for feedback too … we received the 2010 Outstanding Kindergarten Innovation Award for developing our own teaching-learning aids with built in self check devices so that children can be engaged in independent play and learn at their own pace. (Mrs. Chan, 2011, http://imagesofteaching.rdc.nie.edu.sg/)

The Dogwood Kindergarten in China encouraged the use of teacher-made materials and learning aids influenced by a curriculum that was grounded in traditional Chinese culture. Children's art and crafts reflected skills, objects, and ideas that were taken from age-old cultural customs and activities such as the art of paper cutting, the traditional and extensive use of fans and umbrellas, the blue and white pottery-influenced paper plates, and masks and weapons influenced by the Beijing Opera. Very few commercially made posters, toys, or games were noticed in the classroom. These images presented a definite contrast to many early childhood classrooms in which may be seen store-bought posters and charts that "teach" academic skills such as number and alphabet charts, maps, rhymes, and poems, and display photos and pictures on a variety of other topics. Even though such classrooms may place a strong emphasis on displaying children's work and their art, the teaching aids and classroom materials are mostly store bought. Use of store-bought learning materials in classrooms does not nurture teacher creativity. Moreover, when teachers are not encouraged to use their imagination to create materials for their classrooms, the full potential of their students' creativity and imagination is curtailed as well. Children learn from their teachers' attitudes to work and from the way teachers do things in the classrooms.

With regard to classroom materials and teaching strategies that incorporate local funds of knowledge and reflect children's cultural backgrounds, research has strongly established that the culturally responsive pedagogy approach situated within the larger paradigm of multicultural education is critical to addressing issues of diversity. Scholars, such as Gay (2002); Moll et al. (1992); Banks & Banks (2004); Irvine (1992, 2003); Grant & Sleeter (2007); Delpit (1995); Nieto (2009); Ladson-Billings (1994); Williams & De Gaetano (1984); Villegas & Lucas (2002), argue that classrooms need to reflect materials and pedagogies that resonate with the sociocultural backgrounds of the children in the classroom. Culturally responsive pedagogy essentially has three components: *organizational* or institutional, which reflects the administration and its values and policies; *personal*, which accounts for the emotional and cognitive processes that teachers must engage in to become culturally aware and responsive; and *instructional*, which represents the materials, activities, and strategies that form the basis of classroom instruction (Richards, Brown, & Forde, 2006). Although the practices described in this book touch upon all three components, this chapter most prominently dwells on the instructional component through its detailed descriptions of the classroom materials observed. But it is imperative to remember that for any educational system to address issues of diversity, the very ethos of the educational system needs to be culturally responsive—and that necessarily includes institutional policy as well as teachers' dispositions.

An additional consideration in this context is Singapore's Ministry of Education's revised Kindergarten Curriculum Framework (2013), which reflects a distinct Singaporean flavor that

> allows children to learn in an authentic context. The teaching and learning resources incorporate local topics, stories, fables, visuals, songs and dances so that children can learn about things and places around them, such as local food, celebrations of festivals and hawker centres. Not only will children be able to relate better to what they are learning, they will also learn about Singapore traditions and community values to help them build a strong sense of cultural identity. Through the use of local songs, dances and movement, children also strengthen their social and emotional, aesthetic, physical, and language and literacy development. (Accessed on 10/15/13 at www.moe. gov.sg/media/press/2013/08/moe-kindergartens-curriculum-features-distinct-singapore-flavour-and-flagship-programmes.php)

The Impact of Globalization

Globalization and internationalization have unfortunately also brought a new form of neocolonialism. The emergence of English as a global language is leading to linguistic imperialism. In addition, the compulsion to learn and teach English, as well as the compulsion to adopt a Western discourse of ECE, can be seen as forms of colonization leading to yielding control of local forms of knowledge production and research. The perception of English as a global/international language and its spread are very apparent in countries such as India, Sri Lanka, and the Maldives. Significant efforts are being made to promote the English language in education and teacher education. In large urban centers, small hill towns, rural villages, and along narrow roads through the vast countryside, hand-painted signs and commercial signboards frequently appear, as do fliers plastering alley walls, lamp posts, bus stands, and buildings that advertise private classes and tutoring agencies claiming to teach spoken English. The most striking occurrence in every city I visited in all three countries was the visible mushrooming of schools being described as international, world-class, or global, and there is a widespread push for teaching and learning the English language, particularly spoken English. English classes and the rapidly growing international schools are marketed as being necessary to level the playing field by preparing Asian children in the language and skills that dominate the global job market.

During my visit to the Iris School, another primary government school in Malè, I observed all six first grade classrooms in the afternoon shift. These classrooms are used for the eighth graders during the morning shift. All the classrooms looked similar in terms of themes being studied and activities being done. The first grade supervisor explained to me that this school had changed its mission statement recently and was now positioning itself as a world-class school. When I asked her what she meant by world class, she explained that it implied an extended school day, a single-shift system, providing meals to the children, and more activity-based teaching.

Painted on a wall along one particular stretch of an inner-city road in Pune, a city in central India, was a striking example of announcements and advertisements for new preschools combining modern with traditional, and English-language classes with contact phone numbers:

> Smiley Nursery: Modern concept with *Bhartiya Sanskriti*
> Kidz Kingdom: child enrichment center—Playgroup, Nursery, Mental Maths and Abacus classes
> Roots to Wings: Playgroup, Nursery, KG—Admission open
> Divine Child Nursery and Creche: Playgroup 1½ years and above, Nursery 2½ years and above—Rikshaw facility available
> Elite English Speaking Course: Personality development, Fluency development course

In Puducherry, a city in the south of India, similar examples were posted along city streets and in narrow alleys in a congested neighborhood:

Century Academy Primary School: Admissions open for Pre-KG to IV Std—Nurturing every child to flourish … through learning the right way.
PS Consultancy Services: English Language Development Program with "American/British Accent"
Achariya Bala Siksha Mandir: Indian School, International Schooling

The clearest articulation of current challenges with regard to the English language came from Sneha, an early childhood teacher educator and head of the early childhood department in her university in Sri Lanka. She expressed her dismay by saying:

> Now we are trying to introduce English medium to schools and they are going to introduce English teacher training and also we are training graduates in English medium. Now it's a new trend – English … it's a big problem now. All the graduate books are in English. After we came to universities we started reading English. Somehow we managed it in English. So we are not perfect

in English. … And teachers who teach in English medium, they are not fluent in English. So they teach all wrong things. … And the biggest problem is now because of the importance of English, parents want their children to be educated in English. International schools are like mushrooms, everywhere in Sri Lanka all cities, there are international schools. … So they are conducting classes in English medium and also they have their own curriculum, some have imported curriculums—British curriculums, Scotland curriculums. So they are teaching children about pounds, about berries.

Similar concerns about this neocolonial phenomenon of English being viewed as the global language and permeating Asian cultures were voiced by several other research participants who spoke about the desire of families to have their young children learn English. Yamini, the head of a policy-making institute for young children in Sri Lanka, spoke of the pressures and debates surrounding the language of instruction: "some thought that the preschool education should be in the mother language … still this dialogue is going on … and there is some research evidence in this also … we thought of introducing some other languages but this dialogue is still going on. But at the national level and my personal view is I think that these children, in 21st century and globally, need the communication language [implying English]."

Manju, an early childhood teacher educator in Sri Lanka, voiced her own concerns about this trend as she explained this push for teaching English in all grade levels, including preschools. Families, she said, viewed knowledge of the English language as a way to achieve social mobility in this global economy:

> That is I think people are over anxious about learning English and they are forcing their children to learn English. … Even for that how can you blame the parents for not knowing? They don't know what to do except for pushing the child to some crash course where if they don't pick up a few words then they [parents] think that the class is very bad. Then they put the child into another class. They always hunt [search] for a class which sort of brings an output [outcome] where the child speaks few more words than before. The dimensions on which people gauge the value of English is also a problem … about what do they want? Do they want their child to speak English? Or just to learn in English? I am not too sure. But I think if they [themselves] don't know English they want their child to learn English to penetrate the social strata.

She also pointed out that in view of the country's 30-year civil war that had just recently ended, the day-to-day realities in the country still seemed too harsh for the public to achieve reconciliation. As a result, there was a general desire to get out of Sri Lanka, and English would help people get a job in another country.

This perspective was supported by the growing presence of an apparent open market for private classes that offered to prepare a student to go abroad. A couple of examples were the *Australian Education Center* along the road to Galle, or the *Aspirations Education* in Colombo which promised to prepare students to fulfill their desire to study abroad in the United States, the UK, Australia, New Zealand, Malaysia, Singapore, or Canada. Other similar announcements and advertisements for English classes were rampant across several cities in most of the countries included in this study.

Although schools, particularly private schools, have been claiming to teach in English, a wider concern is that the teachers themselves do not know English well enough to be able to teach it. Thus English workshops for teachers are commonly being conducted. A three-day conference in Hyderabad, India, held in 2010 was sponsored by the British Council and the English and Foreign Languages University. The theme of the conference was *Starting, Stimulating, and Sustaining English Language Teacher Education and Development.* State sector trainers, teacher educators, and members of regional and international teacher associations participated in the program. The aim of the event was to provide an opportunity for English-language pre- and in-service teacher educators throughout South Asia to meet and share best practices and experiences in teaching the language. The conference was based on the rationale provided by the British Council according to which teacher educators need to be empowered and attain the necessary training and support to acquire the skills and strategies required to design, develop, and conduct quality teacher education programs.

According to a report in *The Hindu* (Empowering English Language Educators, November 2, 2010, available at www.thehindu.com/features/education/empowering-english-language-educators/article864927.ece and last accessed on 8/27/13):

> The conference will have discussions on themes that include developing English language primary teachers; teacher education in difficult and rural contexts; curriculum and materials development for teacher education; role of technology (radio, Edusat, mobiles, ICT) in teacher education; distance teacher education; continuous professional development (CPD) for teachers and teacher educators; and challenges of evolving and implementing English Language teacher education policy. ... British Council has offered several programs to step up the quality of English language learning in the country and abroad. The "Project English" initiative was launched in November 2007 with the aim of improving English language learning opportunities across the region. ... The council has been working with State governments to design and run large scale teacher training and curriculum development projects that are helping to improve English language teaching in State schools.

The influence of globalization was also quite evident in the curriculum of some schools. The study of a unit on Keith Haring's art in Singapore's Jasmine PCF classroom and the exploration of Jackson Pollock in India's Sonakshi School are a couple of examples. The art project in a 5's classroom at Jasmine PCF was an exploration of Keith Haring's work. The teacher had displayed several prints of Haring's work on a bulletin board, including works titled Radiant Baby, DJ, and other untitled works and murals. After studying the colorful and child-friendly prints through careful observation, the children were encouraged to make their own version of any print they selected to represent. In the second example observed in Sonakshi School, a large bulletin board in the hallway conspicuously displayed artwork done by the students that had been inspired by the techniques of Jackson Pollock. The large chart paper with colorful splashes of paint could very well have been a Pollock masterpiece! In yet another private school in India, the Oxford School, prints of artwork by Picasso and Chagall were displayed on the walls along one of hallways in the school. Alongside these prints were also displayed photographs of two of the masters of Indian classical music, Bhimsen Joshi (the famed Indian vocalist in the Hindustani classical tradition) and Bismillah Khan (known for playing the *shehnai*, an instrument of the oboe class). This certainly indicated that the arts, both local and global, were appreciated and valued by the administration and teachers, and they were openly exhibited as students and their families walked through the school corridors.

Although the currents of neocolonialism underlying globalization cannot be ignored, there is an additional idea to consider here. As is well understood and widely acknowledged, using materials and behaviors that reflect the local cultures and the backgrounds of the children adds a relevancy to the classroom curriculum that serves to facilitate children's learning experiences. Developmental and learning theory well support the premise that new knowledge is better learned and comprehended if it builds on children's prior experiences and knowledge base. Because urban classrooms of the 21st century happen to be situated in a highly globalized context and many are in large global cities, marked by easy access to information technology, children's experiences today include real and virtual interactions with sounds and images along both a local and global scale, and they grow up being exposed to many instances of "differences." It may not be unreasonable to infuse into the classroom some curricular materials and practices that may be culturally unfamiliar to children. This might not only further enrich the classroom curriculum but also provide an additional opportunity for children to share experiences with children around the world. Young children benefit from exposure to ethnic and cultural diversity (Genishi & Goodwin, 2007), and they need more than a one-time holiday celebration or a parent coming in to read a story at circle time to feel connected to people outside of their worlds (Grieshaber, 2008; Gonzalez-Mena, 2008). Adair & Bhaskaran (2010) describes a preschool classroom in the city of Bangalore in southern India in which traditional Indian practices like silent meditative sitting, the art of rangoli (creating designs on the floor using either flower petals or colored powder), and eating meals while seated on the floor were infused into the daily curriculum. Whereas Adair recognizes the importance of these customs in schools in India, she goes one step further to suggest that these practices might be appropriately included in the classroom curriculum of other countries such as the United States:

> Gradually engaging young children in new (to them) versions of everyday practices like eating can flex their global muscles and help them feel comfortable with difference. Young children do not necessarily need to remember that Diwali is an Indian festival to be more globally minded. The important point is for them to understand that people around the world eat, dress, invite guests to visit, and celebrate holidays (among other activities), but that in different places people do these things in different ways. The opportunity to experience a way of doing something that differs from what happens in their everyday lives at home will help children to respond positively to cultural and other differences they encounter later in life (Nieto, 2004, as cited in Adair & Bhaskaran, 2010, p. 54).

This lends support to the idea of designing a curriculum that is infused with globally diverse elements reflecting cultural ideas, people, and practices from around the world. The premise here then shifts from the perspective that new knowledge builds upon what children already know to the perspective that new knowledge can build upon the somewhat unfamiliar if approached within a spirit of meaningful exploration and discovery. This premise would support the teacher's decision to offer children the opportunity to learn and do something new in the classroom.

The juxtaposition observed of familiar and unfamiliar, of Western and local, of creative and academic, and of structured and unstructured with reference to pedagogy and curriculum in many classrooms across Asia is interesting. Although, on one hand, the focus on Western art and artists in a Singaporean preschool classroom seems an unfamiliar concept and one that is far removed from the local context experienced by Asian children on a daily basis, it does, on the other hand, seem to indicate a willingness and curiosity to know the "other." Bhabha (1994) speaks of the third space of cultural hybridity that occurs during postcolonial transactions when cultures with fluid boundaries come together, absorb elements and ideas from each other, and become transformed in some way. Within this space of cultural hybridity is the potential for the emergence of a pedagogical hybridity that may occur when diverse ideas on teaching and learning come together and produce a third kind of pedagogy that can be seen in teachers' classroom practices (Gupta, 2013).

In a globalized world, it is important to move away from an either/or approach. It is no longer sufficient to base a curriculum solely on the local, as aspects of a more connected and communicative world are already integrated into children's reality and daily lives. This is especially the case if they are being raised in metropolitan urban centers. It is also inappropriate for a school curriculum in Asia to be dominated by global discourses. Curricula designed and implemented in the West are based on the understanding of the development and lifestyles of young children growing up in the West. What gets overlooked at the local level is that most of the desired behaviors deemed "appropriate" in these curricula are those that are valued by the socially, racially, and linguistically privileged who most resemble the West. A "form of civilized oppression" is enacted when a particular set of beliefs about children gets imposed upon diverse cultural contexts in this manner (Viruru, 2005).

Pedagogical hybridity may be viewed as positive only if the practice stems from a desire to be open-minded to diversity. It becomes a concern, however, if it is propelled by educators' or parents' compulsion to have children possess a Western knowledge base. The colonized condition can certainly be found in early childhood classrooms when school quality in the non-West begins to be measured in terms of Western standards. There is a widespread perception in Asia that a good school is a global school—one that employs an early childhood pedagogy based on early childhood methods and materials as used in progressive classrooms of the West. Thus many in the emerging economies of the world feel compelled to use versions of Western curricula and teaching strategies so as to ensure that their children develop "appropriate" social and intellectual behaviors. Educators need to be aware of this trend and must exercise caution when designing classroom curriculum. A resolution is inspired by the third space of cultural hybridity that reflects the daily lifestyles of people currently living in global cities around the world, a lifestyle in which the local and the global are intertwined. A similar third space of teaching and learning may produce a hybrid curriculum and a pedagogical hybridity in the classroom that is created by a balanced two-way transaction between the local and the global. The early childhood education discourse needs to be reconceptualized to reflect this cultural and pedagogical hybridity.

6

PARTNERING FOR TEACHING AND LEARNING

Schools commonly partner with cultural organizations and museums to enhance the curriculum and learning experiences of students. In this chapter I highlight some uncommon and innovative partnerships observed in Singapore and India. These partnerships include (1) a technology collaboration between a primary school and a teacher education institute in Singapore that focuses on a project on action research using information and communication technology (ICT); (2) a web-based digital collaboration between several community preschools and a teacher education institute in Singapore to create a portal called *Images of Teaching*, which showcases early childhood classrooms by having teachers engage in self-reflection in their classroom practice and curricular decisions; and (3) a citywide media collaboration between schools and newspapers in India.

A Partnership for Information and Communication Technology in Singapore

Primary schools in Singapore start at the first grade level; this practice is unlike that in U.S. elementary schools which begin at the kindergarten level. Primary and secondary schools in Singapore are under the jurisdiction of the Ministry of Education, whereas programs for younger children are usually run by private or semiprivate agencies such as the People's Action Party Community Foundation (PCFs) and preschools. Since Grades 1 and 2 are technically included in the domain of early childhood education in the United States, it seems appropriate to include a description of this primary school partnership here. But first, it would be helpful to present more information on Singapore's Five-Year Plans that address the topic of ICT.

The Ministry of Education's Masterplans for Information and Communication Technology in Education drive the use of information technology in educational institutions in Singapore. The underlying philosophy of the Masterplans is that education should continually anticipate the needs of the future and prepare pupils to meet those needs. The essence of recent Masterplans for ICT in Singapore can be found on the Ministry of Education (MOE) website. Brief highlights for each Masterplan are as follows:

1997–2002: Providing the infrastructure in every classroom: LCD projectors, computers, wireless in schools.

"The first Masterplan for ICT in Education (1997–2002) laid a strong foundation for schools to harness ICT, particularly in the provision of basic ICT infrastructure and in equipping teachers with a basic level of ICT integration competency, which achieved a widespread acceptance for its use in education." (MOE website, 2011)

2003–2008: Promoting higher-order thinking skills through the use of ICT.

"The second Masterplan for ICT in Education (2003–2008) built on this foundation to strive for an effective and pervasive use of ICT in education by, for example, strengthening the integration of ICT into the curriculum, establishing baseline ICT standards for students, and seeding innovative use of ICT among schools." (MOE website, 2011)

2009–2014: Promoting collaborative and self-directed learners through the use of ICT.

"The Ministry of Education has developed the third Masterplan for ICT in Education (2009–2014). The third Masterplan represents a continuum of the vision of the first and second Masterplans i.e. to enrich and transform the learning environments of our students and equip them with the critical competencies and dispositions to succeed in a knowledge economy." (MOE website, 2011)

The training of teachers in ICT is woven through each step of the Masterplan, with the full support of the MOE.

The partnership described here as an example was developed between the Neon Primary School and a teacher education institute. The school and the teacher education institute are located at opposite ends of the island of Singapore, so distance was not a deterrent to the active institutional partnering that occurred. The partnership was established as a center that was named the Center for Educational Research and Application (CERA). When I visited the school, the principal, assistant principal, and head of technology were very welcoming and hospitable and presented a comprehensive PowerPoint to explain the concept of CERA. At the start of the partnership, a special room in the school was cleared and was designated as the CERA room. No extra help was hired to staff this center, but the availability of this room as a CERA office and designated space for the researchers to meet with and interview teachers and students was in itself an important step in the success of the program.

The Neon Primary School has developed a niche in innovation and ICT. According to the school's underlying philosophy, school learning is not confined to the classroom but can take place at any time and in any place. To facilitate this concept, mobile teaching and learning at this school occur through use of a range of hand-held devices, including pocket PCs, iPods, and mobile phones. The partnering teacher education institute website contains the following explanation: "students are allowed to engage in contextualized learning, making connections between the different spheres of their learning, between what happens in class to what happens outside the curriculum hours" (National Institute of Education press release, 2009).

Singapore's Five-Year Plan for 2015 includes a plan to strengthen the school curriculum around a framework of 21st-century competencies, such as global literacies and cross-cultural skills, and to move toward a more flexible and decentralized curriculum that would consist of a 70% nationally prescribed curricular component and a 30% school-based curricular component designed and developed by teachers in the schools. In the kindergarten framework, the MOE has consciously included the role of kindergarten teachers as being curriculum planners. The current problem facing the MOE is that in its teacher education programs teachers have not been trained to deal with the flexible part of the curriculum where they are expected to create, design, and develop classroom curriculum. Thus they now need intensive training in order to be able to plan and develop curriculum and position themselves as better informed and trained practitioners.

The Neon School's dynamic principal observed that the first step was to make teachers more informed and empowered and to equip them with the skills for curriculum planning and development. Thus CERA had been set up as a collaborative effort between the researchers at the teacher education institute and the teachers in this school to benefit all the participants who were involved. The primary aim of CERA is to make research more grounded in the field by locating and allowing the researchers to conduct research with the teachers at the school. At the same time, teachers at the school are guided during the research process to reflect on their pedagogy and curriculum, and to conduct action research in their own classrooms along with the researchers. The underlying intention is geared to helping primary school teachers translate cutting-edge research findings into meaningful classroom practices and subsequently deliver higher quality teaching and learning outcomes. The hope is that this will better prepare teachers with the skills needed to develop curricula more autonomously in keeping with the objectives of the current Five-Year Plan: "Through CERA, the school can better co-ordinate and promote research, innovative pedagogy and teachers' long term professional development. The coming together of classroom practitioners and educational researchers will develop critical insights into the use of educational technology and enable research to be closely aligned to real classroom practices" (NIE website press release, 2009).

Since CERA was first established, it has expanded as a primary school-based research center and has attracted other players. As of June 2012, Microsoft has joined the partnership at this primary school, resulting in the creation of Microsoft CERA, "a world-class centre of innovation in Singapore, where new technologies are harnessed for teaching and learning for educators locally and in the region … a platform that leverages Microsoft technology and expertise from the educational institutions to enhance the teaching and learning of the Chinese language beyond the four walls of the classroom."

Several Asian nations are leaders in technology and have been far ahead in technologies such as the cell phone for years, but they still have a long way to go with regard to developing and expanding primary education. CERA is a model that could be implemented in other countries in Asia, as well as in other parts of the world. Government educational initiatives for the use of technology in classrooms supported by a partnership between schools and teacher education colleges can go a long way toward bridging theory and practice.

A Partnership to Showcase Images of Reflective Teaching in Singapore

This section describes briefly a collaboration between a teacher education institute and local preschools in the form of web-based documentation of best classroom practices by local preschool teachers. According to two teacher educator advocates of preschool teaching at a Singapore teacher education institute, the work of preschool teachers is complex in its deliberations and planning of day-to-day classroom life. This work should be made known to the public in order to gain recognition for the hard work of preschool teachers, and to other early childhood educators who can reflect upon improving their own classroom practice. The project focuses on a total of 11 teachers, 4 Chinese-language speakers and 7 English-language speakers. All the teachers had been nominated for the Outstanding Kindergarten Teachers' Award organized by the MOE Preschool Branch. The primary sources of data for this qualitative study were in-depth interviews with each teacher, their written reflections and other email communications, and a collection of lesson plans. With selected video sections and interview data, the researchers coconstructed the *Images of Teaching* website with the teachers/principals so that the website would be publicly available for use in professional development sessions and whole-school conversations, as well as for sharing across schools (Lim & Lum, 2012).

The website shows "preschool teachers in action, and opens up the preschool classroom for all to see … who came on board with the desire to improve their craft … and were video-recorded in their classrooms" (Lim & Lum, 2013, p. 8). One of the primary aims of this project was to dispel the notions of best practices as they have been defined and conceptualized within the context of the discourse of early childhood education in the West. As the researchers of this project note: "As early career educator-researchers shaped by discourses that have originated from North America and other English-speaking nations, we were critical. Yet there were times when our Singaporean sensibilities made us pause and reflect on whether our critique was based on culturally relevant considerations" (Lim & Lum, 2012, p. 124).

The website features the videotapes of 11 preschool teachers' classroom practice, each accompanied by details of the context of the preschool, lesson plans, the teachers' reflections on their teaching, professional, and educational philosophies, explanation of their lessons and teaching activities captured on video, and general information about the children, all of which help the viewer contextualize the teacher's classroom decision making and practice. The following quotation by a teacher as she reflects on her classroom decision making illustrates reflective teaching:

> I realised we could use stamps as well. The stamps sold in Chinatown were so expensive but I wanted the children to have the feeling that after they finished the calligraphy, they can sign their work. Then I remembered seeing the soap seals when I visited the preschools in Hong Kong. My idea came from there. So I went to the supermarket to find those big, square and hard soaps. I brought one back to try first. My colleague used a saw to cut it into smaller parts. Then I tried engraving on it. For the engraving tool, initially I was thinking to use the satay stick, but was worried it was a bit too sharp and would break easily.

Another preschool teacher composes her teaching commentary by reflecting on the relationship she has observed between children's interest levels and the level of self-confidence they demonstrate in the classroom. During a lesson on the evolution of Chinese characters, one of the students was assigned to be the "teacher" and to indicate, by nodding her head, when the answers from her peers were correct. Having the little girl enact the role of teacher also gave her a sense of responsibility, thus deepening her attention and interest in the activity and increasing her self-confidence. The teacher's reflections draw on her classroom experiences as well as on her conceptual understanding of learning theories, thus connecting theory and practice in her work:

> Interest is very important. Once children are interested, they show more self-awareness, spontaneity and self-confidence in whatever they learn. If a child has self-confidence, he will take more initiative in whatever he does. We always say that interest is the best teacher. When children are interested in something, they will take the initiative to learn about it and they are willing to try even when met with difficulty. After trying, their confidence level will increase accordingly. The environment and adult instruction are

very important to children's learning too. Personally, I agree with Vygotsky's theory of "zone of proximal development." A teacher has to first understand the ability of children and then provide "scaffolding" based on the foundation of their current ability so that they can reach a higher level of ability. I support this point of view.

A segment in the summary report demonstrates how teachers can inform themselves and become more aware of the nature of their practice by reviewing their own videotapes. This summary is based on a teacher's unit about an introduction to Chinese culture through Chinese calligraphy. The instruction patterns noticed were:

- Large-group activity: The teacher introduces a Chinese painting with some Chinese characters and a stamp.
- Large-group activity: The teacher introduces the rice paper, ink, and brush; she demonstrates how to write with the brush.
- Individual activity (20 min): The creation of a Chinese character using the brush and ink.
- Large-group closure and some individual students to share their work.

Video clips focused on teachers' instruction of learning experiences, accompanied with their detailed reflective narratives regarding the decisions made during the course of their teaching every day, provide mirrors not only to the teachers themselves for self-evaluation but also to other teachers to learn about the intricacies of diverse classrooms.

In summary, "The Images of Teaching is but one avenue in which we can contribute towards an internationally polyphonic texture in the discourses of early childhood education" (Lim & Lum, 2012, p. 125). The authors see the need for continued public postcolonial critique and reconceptualisations of early childhood education so that practitioners with local problems and homegrown solutions need not be marginalised in the international academic discourse. Such a collaboration between early childhood teachers and teacher educators is an invaluable teaching resource for both local and global audiences. The important point is not to view the showcased instances of early childhood teaching as final best practices, but rather to consider them as mirrors into which other educators can peer to reflect on their own beliefs and practices, with the intention of being open-minded, and to strive for broadening their understanding of early childhood teaching and learning theories.

Currently in the United States, teacher certification requirements have been revised to include an Education Teacher Performance Assessment (edTPA) in which teachers and teacher candidates have to proceed in a manner similar to the above study: planning. They need to implement a learning segment of three to five experiences, videotaping their instruction, assessing children's learning, and writing a detailed commentary that reflects on the curricular decisions they made during this process. If colleges of education collaborated with schools to create a showcase like *Images of Teaching*, then teacher candidates and students of education would be more confident and better prepared to create and submit their own edTPAs.

A Partnership between Local Media and Schools in India

The media in India has had an interesting influence on education for decades. One illustration is provided by the role that leading newspapers play in the life of schools in New Delhi. Everyday activities and events in both private and public schools are covered by newspapers and reported in a special section on schools and education. The reporting covers a range of events such as interschool and intraschool academic quizzes and competitions on debates; athletic and sporting events; creative activities within the arts such as painting and drawing, music and dance performances; and so forth. Other education-related news, such as exchange programs, conferences, workshops, and seminars for teachers, are also reported on a regular basis.

One specific example is the PACE program, which is an initiative of the Newspaper in Education Department of a leading daily. PACE, or Partnerships for Action in Education, is spread out across four cities in India, and its aim is to provide curriculum support; conduct exclusive interactive sessions for students, principals, and teachers; and organize numerous events such as interschool competitions and contests that focus not only on academics but also on the arts, sports, and other fun-filled activities. What is striking is that news about schools and schoolchildren gets reported on a regular basis in widely read leading dailies and is not confined to any particular publication that is designated for only educational news. The events thus reach a wider audience, and there is a greater and deeper awareness that everyone has about school happenings: the public, educators, families, and children in school, teachers, and other educators.

The following excerpts are from popular newspaper dailies published between 2005 and 2013, and the reports highlight school activities in New Delhi (the names of schools and of students have been kept anonymous). Two points are of interest: First, schools as well as students compete with each other in all kinds of competitions, both academic and nonacademic; and second, a postcolonial hybridity is present in the school curriculum and in school activities in general as Western and Indian elements become closely integrated (Gupta, 2006/2013):

> XY School held its annual function. The students presented a variety cultural program that included the saga of *Rani Lakshmi Bai* [a historical warrior queen], elements of nature, living heritage, a dance drama on "composite culture" and fusion dances. Scholarships were awarded by the school director and founder principal. (*The Times of India*, Education Times, January 17, 2005)

MN School … held its annual day with the theme Unity in Diversity. … The programme started with an invocation to Lord *Ganesha*. All 12 names of the god were depicted through dance. The school orchestra performed to a rapt audience with *sitar*, guitar, *tabla*, flute, *mridangam*, banjo, and other instruments. The school song *yeh desh mera jaage* [may this country of mine awake] reflected the spirit of patriotism. The highlight of the day was a play "I am the people" based on Carl Sandburg's poem by the same name. (*HT School Times*, January 17, 2005)

The students of NA School displayed excellent oratory skills by winning both senior and junior trophies in the Interschool Debate Competition. … In the Junior category, surfacing their thoughts on the topic "Information Technology is necessary in School Education," SG and CG bagged 1st and 2nd Best Speaker prizes respectively. (*HT School Times*, January 17, 2005)

Students of EF School participated in the Science Symposium and Computer talent hunt at Vishwa Expo 2004. Over 20 schools of Delhi … participated in the various events … S. and A. of EF School brought laurels to the school by winning the first prize in the junior science project display on "winter harvesting." (*HT School Times*, January 17, 2005)

B School organized a cultural extravaganza. … The students staged a play "*Ram- kal aaj aur kal.*" Other acts included *Bharatnatyam, Kathak* (both Indian classical dances), Yoga at Gurukul, and a fusion of yoga and ballet projecting the question '*Kahan hai aaj ka Ram.*' The programme concluded with a Bhangra performance. (*The Times of India,* Education Times, January 9, 2006)

ABCD Public School celebrated its 50th annual sports day. … Vice Chief of the Air Staff gave away prizes to the students for excellence in sports at the Zonal, State and National level during the year. School principal highlighted the sports achievements of the school. 2200 students participated in various events like athletics, aerobics, mass physical display, and a skating presentation. (*The Times of India*, Education Times, January 9, 2006)

The students of H School presented a colorful, soul-stirring show, Music of Skies. The spirit of monsoon was celebrated in different dances and songs. … A comedy play with the serious message of water conservation was appreciated by all. (*The Times of India*, Education Times, July 14, 2008)

GS, a student of RR Public School, participated in the Violin *arangetram* (recital) organized by Delhi Tamil Sangam. GS has been learning to play the strings since he was 11 years old under the tutelage of Guru KVSKC, preeminent violin virtuoso. (*The Indian Express,* July 24, 2013)

An inter-house English debate competition was held in MG Public School. The topic for the junior category was "Should junk food be banned in schools" while the seniors debated on "Should careers be based on academics or interest-areas?" SG of Gandhi House and ST of Nehru House stood first and second respectively in the junior category. CJ of Bose House and AS of Nehru House won the first and second place respectively in the senior category. (*The Times of India,* July 29, 2013)

ST and SA of U School for Girls bagged the second position in the All India NSE Young Pioneers contest conducted across 500 schools. The competition that aimed at generating innovative business was judged by an esteemed panel of judges. (*The Times of India,* July 29, 2013)

RIG School participated in the World Scholars Cup held at Dubai. More than 33 countries comprising 1600 scholars participated in the event. NA stood third in the collaborative writing among juniors, KA bagged the gold medal in the debate showcase (junior category). (*The Times of India,* July 15, 2013)

The Eco Club of BVB School celebrated *Vanmahotsav* (forest festival). It was inaugurated by a tree plantation drive on the school premises. … A poster making competition and slogan writing competition were organized in the school on the topic "Make the earth green." The *Vanmahotsav* concluded with a prize distribution ceremony. (*The Indian Express,* July 29, 2013)

To commemorate World Population day PPI School initiated a campaign to sensitize the youth about the urgency and importance of population issues. … like those of extreme climatic change due to global warming and its repercussions on human life. (*Hindustan Times,* July 29, 2013)

These reports on competitions that are both academic and nonacademic are read widely by the general public, and there is an attempt to promote healthy competition in all aspects of a child's education at all grade levels. Interestingly, in the United States interschool meets are often held but focus on sporting and athletic events. The most well-known publicly broadcast "academic" events are the National Spelling Bee Championships, in which children of Indian families excel (Lipman, 2013) judging from the winners of the Scripps National Spelling Bee Championships for the last six years who have all been students of Indian origin (www.spellingbee.com/champions-and-their-winning-words). These contests, however, stir up plenty of controversy within the United States and are viewed by its critics as being unhealthy for children.

Discussion

Two issues might be of concern with regard to the open competition and report-ing of school events by the media, as well as with regard to showcasing teaching practices. The first touches on privacy and confidentiality, but does not seem to be a problem to many in Asia. Private space and public space are not as rigidly established in many Asian worldviews as it is in the Euro-American. For instance, there is a greater tendency to open up one's home and heart to strangers in India, whereas to do so in the United States prompts greater wariness and reluctance. In the United States children are raised to be cautious of strangers, whereas in India and many other Asian countries children are raised to be polite and respectful of strangers, and to warmly and enthusiastically welcome all who visit their home and treat them as honored guests. In Indian philosophy the Sanskrit phrase *atithih devo bhavah* means a guest is like god and should be accorded the same respect and honor. It is a fundamental spiritual idea that is taken seriously by Indians across ethnic, religious and socioeconomic divides. A similar sentiment applies to teach-ers as they open up their classrooms to visitors. Asian teachers may be more will-ing than Euro-American teachers to be observed while instructing and teaching.

The second issue is the sense of exclusivity that results from competitions and competitiveness, and how that sense impacts children's self-confidence and self-esteem. A public announcement of the results of school competitions does pitch school against school and children against children on a regular basis. In a similar way, teachers also feel the stress of competition when the pedagogy of some is recognized and showcased for others to view. The question is whether this kind of competition that motivates individuals to constantly do their best and keep raising the bar for themselves is viewed as healthy or whether it is viewed as a stressful experience detri-mental to their self-esteem and results in discouragement and depression. These two perspectives may be couched in two different worldviews. In their study, Li and Wang (2004) provide a lucid description of the contrasting views of Chinese and American children toward their peers. According to Li & Wang (2004, p. 419):

> Chinese children are often encouraged to focus on others' strengths rather than weaknesses, which is intended to promote constant learning from oth-ers. Children are socialized to remain humble toward those who achieve and be helpful to those who do not ... 73% Chinese students expressed respect, admiration, and appreciation toward those who achieved well. ... In contrast, US children would perceive more negative reactions to their achieving peers.

Studies have evidenced a correlation between increased competition and higher educational quality and modestly higher educational outcomes (Belfield & Levin, 2002). Certainly, this discussion is not about advocating for more stress or competition in children's lives, but rather about attempting to contextualize and understand why and how students in many developing countries are able to demonstrate high learning outcomes despite being in classrooms with very large numbers and relatively few resources. At the same time, it is also relevant to keep in mind that work habits and attitudes form early in life.

Recent research findings on why some individuals perform better under stress than others indicate that several factors are responsible, including social-cultural experiences, parenting modes, genetics, and the nature of the stress (Bronson & Merryman, 2013a). The thrust of this argument is that the individual has more control in handling stress than was previously thought, and it is the presence of short-term stress that provides an antidote to stress anxiety rather than its absence. The authors of this book provide scientific support for their argument. Jeremy Jamieson, a social psychologist at the University of Rochester, found that the performance of people who were told stress is negative declined, whereas people who were told being anxious is good felt more energized, had a higher blood flow and higher levels of oxygenation, and turned in a better performance. Rena Subotnik, a psychologist at the American Psychological Association, notes that scholastic competitions can raise the social status of academic work as well as that of the contestants.

> Competitions like these are certainly not without stress, but the pressure comes in predictable ebbs and flows, broken up by moments of fun and excitement. Maybe the best thing about academic competitions is that they benefit both Warriors and Worriers equally. The Warriors get the thrilling intensity their minds are suited for, where they can shine. The Worriers get the gradual stress inoculation they need, so that one day they can do more than just tolerate stress—they can embrace it. And through the cycle of preparation, performance and recovery, what they learn becomes ingrained. (Bronson & Merryman, 2013b)

Related studies point to other benefits that can accompany some levels of stress associated with events such as test taking, interviewing for a job, and competing against others. Mark Seery's research is based on the premise that some degree of cumulative adversity is associated with optimal well-being (Seery, 2011; Seery et al., 2010). His most recent study directly tested the relationship between the history of adversity and resilience to stressors. Findings indicated that "relative to a history of either no adversity or non-extreme high adversity, a moderate number of adverse life events was associated with less negative responses to pain and more positive psychophysiological responses while taking a test. These results provide novel evidence in support of adversity-derived propensity for resilience that generalizes across stressors" (Seery et al., 2013, abstract).

Dienstbier & Zillig (2012) write on the concept of toughness and provide a physiological explanation of the relationship between toughness theory and the neuro-endocrine systems that promote tough experiences in helping to develop resilience and the ability to pick oneself up again. According to these authors, toughness appears to be a promising concept as it helps to explain how psychological and somatic processes interact to produce positive outcomes.

It thus seems that low degrees of age-appropriate failure within a competitive environment would actually help children perform better in the long run. However, there is a caveat: The outcome will be positive only if failure is *not* seen as an indication of low intelligence and incompetence but in fact only indicates that the individual has to work harder to reach those goals. The study by Autin & Croizet (2012) was conducted with 111 sixth graders who were presented with academic tasks. They found that when they reframed the notion for the students, showing that the concept of difficulty was not an indication of intellectual limitation or inability, the students demonstrated cognitive gains:

> We also found that these cognitive gains were especially observed when the cognitive demand of the task was high, that is, when difficulty was at its maximum. … This study also indicated that re-framing difficulty was more beneficial for cognitive performance than a prior experience of success … and children's academic level, gender, and socioeconomic background did not moderate the gains in cognitive performance across the three studies. (Autin & Croizet, 2012, p. 615)

Similarly, the work of Carol Dweck supports the fact that students who thrive are not necessarily the ones who have the highest scores but the ones who love what they're doing and work hard at it. Dweck's study with fifth graders revealed that children performed better when praised for their effort as compared to when praised for their "smartness" or intelligence. In other words, people did better when they believed they could control their behaviors and were responsible for outcomes. Dweck refers to two kinds of mindsets—fixed and growth—which begin to form in childhood (Dweck, 2007). People with a fixed mindset fear failure and view challenges as negative experiences. People with the growth mindset regard failure as an opportunity to learn from it and continually improve themselves. A culture that highlights competition but also views challenge as an opportunity to grow further will nurture children who are confident and successful.

Two points should be made with regard to this research. In Asian countries such as India and China, the large populations create a culture that is overcrowded and intensely competitive. At the same time, in these societies the perception of failure is linked to the individual not working hard enough rather than to a lower level of intellect or intelligence. Most people believe that children will succeed if they work hard enough. In Western societies, on the other hand, achievement is mostly equated with intelligence and competence.

In populous societies such as India and China, large numbers and overcrowding necessarily lead to fierce competition for the few available resources and opportunities at every level—in classrooms, schools, colleges, job markets, and even within families. The educational environment in dense urban centers is high-pressured and competitive, characterized by high academic standards, high-stakes assessment, and tremendous pressure on students and teachers to produce results. The basic nature of Asian education systems has long been exam-oriented and based on rote memorization of prescribed textbooks. This high-pressure environment is not ideal, but in Asia it reflects the reality of people's professional, social, educational, and personal worlds. People in underresourced and densely populated regions, therefore, must develop a set of specific skills and competitive attitudes that will allow them to not only survive but also succeed. Because things don't come easily, the general public aspires to what they don't have, as a result of which students become more competitive and hardworking, and families more determined to support their children's success in schools. Unfortunately, this has also led to the exclusion of many children who are unable to compete for various reasons.

In Euro-American societies, with much smaller populations and stronger economies, the public has more access to basic resources and more institutional support. Lower population numbers support smaller class sizes, and provide easier access to public schools and colleges. Smaller class sizes in the United States have led to a *relatively* higher rate of inclusion and lower competition between American students for college and career opportunities. In the current world order, where people are globally connected by the Internet and telecommunication, American students are for the first time experiencing direct and instant competition from students and graduates of other countries.

With regard to the media, the role that it plays in schooling and education takes very different forms in countries such as India and the United States, for example. In the highly competitive educational environment in Indian cities such as New Delhi, not only are students competing with each other but schools are competing with each other as families seek out the best schools for their children. Schoolchildren compete with each other not only academically but in frequent interschool competitions in the areas of art, dance, music, debate, declamation, sports, science, poetry, athletics, drama, chess, and so forth. All these events are covered and highlighted by the media: They are reported in the national dailies on a weekly basis and are read by millions of readers, whereby education and schooling necessarily become very much everybody's business. This seems to bestow a priority and value on what is going on in children's educational lives at the level of community involvement far beyond the usual parental involvement one sees in schools in the United States. U.S. newspapers have educational sections, but these include general reports on topics such as the state of education and educational institutions, current educational policies, political viewpoints on educational issues, and so forth. Actual school experiences of children and school activities in local schools are usually reported in school newsletters or local educational publications that are not read by the general public, or as occasional articles in newspapers. Further, the interschool meets and competitions focus mostly on sporting and athletic events; thus, a healthy competition in physical activities is seen as acceptable but not in other areas of learning.

The open competition and recognition of accomplishments in many parts of Asia is a societywide phenomenon that puts pressure on schools to maintain their standards, encourages children to participate, and sends students the message that the whole community is interested in what they are doing. *The Economist* reports that according to Andreas Schleicher, who runs the Programme for International Student Assessment (PISA), the one thing that high-performing nations like Finland and South Korea have is a "high level of ambition for students and a strong sense of accountability" (PISA envy, *The Economist*, 2013). In this way, the larger national culture has more to do with how well students perform than does the specific structure of an educational system. From that perspective, the public reporting of school events and students' accomplishments, and the showcasing of selected teaching practices as described above, contributes to a larger social culture that is interested in and supports children's educational achievements, both academic and nonacademic.

The three partnerships highlighted in this chapter represent the building of concrete bridges between teacher education and the three sectors critical for the improvement of education and teacher education: technology, media, and community schools.

7
CURRENT THEMES IN TEACHER EDUCATION

As discussed in Chapters 1 and 2, the work of world governments, private sectors, and nongovernmental organizations (NGOs) since the early 1990s with regard to the field of primary education has been impacted by the widespread ratification of the Convention on the Rights of the Child (CRC) and Education for All (EFA). Much attention has been given to the development and expansion of pre-primary and primary schools to ensure access to schooling for all children. Thereafter, the quality of education provided also came under scrutiny, and recent revisions to policy documents reveal greater emphasis on "quality" early childhood education to incorporate more play and child-centered experiences. Nation governments in Asia are denouncing test-based and teacher-directed academic learning in pre-primary and primary schools, while urging a more child-centered pedagogy. This mindset in turn has created another critical need: the appropriate preparation and education of early childhood teachers who will be qualified and adequately prepared to adopt the new pedagogy that is being urged. Thus far, all teacher preparation in most of Asia has followed a traditional, teacher-directed, content-based teaching approach.

Because pre-primary education in most Asian countries has not been in the purview of the governments, there has been no formal pre-primary teacher education degree program that is affiliated to a university. With the current global emphasis on early childhood education as an independent field, Asian governments and policy makers now widely recognize the need for universities to offer "high-quality" pre-primary or early childhood teacher education degree programs, as opposed to the currently available diploma and certificate programs that are offered mostly by nonuniversity-affiliated institutions. This is a distinct shift from the earlier thinking that teaching young children did not require teachers to be professionally qualified in university degree programs. Therefore, the need for a nationally organized and professional field of pre-primary or early childhood education has now become a high priority for nation governments and international organizations. Ministries in Asia are scrambling to launch formal degree programs at the undergraduate and graduate levels to prepare teachers professionally and appropriately in "best practices" within the field of early childhood education. In the interim, and until such degree programs are ready, the training of early childhood teachers continues to be taken up by three different sectors: nondegree programs offered by government, private bodies, or NGOs. Sneha, an early childhood teacher educator in Sri Lanka, explained that "now in Sri Lanka preschool education is not handled by the central ministry so different people run their preschools. They are run by NGOs, different people, there are international schools. They run their own schools and preschools." Additionally, distance education teacher training programs exist on a massive scale, especially in India, Sri Lanka, and the Maldives, where the primary goal is to reach teacher candidates in remote areas of these countries. The heads of the early childhood departments in the open universities in these three countries described their distance education programs as being highly organized and carefully planned programs based on a large network of professionals and schools.

In many instances, the quality of the diploma-awarding programs is substandard, outdated, and not recognized by the government agencies that evaluate schools. Schools thus hesitate to hire teachers credentialed by such programs. Aruna, a private school principal in India, explained the dire need for teacher training but lamented that there were no institutions to depend on except "private companies, private agencies, and not all of them are very authentic. There is a lot that is available, but what is really authentic, not so commercially driven, one might not even mind paying for it. It should be good quality."

This chapter does not seek to provide detailed descriptions of the current systems of teacher education in India, China, Singapore, Sri Lanka, and the Maldives as that is not in the scope of this book. Rather, this chapter will present the reader with the voices of teacher educators, policy makers, and school administrators from diverse groups concerned with early education. These voices illustrate some of the concerns, questions, and challenges that lie at the heart of the current debates surrounding early childhood teacher education in Asia and as experienced by the participants.

The main findings that emerged during the course of this study specifically with regard to teacher education are as follows:

- A dissonance exists between preparation and practice which echo similar findings in the author's earlier study (Gupta, 2006/2013): Teachers seldom implemented the pedagogies they had learned in their teacher education programs, which had been largely informed by Western theories of learning and development.
- A dissonance also exists between the child-centered pedagogies urged by the new and revised educational policies and the ways in which teachers are still being prepared in teacher education programs in traditional teacher-directed methods.

- There is an acute shortage of teacher educators who themselves are skilled in these new pedagogies that are being called into play in early childhood education.
- Teachers are not prepared in culturally responsive pedagogy and are not ready to address issues of diversity that are increasingly emerging in integrated classrooms.
- It is widely believed that good teaching depends heavily on affective qualities and a teacher's dispositions and attitudes, such as commitment and dedication, none of which can be taught in certification programs or evaluated by certification tests.
- Colonial influences on notions of child development, pedagogy, and curriculum continue to impact the field in formerly colonized nations.
- A great deal of interest has arisen in professionalizing the teaching profession.
- There is an acute paucity of qualitative research in early childhood education conducted at the local level and disseminated in local and global forums.

Current Concerns and Challenges in Teacher Education: Voices from the Field

Government Efforts

Sarva Shiksha Abhyan (SSA) is the government's largest program for the universalization of education from grades 1 through 8 for children 6 to 14 years of age. SSA began in 2001, and its framework was revised in 2011. The SSA has four major roles: increasing access to education; increasing enrollment across social groups; promoting retention of students; and ensuring quality of education. Part of the last goal is to ensure teacher quality. Selina, an early childhood consultant working with SSA, described how this goal was being approached:

> For example, teacher training is a big one [goal]. Like, almost all government teachers are required to go on up to 20 days of in-service training a year, under this program. That is one major component. Then things like trying to revise the curriculum, especially in light of the national curriculum framework of 2005. So we are trying to revise the curriculum in tune with that. And then we are also looking at teacher learning materials that are available in the classroom; the learning process; obviously serious learning outcomes … to make sure that improves. So our role is; we are a team of consultants; a link between the ministry and the implementation of this program. So we are the ones to build the capacity. We do training programs, orientations to expose them to good resources, and also monitor the progress against the targets, appraise their budgets and annual plans, things like that.

She went on to describe how this large-scale training was being planned, managed, and implemented across the country to reach all teachers:

> Usually, within a state, there is a cascade model. There will be a core group of master trainers at the state level. These master trainers will then train trainers at the district level. Then [there is] another round at the block level. Those block-level persons will then train teachers regularly. Usually, at the state level there would be professors, faculty, and resource persons from outside, things like that. At the district level there are these institutions called DIETS (District Institute for Education and Training). And at the block level ... Block Resource Centers (BRCs) and Cluster Resource Centers (CRCs). So every block has resource centers that provide academic support to teachers. Each BRC reaches out to about 20–30 schools and each CRC [has] about 15 schools. So they are the ones that do training and give on-site support.

Selina also explained that the funding for this mammoth process came not only from the Indian government but also from bodies such as UNICEF, the World Bank and the European Commission.

School Administrators

One set of administrative voices emerged from within the context of the Kendriya Vidyalayas (KV) or Central Schools, which are a system of schools in India attended primarily by the children of government employees who undergo frequent job transfers and postings across the country. These schools provide a stable and consistent educational system for the children who move from city to city with their families. The KVs are not private schools, but at the same time they do not quite belong in the category of government schools either. Most KVs start with Grade 1, although some KV schools are now beginning to offer kindergarten for children 4 to 5 years of age. The pre-primary curriculum that had been implemented across the KVs included the Common Minimum Program (CMP), a curriculum that had been developed and prescribed for primary grades in all KV schools and addressed the teaching of minimum competencies. The published CMP book presented the prescribed curriculum to the pre-primary teachers in the form of a collection of poems, stories, fables, historical tales, science lessons in both English and Hindi, accompanied with questions and activities. This bilingual approach did not present every story or poem in both languages simultaneously; rather, some of the content was in English and some was in Hindi, in no particular order or pattern. Teachers and children were expected to go back and forth between English and Hindi throughout the instruction and learning experiences.

At a 2010 principals' meeting in a KV site in New Delhi, I met with a focus group of 12 principals (including 5 women) from KVs in various cities across

India, including Hyderabad, Ahmedabad, Bokaro, Garwa (Jharkhand), Dehradun, Patiala, Ambala, Pathankot, and Jammu. The hosting principal had arranged for us to meet around a conference table over tea, biscuits, and savory snacks to discuss issues concerning pre-primary and primary education and teacher education. During the course of our conversations, the principals shared their perceptions on the roles and preparation of early childhood or pre-primary teachers in their schools. They were forthcoming with information, enthusiastic about answering, and demonstrated a deep understanding of teacher education and the most urgent needs facing pre-primary teacher education.

With regard to the basic qualifications for pre-primary and primary teachers, they unanimously agreed that the early grades represented the most important level of education because, as one principal stated, "it is class 1[grade 1] where a nation is made." Another principal shared his belief that "teachers are by choice and by chance," implying that some of the preferred qualities teachers should possess were inherent in the teacher's personality and character. With reference to the qualities this group of principals considered most important for teachers of young children, they mentioned the following: having communication skills, displaying the ability to handle children, being creative, understanding that young children are self-centric, believing that education happened outside the classroom as well, not curbing a child's play, and possessing a teaching attitude whereby the "teacher should not say no but must provide options."

One of the principals reflected on what young children should be learning in school: to be self-sufficient, to learn the dignity of labor and to do things by hand, to be prepared for formal learning, and to learn values. The importance of this last point seemed to resonate with all of them since, as one of them observed: "ECE is the most impressionable age and what is learned then has a long-lasting effect." They proceeded to qualify the values they considered important and named, among other qualities, honesty, sharing, cooperation, selflessness, and personal hygiene. In response to my question about what needed to be different in the existing models of teacher education, the principals collectively came up with a wish-list for reconceptualizing teacher training. Their general concern was that the teaching profession did not draw good teachers since the best candidates entered programs for professions that paid higher salaries. According to one principal, attitudes to teaching could not be changed, but they could be modified a little. Some mentioned that Sri Aurobindo had addressed the issue of primary teacher training extensively and that much could be learned from his ideas. Sri Aurobindo was a prominent spiritual leader and philosopher in India based in Puducherry. His educational philosophy formed the basis for the school that was founded in his ashram in Puducherry. Briefly, he urged that

> the aim of education should be to help every individual child to develop his own intellectual, aesthetic, emotional, moral, spiritual being and his communal life and impulses out of his own temperament and capacities. ... In a true

education, one should not regard the child as an object to be handled and molded by the teacher according to the conventional ideas or the individual interests and ideals of the teachers and parents. (Mukherjee, 2008, p. 12)

The Central School Society (KV Sangathan) has taken several steps toward drafting a primary education pedagogy, but the challenge the Society faced was how to translate this pedagogical theory into actual practice in every classroom. Here emerged the age-old and universal conundrum: the sense of dissonance between the theory of teacher training and the actual teaching practices in classrooms (Gupta, 2013).

Aruna, the principal of an elite private school in India, expressed her own concerns about the current teacher training situation and the unsatisfactory way teachers were being prepared:

> Education has a very dynamic character here in India. It is changing. A lot is happening and because of that the need for teacher education has been felt greatly. We all know that teachers have to be trained; there needs to be in-house training, enrichment programs.

One of the biggest needs, she said, was to prepare teachers in qualitative assessment techniques and tools because, as she explained,

> Assessment is becoming very broad based in which we are looking at assessing life skills … assessing values; nobody ever thought about how to assess that. Even now we are thinking how to assess values. It's a big problem, and how do we grade values. Plus the role of co-scholastics; music, dance, all that was there in schools and we were grading our children but there was no accountability for that. Now it has repercussions on their careers, so now we have to revamp that too.

Part of her concern was the challenge of the *privatization of teacher training,* with centers mushrooming everywhere: "But you know a dangerous trend that has started is that, the moment a need for something is realized and felt, immediately people want to cash in on it. So what is happening now is that everybody finds that there is a fast buck to make in it." This sentiment was echoed by Saha, the head of the education department at an established university in India, who observed that education has shifted from being a philanthropic enterprise to a service that charges and people pay for, "and by way of market intervention anyone who is able to invest can provide education." He emphasized this growth in privatization by explaining how, through a complex process of networking and collaboration, market intervention was also spreading to towns and villages across rural India. In China as well, the privatization of educational institutions, especially schools, has become a significant trend. The number of private early childhood services jumped from 40% to 60% between 2001 and 2007 (Liu, 2010a, as cited in Zhou, 2011). Gu (2006) notes that the number of private kindergartens in China doubled between 1994 and 1999. He also observed that some private educational institutions may offer better quality educational experiences with regard to lower teacher–child ratios, higher autonomy and flexibility in curriculum, higher income for teachers, and more classroom learning materials for children (Gu, 2006). At the same time, there is "evidence of profiteering in running kindergartens, charging improper fees, concealing and pocketing funds, and infringing on children's and staff's rights and interests" (Gu, 2006, p. 34).

Teacher Educators and Policy Makers in India

At a citywide seminar in New Delhi on *Preparing the Early Childhood Professional for the Needs of 21st Century India,* several early childhood teachers, teacher educators, and policy makers from numerous educational institutions and universities presented their views on current issues regarding early childhood education and teacher education. Among their concerns were the age that children should start school, the challenges of teaching in slum-area schools, the use of technology in the education of young children, and the need to train teachers to be culturally responsive.

With regard to the school starting age of young children, a professor and head of a college department on development and childhood studies questioned why pre-primary education and nursery schools were needed in the first place. The context for her question was the fabric of Indian society which is characterized by extended family and joint family systems. In her view, instead of being sent to nursery schools, children under the age of 5 should be allowed to experience the nurturing available to them within the home environment by their family members. Related to this issue was a critical question posed by a professor and head of an early childhood department at another university which invoked the politics of educational decisions. She asked whose decision it was to set an entering age for primary school when there was no arbitrary entering age for either middle school or high school, and no age set for when children must leave school.

Teaching within the constraints of slum-area schools was an enormous issue, challenging the efforts of NGOs which strive to bring education into the poorest communities of the country, while withstanding the scrutiny of being evaluated for "appropriate practices." The director of an NGO-run school for urban slums defended the classroom pedagogy of teachers in her centers, explaining that play looked very different in an NGO-run center because these centers usually have very little space. She emphasized how difficult it was to get her teachers to implement a play pedagogy in classrooms that only measured about 6 feet by 7 feet in size. So the real question is as follows: If classrooms are not offering a "play" pedagogy as defined within a global early childhood discourse, does it minimize, or even negate, the educational experiences that are being offered? The participants put into perspective the scarcity of resources in slum-area schools by explaining that an early childhood teacher in a government school in India earned approximately Rs. 20,000 on an average, whereas an NGO school teacher earned about Rs. 4000, given that their qualifications and the populations they serve are dramatically different. Most NGO-run preschools offer educational experiences to children from underprivileged and marginalized sections of Indian society. The NGO teacher is usually a member of the same community and has no professional training except some schooling (the minimum requirement is a sixth grade pass) and some in-house training provided by the NGO staff. Currently, NGOs provide education to a large population of young children in many Asian countries since early education has not historically been a government responsibility.

A professor at a premier government policy-making institute acknowledged that early childhood or pre-primary teacher training is indeed a major challenge in India and currently exists at a bare minimum, if at all. He also emphasized that the government cannot recognize and approve teacher training programs that prepare teachers poorly. It was imperative, he said, to offer teacher training that was standardized, complete, and at least two to four years in duration as it is in the West.

An executive of an Indian children's television show strongly recommended taking advantage of popular media to reach remote areas and enhance teacher training and educational experiences for very young children. The television media, she urged, was an effective way to reach all children had little or no access to schools. She claimed that the television show has improved visual discrimination skills, enhanced Hindi speaking skills, increased narrative skills, and bettered social attitudes toward early education in general. The show has also worked to train teachers in soft skills such as how to be a better and more effective story teller, how to use body language more effectively, and how to use impromptu materials for teaching when resources are not available. The show offers staff development programs and workshops for the development of these skills in about 6000 early childhood centers across the country.

The show's executive noted that the one of the last frontiers in India is the urban-rural divide, and this divide gets reinforced by the lack of access to information. The media has the potential to bridge this divide because it can reach out to children in inaccessible places. The executive further believed that this digital reaching out can happen not only through television but also through the use of cell phone technology which may some day be able to beam children's television and digitalized books to remote areas. In response to this idea, another early childhood teacher educator cautioned about not succumbing to the habit of teaching children every minute just because cell phone technology is easily available. She emphasized the value of those moments of silence when the focus is not on explicit "teaching" through an electronic screen but when children can instead interact with real people in their social environments or even engage in contemplation.

As a result of India's new policy mandates on inclusion and education for all children, classrooms in all schools have increasingly become more integrated and socioeconomically diverse. However, teachers are not yet sufficiently prepared in multicultural and culturally responsive pedagogies, which has become another area of dire need in teacher education. A lecturer in a college department of primary education recognized this deficiency and described how she encourages cultural responsiveness in teachers in her own teaching. She ensures that each of her student teachers spends at least a day each in diverse settings during their field experiences: with a child in a *basti* (slum), a child from a middle-class family, and a child from an elite class family. She claims that this policy has helped her student teachers understand the daily realities of children's lives outside of their classroom and within their home environments. Often it comes as a surprise that children from both rich and poor families equally struggle with their own challenges within their individual social worlds. The material nature of their worlds may be different, but the emotional challenges they face are comparable. Indeed, a child's happiness and well-being are not necessarily determined by the material wealth of the child's family.

A general concern was also voiced that ECE teachers in India are not being recognized and that the teaching profession is not being valued as a profession. Lack of teacher professionalization in India has deeply impacted teacher professionalism and the traditional notions of teachers and teaching. The underlying question, however, is whether it is possible to professionalize the teaching profession and improve teachers' salaries and image without professionalizing and standardizing their training.

Other Higher Education Faculty in Asia

Similar concerns emerged in the course of my conversations with teacher educators and policy makers in Sri Lanka. The dean and two lecturers at the Faculty of Education in Colombo shared their views on the challenges they face in educating children for the 21st century. This teacher training institution offers two B.Ed. degree programs subsequent to the A Levels: the Primary B.Ed program for grades 1–5, and the Secondary B.Ed program for grades 6–12. The B.Ed has two components: a *professional* component taught by the Faculty of Education, which includes the teaching of educational courses such as Educational Psychology and Evaluation; and the *academic* component, which is taught by the Faculty of Arts and Humanities and includes the teaching of content areas. An optional course on early childhood education is available, and this one course counts toward the pre-primary training of teachers. Thus, currently there is a great demand for a pre-primary training program within the B.Ed. program inasmuch as early childhood teacher education is a gap that needs to be filled and the number of preschools has mushroomed, leading to a further dearth of qualified teachers. Even though most employed teachers may have extensive experience working with young children, they do not have any formal training in ECE pedagogy.

Yamini, the head of a policy-making institution for young children in Sri Lanka, mentioned the lack of quality early childhood centers and professionals who were appropriately prepared to teach in early childhood classrooms. She referred to the prolonged time that young children spend at home and how parents and family members could be helped in providing enriched educational experiences to their children at home: "In Sri Lanka, we are introducing home-based ECD programs. Most of the time children are with the parents 3.5–4 hours in preschools, or 5–6 hours in day care. So we introduce home-based programs. At this time we are piloting. We identified some families who can do these things in their homes." She added that 100 early care and development officers had been recruited across the country to develop activities that would be taught to the parents at the village and district levels.

Technology was definitely an issue in early childhood education as well as teacher education. Although high technology was widespread in society at large, it was still not emphasized enough in schools, especially in the primary grades, or even in teacher education programs. At the same time, current primary education in Sri Lanka was of higher quality than secondary education because the new innovative practices and policies were mostly being implemented at the primary level. The Sri Lankan educational system has been gradually changing to a competency skills-based educational system, including competency skills such as communication and listening skills. Yamini described how the media and technology could be used to supplement the role of teachers in teaching children about appropriate behaviors, attitudes, and skills and illustrated a recent project that the policy institute had launched:

> When we launched our own media campaign we used only the good things—all the positive sides. We made a docu-drama—22 minutes long, with Tamil subtitles. It shows the importance of early childhood and we focus on birth to 5 years—from pregnancy onwards … how you have to behave … take the children to what you're doing … what are families … what are the correct things to do. Finally we didn't show the child who was badly affected, but we showed a child who did all the good things. This year we are planning a huge media campaign. UNICEF has funded for that— "Care, Protection and Development for child". … this will be our media campaign with three main strategies—one is ECCD, one is care and protection, and the other is development. … Totally integrated.

As in most of Asia, the position of teachers is not satisfactory, and teaching salaries are low. However, as is also the case in most Asian countries, teachers are highly respected, although not as much as in earlier periods of history. In 1971, the Sri Lankan government introduced an open economy, and with that other professions became more valued and lucrative; subsequently teaching became devalued. The minimum qualifications to enter primary teacher training is a Pass in GCE (General Certificate in Education). But there are a large number of teachers with graduate degrees as well as many colleges of education where an Advanced Level of teacher training is available.

Diversifying the teacher's training experiences and ensuring that all teachers are exposed to socioculturally diverse student populations as well as settings are important goals in Sri Lanka. Manju, an early childhood education lecturer at a university, expressed this concern about preparing teachers in one "mold" and then expecting them to teach in diverse settings:

> About teacher preparation ... schools in Sri Lanka, they are of different nature ... there are big schools, there are huge ones, medium size, small ones, and then very very tiny ones. All things are there. But we have a one sort of thing ... one jacket where we ask the teachers to fit this jacket to every unit. Each and every classroom ... maybe school ... we need to identify differences between these classrooms in the schools but we don't do that. We cater to them with one model. Teachers fail when they go there because the adaptation they have to do is too messy. A little bit of adaptation is fine, they will have to do that anywhere in the world but it's too messy. So they find the training not related sometimes. So there are many challenges. There are some good practices that we try to inculcate in them, but some critical things prevent them from making use of those good practices. So, one such example would be student number. Student number in one extreme would be 50 or 60. At the other end it's about 2 children or 3 children in one class. But they go through same training.

Sneha, the head of a department of early education in a university in Sri Lanka, echoed the same sentiment about teachers being born teachers:

> The other problem is the entry criteria of teachers ... there should be some sort of entry criteria where we can identify their talents, their attitudes, their skills. Actually my idea is that there should be a born talent. All cannot be teachers. They must love their profession. They must love their children. Patience, commitment ... but earlier we had a set of teachers like that. So maybe teacher training programs are not so [effective] ... we should ask are we teaching them properly? They are getting the certificate, but I think we have failed somewhere.

Members of the Review Committee for Teacher Education Institutions in Sri Lanka shared their findings with me. The evaluation of teacher education colleges by the Review Committee has revealed two critical gaps, and filling both of these gaps needs to be a priority: (1) research, specifically to build a body of qualitative and quantitative research on preschools and early childhood education within the Sri Lankan context; research is important because it is a source of knowledge and it is important to build up a local source of knowledge rather than continue to rely on a Western body of knowledge; and (2) closer coordination between the different factions and stakeholders of early education such as the Ministry of Child Development, Child Protection authorities, Health Ministry, departments of primary and pre-primary teacher education institutions, and NGO-administered preschools to form an umbrella ECE network.

This issue is of concern in India as well. Priya, a faculty member from a college of education for girls in New Delhi, described the wide-ranging curriculum of the four-year B.El.B.Ed program at her college that prepares teachers for primary school:

> Interestingly it has courses in the Sociology of Education, in understanding the current sociological, political, ideological trends in India; so in understanding the country well there are a couple of courses in that. There are even courses in curriculum planning, gender studies, and lots of pedagogy courses. So they do pedagogy courses in science, in language, where they mostly look at reading and writing, the acquisition of reading and writing.

But she expressed her own concern about the paucity of locally published research for students to consult:

> Unfortunately, there is not too much research or material available. ... What we do is that we look at Western studies and ideas like emergent literacy and those kinds of concepts. And we see how they would work in the Indian context. So what girls do is that they read material which is written mostly in the Western context, but then they collect data from the classes they go to or the data from neighborhood, or from children in the family, and then they try and see what are some of the ideas that work in the Indian context. What are some that don't?

Priya provided a specific example of how her students in the elementary education program would often confront cultural and pedagogical dissonances when they were using a Western research base and scholarship:

> For example, there is this girl called Shalini; she worked on miscues, looking at what kind of reading errors children make and what does that tell the teacher about how they are reading and what comprehension level they are at. Do they comprehend well at all? She found that there were differences. But she could not quite place some of the miscues because the reading she had done was in the Western context. Then some miscues came out from the fact that children spoke a different language at home and the classroom language was standard Hindi. So errors that happened because of the interference from home language, those were the errors that she had to figure out how to deal with and what to make of those errors, whether the child was comprehending or whether she was not.

Until recently, children in the Maldives were being largely raised by extended families, which minimized the need for day care. Laila, an early childhood faculty member, explained that

> the reason why [ECE] has not yet started is because the set up of Maldives … we don't seem to have the need for day-care. Because we live in extended families and you have all these support systems helping you with children. And you have your maids at home. So the need has not been there. … But now because people are starting to move out of families and starting to live independently. It's changing and people are now realizing the importance of early years. So I think this is why we have started this move.

In the Maldives, early childhood teacher education is even more dire as, according to Laila, the "majority of the teachers in preschools are untrained. A lot of untrained teachers but highly motivated. If we can have them trained then it would be a good step for taking forward our society… political parties are addressing this issue about training of preschool teachers and setting up of daycare." The Maldives National University (formerly known as the Maldives College of Higher Education) started the country's first ever program in ECE teacher education in 2009, which was initially approved as a two-year diploma program. It has been recently approved as a four-year degree program and is scheduled to grant its first degree in ECE in 2014.

Ahmed, who is in charge of a distance learning program in education in the Maldives, outlined a pre-primary and primary teacher education program that was being developed. He spoke about the first two years that had been initially approved as a diploma program in 2009, prior to being approved as a four-year degree program:

> The basic outline is that every year they do a main education module, like instructional psychology, developmental psychology, and then there are two others. Then they also do curriculum studies or pedagogy kind of subject. In addition to those we do have maths, two languages, social sciences, and then we have things like assessment and evaluation. Every year there is a practicum. The reason why we had to include a practicum every year was that if they exit at any point they would have their practicum. And our course is targeted for two groups: One is the school levels, the O-levels. The other, we have a lot of trained professionals up to the advanced levels. The CCE—Center for Continuing Education, they run an advanced certificate in Early Childhood course which actually is not adequate [for preparing teachers] to go in schools and teach. So we want to upgrade them as well. … We don't do, from our side, any supervision. The school does the supervision for the first year, wherever they might be. Second year, that's a diploma, a major exit point. So we do the external supervision, the examination as well. It's a five-week practicum where we will be testing their skills on handling different types of students.

School-based Teacher Education and Training

Although early childhood teacher education is garnering much importance, it is clear from discussions in earlier chapters of this book that most countries in Asia lack organized university related pre-primary teacher education degree programs. Most often, pre-primary teachers are either untrained formally or have earned diplomas and certificates from alternative institutions. Student teaching and field experiences constitute one of the most important aspects of teacher education, and yet that is one area that needs careful attention in teacher preparation programs. Strong and diverse clinical and field experiences combined with readings on research not only clarify theoretical ideas for the teacher candidates but also provide valuable opportunities for them to get hands-on, practical experiences in how to address issues in classroom management, find effective ways to set up a classroom to facilitate children's individual and group activities, learn how to facilitate smooth transitions, and schedule the school day for both quiet and active activities—in short, how to create an efficient and meaningful classroom environment in general. Frequently, full-time student teaching requires graduate students to either give up their current jobs or take leave without pay for an extended period of time. As a result, the candidates do face financial challenges, and the concept of student teaching is viewed as a hardship rather than an exciting opportunity to embrace. Thus, the student teaching experiences in many colleges often get telescoped into shorter, less intensive, and less diverse experiences in the field.

Additionally, the focus of student teaching may often be limited to technical skills such as writing lesson plans, creating rubrics for assessments, and designing visual aids, and not enough attention is given to teaching dispositions and the actual teacher–student dynamics and interactions. Internship programs could be set up between teacher education institutes and schools that could pay teacher candidates a stipend as they are placed in a particular setting for a year of student teaching. A juxtaposition of practice and theory of teaching over an extended period of time would help narrow the gap between teacher preparation and practice that exists globally.

One solution that numerous schools in Asia have come up with is to offer in-house workshops for professional development. Aruna, the principal of an elite and well-resourced private school in India, described how her school offered professional development experiences to the teachers. She provided an example of such a workshop that was based on the topic of Howard Gardner's Theory of Multiple Intelligences, a Western concept that is rapidly gaining popularity in Asia:

> And yes, we have to train our teachers. It is easier said than done. It's not very easy to [implement] MI strategies in the classes. …We went ahead and we started using different strategies. We did role play, we did theater, we did a little bit of some visuals. Of course we got our own in-house resource, we have a resource center. So we got a teacher who was specially trained. And we got great results. It is the need of the hour … in schools we have to address this. Again, sensitizing of our teachers, training our teachers.

Another method of teacher training and development observed in this study includes the use of private resources, such as consulting companies that work closely with schools or entire school districts. Yet another program for teacher education and development is the diploma program offered by a private school system for the teachers already employed in the school.

In the NGO sector, I observed an instance of an in-house teacher training program in a slum-area school system that aimed to train teachers who belonged to the same poor community and most of whom had no more than a high school education. The Kamalika School began as a lab school with a handful of children in a slum community in New Delhi, where families earned about $12 a month. Today Kamalika is an extensive network of dozens of schools with thousands of children. The early childhood centers of Kamalika enroll children between the ages of 3 and 8. Over the years the school system has developed a three-pronged learning system for the child and community based on the 3 E's: Enjoyment, Engagement, and Employment. It adopts a community-based education model where the goal is to educate the children within a poor community while supporting the economic resurgence of the community.

According to Asha, one of the school system's senior administrators, the teachers for these schools are selected from the same community as the children and are mostly untrained and have no formal knowledge of early childhood education or child development. The educational levels of the teachers vary from completion of 10th grade or 12th grade; only a few of them have completed a basic three-year college degree. The school administrators recognize that the teachers need some formal training in early education and have thus created an in-house system of teacher training. On two Saturdays a month, full-day training workshops are offered from 9:00 am to 5:00 pm that include classes on various topics such as the administrative functions of teachers, issues in early childhood care and education, and the pedagogy and philosophy at the core of the school's mission. The teachers are also taught how to handle mixed age groups and mixed abilities, as that is how children are grouped in the classrooms at this school. Administrators and senior educators in the school system help teachers learn how to develop a curriculum unit, design worksheets, and create learning materials for their classrooms. A weekly curriculum unit is developed and designed collaboratively, photocopied at the main school office, and thereafter distributed to all the teachers who implement these duplicated worksheets in their classrooms across the school sites all over the city. Although the content of the curriculum with regard to the units or topics is common, the teaching strategies may vary from teacher to teacher but nevertheless are informed by the overarching school philosophy. The pedagogy of the school system is based on the oral tradition method and incorporates narrative and story-telling techniques. Thus teachers are also taught how to make the art of story-telling central in the teaching of all content areas in the curriculum.

In addition to the Saturday workshops, the teachers attend an intensive summer training program for 160 hours during the month of June. The summer program is held five days a week, from 9:00–5:00 each day, breaking only for tea and lunch. The summer program includes the teaching of the basic concepts of early childhood education, and the pedagogy and philosophy of the school. The teachers visit the original Kamalika flagship school in order to observe the pedagogy being enacted in the classrooms. Often teachers from the flagship school are invited as guest speakers for various sessions during the teacher training. Sometimes, external speakers as resource persons are invited to speak, and they discuss issues related to current trends in the field, the topic of global warming, policies such as the Right to Education Act, and so forth. Although some of these topics may not directly impact teachers' classroom practice, the school administrators felt strongly that these discussions deepened teachers' awareness and knowledge of the field and enhanced their professional stature. Asha described the content of the training curriculum that was covered in the 160-hour summer session:

> Basic topics such as the principles of development, the domains of development, curriculum planning, web-chart designing, monitoring, resource management, stages of development. … We did talk to them about disability, inclusion, even learning disabilities for that matter, even if we don't go into details, we do talk about all these aspects. Assessments, evaluations, all these basic things … at least to be able to know that they have to take care of all aspects of development and not just do *ka-kha-ga-gha* [these are some letters of the Indian alphabet] the so-called academics that we generally have in our education system. Because even the [parents of the] community tell that *"arre hum ne toh bacchon ko padne ke liye bheja tha, aap yeh kya karane lag gayi hain"* [We sent our children here to study, what are you doing playing with them?] So they should know why they are doing what they are doing. Why do they have to do activities, what is activity-based, what is play-based? In fact, we did tell them about the basic philosophies of education. We talk about Maria Montessori, Gijubhai, Gandhiji, though not in detail because this is not a full-time course. But we sensitize them to all these aspects so that when they are with younger children they should at least know the right from the wrong.

Thus far, the language of instruction in all the Kamalika schools and teacher training programs has been Hindi. But recently attempts have been made to include the English language. This change reflects the larger and wider trend that favors the teaching of English in schools across Asia, as described in Chapter 5. I observed with mixed feelings a Kamalika classroom of 3- to 4-year-olds in which the teacher was teaching the children the English language by using flash cards in English that contained groups of rhyming words like *hay, say, way, gay*; and another card with words like *mug, rug, jug, bug*. Parents of children at the school have exerted tremendous pressure to provide English language instruction. Many of the posters displayed in the school were made by the students using both languages: English and Hindi.

This kind of parental pressure was consistently found to be the case across countries such as India and Sri Lanka, as described in Chapter 5. A high percentage of poor families in developing countries in Asia and elsewhere in the world are choosing to enroll their children in private schools rather than public schools for this and other reasons (Tooley & Dixon, 2003; Tooley, 2009).

Asha also spoke of the challenges encountered by the teachers and those administering the teacher education workshops, based on the feedback from the teachers who tried to implement what they had learned in the workshops. Examples of such challenges are apparent in Asha's summary comments:

> Some of the activity sheets that we designed here, they [the teachers] went back and tried to do and they said that it was too difficult for the children or that it was too easy and not challenging enough. Then at times when we said about things like free play, they said "where is the place for outside free play in my slum community?" Then in one of my projects they were told to go out with children and count the number of trees, so they came back and said that there is no tree in my community at all. So there were lots of issues. We talked to them about hygiene and sanitation and they said "you should come and see there is so much filth." Just taking the name of hygiene and sanitation I feel that this will not work here because this is not happening.

Other examples of in-house teacher training in the absence of a university degree program were seen in schools such as the Play School in Goa, the Delphinium School in New Delhi, and the Dogwood Kindergarten in Hangzhou, which offered apprenticeship programs, diploma programs, and professional development workshops for early childhood teachers.

Hopes and Visions for Teachers and Teaching

During the course of the interviews, participants were asked a question regarding their hopes and visions about the future of early childhood teaching, teachers, and teacher training. Presented here are some of the responses of the teachers, teacher educators, and policy makers.

Asha, the early childhood teacher educator quoted at length earlier in this chapter, expressed her opinion as to what makes a good teacher and how the teaching profession could be improved. Her response echoed the sentiments on the critically important role of dispositions in teaching:

> There is something intuitive about being a good teacher. Something very social about it, that you have to be interested in people. You have to be awake to pick up the cues from different people. Yes, you have to be trained, but you have to be intuitive. The training may be very good, but you may

become very rigid with that good training also. That openness to adapt and respond to students' needs, all those aspects make a good teacher. That openness and that interest in human beings. … Teacher training should focus as much on subject matter content as on personalizing, creating, and sustaining that will to learn. Task persistence. Those are the elements that should be drilled in teacher training, especially at the young children stage.

Kala, a veteran teacher and teacher educator, and one of the first to lead a national effort to formalize primary and pre-primary education and curriculum in Sri Lanka in the 1960s, expressed her thoughts on the freedom that a teacher needs to be a good and effective teacher, suggesting the disadvantages of mandated and scripted curricula:

> My experience is you have to know the children, you have to know about teaching, how to teach. But you cannot be dictated as to how to teach a child because each child's learning style is different, learning requirements are different, learning levels and rates are different. So the teacher has to have so much freedom as there is no set pattern to deliver a lesson. If I deliver it this way and it does not work then I must be able to deliver it in another way.

Aastha, an early childhood teacher educator in Delhi University in India, presented her wish-list for teacher training on the pre-primary and primary levels:

> Teacher training, vibrant classrooms, color, playfields, activity, teachers running with the children. If education for the young child becomes compulsory for the 3–4–5 year old, that joy of being … freedom to go and question. Teachers who are trained well and who respond to children's needs. Children are not just students in a class but children who are growing up.

In the Maldives, Laila asserted that there was a need to create awareness of the importance of early education and early childhood teacher education in Maldivian society. She was very excited about the first undergraduate early childhood degree program that will be offered in 2014, but she was also deeply aware of the challenges:

> I think even still the thinking is not as strong as we would want it to be. Thinking in terms of importance of early years. We still think that primary is where it all starts. Now that people are realizing. I think the reason why thinking has not yet started is because [of] the setup of Maldives—we don't seem to have the need for day-care. Because we live in extended families. … But now. … It's changing and people are now realizing the importance of early years. So I think this is why we have started this move. … Right now there is no policy, there is no curriculum. So we have to work on all these things before we can run a program at the college. So it is all taking place at the same time so it is pretty slow.

Ahmed, the head of the distance learning program, also expressed his concern about a structural and ecological challenge that the Maldives faces in terms of teacher training:

> We have 200 islands and untrained teachers in each one of those islands. We cannot afford to send people [to each of these islands] or afford to bring them [all] to Malè, so we have to reach them in Open and Distance mode [referring to the distance education approach]. … We have currently 17 centers in the islands so it's a similar model as India. The difference is that we actually hire staff from local schools. … But they may not have the expertise to do an external examination or supervision for early childhood course because we don't have early childhood trained people. That might be an issue but that's something we'll have to plan well. The practicum is really of essence to us because that is where students will show whether they can do it or not.

Aruna is the principal of a leading N–12 private school in New Delhi. I asked her what teacher training needed to be addressed in order to prepare teachers to teach effectively in today's world. She had the following thoughts on what she believed a core curriculum for teacher training should include:

> "Definitely multiple intelligence. Definitely how to handle slow learners … how to incorporate co-scholastics in their teaching. But definitely integrated curriculum; definitely assessments. And assessment in a big way."

Aruna continued by referring to a deep shift in teacher image that seems to have occurred in recent years as compared to older times when teachers received much respect:

> A big problem is that we are not finding the right kind of teachers. Very difficult. And people are not coming into this profession any longer. Teaching, contrary to what people think, people have started realizing that it is a job which is a full time job and remuneration is not full time salary and plus respect of the community … respect is more for the status of the school … teachers are just not coming, it's not a preferred job.

Priya, a faculty member in the elementary education program in an all girls' college in India, noted an interesting gender gap in teacher education. She pointed out that currently eight colleges in New Delhi offered programs in primary or elementary teacher training:

> And at the moment these are all women's colleges. That is interesting because guys have been asking for it. Recently the teacher salaries have gone up and even in government schools there is now better pay than what was earlier and the way recession has affected jobs, men are interested in teaching too. And I am hoping that some of the co-ed colleges in DU would offer. There has been some talk but no final decisions as yet.

Priya's opinion on the teacher's current image and role in India was also revealing with regard to teaching in government schools. She expressed her hope that the government will view teaching more professionally:

> In India, the image of a teacher at one level, since you have studied here you would be able to understand, at one level the teacher is a guru and she is unquestioned inside the classroom and you don't question the authority of the teacher. But at another level she is the lowest among all the government workers. So in that sense. ... As far as the government and larger society is concerned, that dichotomy is always there. At one end children are told that the teacher is always right. ... Within the government system she is also expected to conduct elections and help do census duty when census data is being collected. She does a lot of administrative work for the government. She is expected to maintain records on inclusion in the classroom, children coming from various strata in the society; she is expected to maintain all those records. In that sense for the government, how many children in that area are in school and how many are out of school. So right from maintaining that kind of data to managing classrooms she is doing a lot.

The director of Dogwood Kindergarten in China was concerned about how to implement the new policies regarding child-friendly approaches. During our meeting she asked me to suggest some ways in which the school curriculum based on traditional Chinese culture could be implemented in the classroom in child-centered ways. Her eagerness to maintain the rigor of the curriculum and at the same time be able to teach children in a meaningful and interesting manner was another indication of how some educators are attempting to create a hybrid pedagogy that will combine diverse ideas from global perspectives enacted within the local context. They see this as the future of teaching in a globalized world.

Discussion

The concerted efforts of local and global partners in envisioning and implementing pre-primary teacher education reforms in Asia, and the active borrowing of early childhood concepts from the Western discourse face major challenges, as explained in Chapter 3. The prerequisites for a play-based and child-centered pedagogy include plenty of resources in the classroom with regard to space, materials, and time; teachers adequately trained and prepared in child-centered pedagogy; teachers equipped with sufficient tools and time to implement this pedagogy; classrooms with low teacher–child ratios; children entitled to make choices with regard to their engagement with classroom life; children starting school already comfortable with decision-making skills and ability to readily select activities from a wide range of choices.

But as educational policy reform in Asia shifts to include more activity-based learning, emphasis on child-centered teaching, the dropping of annual examinations in elementary schools, and elimination of retention policies, major obstacles to these change initiatives are being experienced: (1) Teachers are inadequately trained in these new teaching methods; (2) it is a challenge to find teacher–educators who have themselves adopted the child-centered approaches in their own practice and who can then train teachers accordingly; (3) class sizes continue to be very large; (4) much of the theory in the coursework continues to be unrelated to the local culture, unlike actual classroom situations; (5) teacher education programs are still performing inadequately in preparing teachers to teach the whole child; and (6) there is limited recognition in teacher education philosophy and pedagogy of who the teachers are as human beings, and how their socially and culturally constructed implicit belief systems determine their classroom practices.

Some of these issues also plague teacher education in the West. Therefore, broad recommendations may be offered for teacher education in general; these recommendations seem to be critical to preparing teachers in any country to be able to recognize both local and global values. These recommendations include:

- Preparing teachers in a multicultural approach to education; in qualitative and quantitative assessment; and in the understanding and implementation of child-centered teaching within the local context but aware of and familiar with global discourses and current research
- Diversifying the teaching force
- Strengthening connections between schools and teacher education colleges
- Raising teaching standards and increasing teacher accountability
- Viewing teacher development as lifelong learning
- Revising teacher education curricula for content and development of materials

Further recommendations are provided specifically with regard to the last point: the content of teacher education curricula. Teacher education programs everywhere can be strengthened and energized only if they formally include knowledge and a deeper understanding of the following topics, among others:

- Local cultural and educational history
- Development and evolution of education in respective countries
- Origin of local belief systems and traditions
- Learning styles with which native and local children are comfortable
- Developmental milestones that are prioritized for children growing up in respective countries
- Significance of the relationships between local childrearing practices and the roles adults play in individual societies

- Social norms, speech and language patterns, and interactional and behavioral modes that are deemed appropriate within local contexts

The process of preparing teachers has long been stagnant in Asia, and the professional preparation of early childhood teachers has been absent. As current educators and policy makers approach the defining and restructuring of early childhood teacher education programs in Asia, it might be pertinent to remember that a variety of teacher training programs are required to meet a range of needs, including short-term in-service programs, longer academically rigorous preservice programs, as well as programs to produce teacher educators who are themselves in short supply. More importantly, policy makers are advised to be mindful of two critical concerns: the issue of *cultural incursions* and the issue of growing *neoliberal incursions* in education.

With regard to the issue of cultural incursions, the local cultural context and worldviews in Asian countries may not necessarily support the core ideas of child-centered teaching, which are rooted in a progressive pedagogy that emerged within the sociocultural-political context of a capitalist and democratic English-speaking, white middle class of Euro-America referred to as the West. For example, in collectivist societies of much of Asia, parents and children live together for a much longer time and the adult–child continuity is much longer than it is in the West. This interdependent worldview largely shapes ideas on child development at the local level. What parents in Asia want their children to learn and develop in terms of skills and attitudes may be different from what parents in the West want for their children; in the West the skills of independence and self-reliance are key to competing in developed, knowledge-based, capitalist economies.

Indu, who was formerly head of the department of early childhood and primary education in a university in Sri Lanka, reflected on a cross-country study she had conducted in her country to survey how parents perceived their children. Information was gathered from urban, rural, and plantation communities across the country. The findings indicated that parents everywhere expected their child:

> to be obedient and to be educated … and when the child grows up, to look after them [parents]. That is the thing they expect. … It has something to do with our own tradition … even the present generation depends so much on parents. … With all the ladies employed they leave their children with parents. Recently, even with all the day care centers and everything, we prefer to keep our children with our parents [grandparents]. Sometimes even our parents say "Servants are there, but we want to be there to help."

Interdependence between generations, and the vital role that grandparents play in raising their grandchildren and helping out their own children is commonplace in Asia and emerged as a strong finding in the author's earlier research (Gupta, 2006/2013). Developmental expectations are quite different in diverse cultural contexts, laying varying emphasis on developmental milestones.

With regard to the second issue, increasing neoliberalism has led to increasing privatization and corporatization of all dimensions in education. A neoliberal approach is rapidly becoming dominant in Western countries such as the United States, leading to increased standardization in the evaluations of not only institutions and students but also of teachers. As Gupta (2012) notes:

> Neoliberalism frames education within the discourse of consumerism; consequently, the learning experiences of young children are increasingly quantified and evaluated in terms of economic profit. Quality of early education centers is measured in terms of the academic performance of its students as a selling point for its consumers. An emphasis on academic achievement often results in "teaching to the test" which dominates children's learning experiences in the classroom, sometimes to the detriment of their social-emotional well-being. (Gupta, 2012, pp. 115–116)

Thus, a neoliberal perspective views schools as businesses and favors an assessment system that evaluates teachers on the basis of their students' academic success. This form of evaluation cannot be used for pre-primary teachers whose success is marked by the happiness and well-being of very young children. The dispositions of teachers who can more effectively nurture a feeling of joy and well-being in 2- and 3-year-olds is different from those who can more effectively guide older students to academically excel in content areas. Their teacher education experiences will necessarily be different as well.

Sneha, head of the early childhood and primary education program at a university in Sri Lanka, captured the essence of how many felt that early childhood teachers should really be prepared and evaluated. She perceived teaching to be "an inborn talent," almost a calling, implying that certain inherent dispositional qualities went a long way toward making a good teacher.

Sneha questions the effectiveness of teacher training programs, and asks whether the increasing emphasis on professionalization requirements, such as test scores and content-based standardized certification exams, will help make a good early childhood teacher. She also recognizes that pre-primary teacher education requires an emphasis on dispositions and affective skills just as much as it does on academic skills—an observation that is supported by many other educators around the globe.

8
REFLECTIONS AND RECOMMENDATIONS

This study was conducted in five different countries in Asia, each dominated by vastly diverse sociocultural-political-spiritual influences. The cultural ethos of every country was palpable during my visits, and I encountered culturally diverse worldviews and practices that helped define educational decisions. I wish to make two points that will shape the discussion that follows. First, it is important to reiterate the caution urged by Mason (2005) against perceiving cultures as monolithic, stereotypical, simplistic, and devoid of complex interactions and hybridity. He argues for a construction of culture that is based in sociological understandings to do justice to culture's complexity "in a world characterized by increasing degrees of plurality, multiculturalism, interdependence, hybridity and complexity" (Mason, 2005, p. 169). Second, it is widely recognized that cultural factors influence aspects of education, and this is evident in the way elements of traditional culture and education continue to linger within educational objectives, images of students and teachers, and teaching practices in these countries. Law (2005) emphasizes this idea when she notes that "what teachers and students do in classrooms both reflects and enacts the values of the wider society" and that studies of pedagogy should be contextualized within a larger context (Law, 2005, p. 321).

Having said that, it should also be noted that one of the effects of globalization is the grouping of people based on their cultural and cognitive schema, and the ability to communicate with like-minded people anywhere. People are being united less by geographical boundaries than by their invisible cultural/cognitive perspectives. Local events, closely shaped by global events, blur the lines between local and global in many societies, but at the same time embedded within this transaction is the inevitable tension between often conflicting worldviews. With regard to diverse educational traditions, in this study there emerged some common themes that distinguished these approaches to education in the Asian context.

Distinguishing Features of Education in the Asian Context

1. *All-encompassing education*: In this study, a distinction was found between schooling and education, and a child was educated both informally and formally, inside and outside of schools and other educational institutions. Education was perceived as a more encompassing and interdependent concept involving the active participation of the immediate family, extended family, and schools, as well as the larger neighborhood and community within which children were raised, including their interactions with their siblings and peers.

2. *Multiple teachers*: Closely related to the preceding point, the child was seen to have many teachers simultaneously, including not only the adults in the child's classroom and school but also the adults in the child's life outside of school, including parents, grandparents, extended family, neighbors, and family friends. It was expected and appropriate for all adults in a child's life to be informally and actively responsible for the child's upbringing and education, and all the adults had the "right" to teach the child.

3. *Cultures of caregiving*: Asian cultures may be characterized as caregiving cultures which, according to Goncu (2010) are those in which nonkin participate in caring for young children and serve as attachment figures, and where children grow up immersed within systems of extended family and friends. However, this picture is changing under the influence of current flows of migration, urbanization, new employment patterns, and increasing globalization (Goncu, 2010).

4. *Parent involvement in children's education*: Parent involvement in many schools in the West is widely viewed as institutional involvement whereby parents volunteer and are physically present in their child's school or classroom to assist with various classroom activities or fundraisers. In Asian cultures, parent involvement was widely understood as being involved in their child's learning experiences by taking a deeper interest in ensuring daily homework was completed, helping when the child needed assistance with academic work, arranging for tutoring for their child as needed, making sure that what was taught at school was reinforced at home, and, most importantly, always giving the child to understand that the teacher was someone to be highly respected.

5. *Large class sizes and competitiveness*: Most classrooms in Asia have large numbers of students in every classroom. Government schools can have as many as 30 to 60 children in each room, whereas even the most resourceful schools have about 25 to 40 students in preschool classrooms. In most urban areas of Asia, large numbers of people are seen in close proximity everywhere, "whether in homes with joint or extended families; on the crowded streets, whether in large cities, small towns, or villages; in the markets, bazaars, and departmental stores; in classrooms on school and college campuses; in the fierce competition for jobs and employment; in cinema houses and malls;

in all places of worship; and in office buildings or other places of work" (Gupta, 2006/2013, p. 153). Thus, it is not surprising that many children in urban Asia are raised in crowded and competitive environments both at home and in schools, and are required to develop the skills needed to flourish in such environments.

6. *Self versus other.* The general importance given to the "other" in Asian cultures is a well-established fact and has been frequently raised in this book with regard to concepts such as interdependence and autonomy, respect, hospitality, filial piety, strengthening community, and harmonious living. Li & Wang (2004) provide a lucid description of how Chinese and American students view learning. Both cultures stress intellectual development, skills acquisitions, and a love for learning but use a different approach. American students tend to value these qualities more as individuals and for their own personal achievement. Chinese students are seen to view these values from a Confucian perspective, and attention is less geared to the self than to "moral self-cultivation through learning and social contribution" (Li & Wang, 2004, p. 415).

7. *Image of the teacher.* The image of the teacher in Asia has been influenced culturally by the traditional image of the teacher as described in philosophical, educational, and spiritual texts, and as has been historically practiced over the ages. A recent study conducted by Varkey GEMS Foundation surveyed the Global Teacher Status Index across 21 countries covering every continent (China and Singapore were included in the survey but not the other Asian countries referred to in this book—India, Sri Lanka, and the Maldives). The findings indicated that teachers had the highest status in the non-Western countries of China, Greece, Turkey, and South Korea; the teaching profession was most respected in China, South Korea, Greece, Turkey, and Singapore; and students respected teachers most in China, Singapore, Turkey, and Egypt (available at www.varkeygemsfoundation.org/teacherindex accessed on 10/19/2013). Gu (2006) notes that esteem for teachers and respect for elders are underlying and consistent characteristics of Chinese traditional culture in Confucian societies, and reflect "a mentality of great reverence for intelligence and knowledge" (p. 37). Respect for teachers and for higher learning has been similarly demonstrated in traditional education within Hindu, Buddhist, and Islamic cultures as well. This finding is consistent with my own findings in which a high degree of respect was accorded to teachers and which automatically gave them a certain degree of authority to establish ground rules in the classroom (Gupta, 2006/2013). This also promotes a higher degree of confidence in the teacher who is then able to address her students with calm confidence and an absence of hostility. The more confidently students are addressed, the more likely they are to respond positively, and conversely, the more tentatively a teacher addresses her students, the less likely they are to respond in the desired manner

(Katz, 1999). In most Euro-American contexts, the democratic values of individual autonomy and the rights of the individual have been traditionally prized. Thus, European and American teachers experience a great deal of confrontation in their classrooms and much more challenge to their educational practices (Alexander, 2000). A more respectful attitude toward the teacher eases classroom management when classes hold anywhere from 25 to 60 or more 4-year-olds, and further, seems to eliminate the time and energy that go into trying to establish a learning environment conducive to constructive and progressive experiences when classrooms have so many students.

8. *Teaching of values*: In the study, definite emphasis was placed on the teaching of character, citizenship, and cultural values as part of the child's education. In all schools included in this study, regardless of whether the school was a private or a government school, there were numerous posters and slogans with phrases, quotations, and reminders about human virtues and preferred behaviors necessary for developing good moral character. Kennedy & Fairbrother (2004) note that citizenship education in Asia is characterized more by moral virtues and personal values, and that teachers are key players in implementing citizenship education in schools. This observation is consistent with findings of an earlier study on early childhood teachers in India indicating that one of the most important aims of education was the teaching of values to young children, such as respect, honesty, caring, citizenship, integrity, compassion, responsibility, dedication to work, humility, perseverance, friendship, strong character, ability to get along with peers, viewing failure as the need to work harder rather than it being indicative of a deficiency, and awareness first of one's duties and then of one's rights (Gupta, 2006/2013). Here too, the preferred attitudes and behaviors are those that give more importance to the "other."

9. *Academic rigor and teaching for academic proficiency*: Simultaneously, this study revealed a strong emphasis on developing academic excellence. Many studies have demonstrated a higher performance of Asian students in academic subjects such as math and science. Li & Wang (2004) indicate that reasons for this may include greater amounts of school work, longer school calendar, the nature of school pedagogies and instructional strategies, greater parental expectations and involvement, motivation for economic advancement through education, and the Asian belief in effort versus the Western belief in ability (Li & Wang, 2004). Alongside activity-based learning in child-friendly classroom environments, the study produced strong evidence for the teaching of academic skills through the use of worksheets, workbooks, readers, and notebooks that could be seen piled on shelves, placed on tables, or displayed on bulletin boards. The teachers did not seem to perceive the use of workbooks as being "child-unfriendly" if the children demonstrated interest and enthusiasm. An earlier study on early childhood teaching practices in India demonstrated how teachers practiced a

hybrid pedagogy by enacting a curriculum that combined diverse elements such as the teaching of values and of academic proficiency in an activity-based child-friendly manner in classrooms with 40 children each (Gupta, 2006/2013).

10. *Standardized curriculum*: Early childhood teachers usually worked within broad curricular frameworks published by the nation's educational ministry or an equivalent agency. But within the general framework teachers at each grade level had varying degrees of freedom to discuss and determine the specific topics and activities that would be implemented in the classroom. Uniformity was observed in that classrooms at the same grade level within any one school would be following exactly the same curriculum with regard to topics, the order of topics, and the time frame for completing each topic.

11. *Long traditions of education and a cultural value for learning*: The value and importance given to education as a way to acquire intellectual knowledge are rooted in Asian cultural and spiritual philosophies in which educational traditions go back thousands of years to ancient times. Educational goals in Asian cultures traditionally were aimed at helping the child to become the kind of adult who would function appropriately and effectively in the society in which they would be living. Developing competencies to become economically independent or successful by getting good jobs was not a primary objective of education, which is mostly the case in the West. However, as is happening in the West, the influences of neoliberalism and globalization seem to be changing the approaches to education in most of these countries.

12. *The practice of memorization*: Educational practices in the Asian countries studied involved learning through memorizing to a high degree. Memorizing for learning has been prevalent in Asian educational systems and has been equally discouraged and criticized in the Euro-American progressive education systems. However, in many Asian contexts, students view memorization as helping them to deepen their understanding of content, whereas memorization in the United States has been traditionally viewed more as rote learning to answer multiple-choice test questions. To take an example from Indian philosophy, ancient Indian texts such as *Naya Sutra* and *Upani-shad* maintain that memorization is a necessary first step toward cognitive knowing, the learning and comprehending of concepts, and the retaining of important factual information. This acceptance of memorization as a necessary step in the learning process is vastly different from the Western attitude toward memorization. Based on her ethnography, Viruru (2001, p. 93) explains that memorization involves a definite engagement of the mind "because all the time an individual repeats information, the subconscious is pondering over and processing what is being repeated, and further, one cannot think about what one does not know."

13. *Recent shifts in policies and pedagogies*: In all the countries studied, the definite intention was to move away from age-old educational policies that reflected an academically rigorous and examination-driven educational system toward a more child-centered method to nurture creativity, imagination, and joyful learning. Innovation, imagination, and inclusion were major areas of emphases in the new policy documents and national educational discourses. This is in apparent contrast to current educational reforms in the United States, which seem to be increasingly moving away from joyful learning and toward more high-stakes testing and standardized assessments for all school levels.

Cultural Incursions: Dissonance between Beliefs and Pedagogy

The issue of cultural incursions encountered during pedagogical implementation was raised in Chapters 2 and 7, with examples provided to illustrate some of the barriers that these incursions pose to the complete implementation of new policy reforms. The findings also presented clear instances of dissonance between the lived realities of children and teachers and the guidelines of appropriate practices as upheld by the dominant discourse in the West. For each situation there emerged a series of questions as to how these differences might create a tension between those who prescribe pedagogical expectations and those who want to implement it. Examples from various countries illustrate this tension.

In a 2010 newspaper article published during the first presidential election held in Sri Lanka in 30 years, a former director of education and primary school curriculum specialist emphasized the importance of the early years and urged that the four divine abidings central to Buddhism be developed in the minds of children: *metta* or loving kindness, *karuna* or compassion, *mudita* or sympathetic joy, and *uppekkha* or equanimity (Abhyadeva, 2010). These qualities are somewhat in contrast to the preferred qualities and behaviors promoted by Western progressive education that emphasize individualism, assertiveness, democratic advocacy, free and open expression of feelings, standing up for one's rights, and so forth. The challenge for educators is to determine how to effectively reconcile aims and philosophies rooted in discourses that lie at different points along the individual–group continuum. Buddhism is the dominant religion in Sri Lanka and in several other East and Southeast Asian countries.

Manju, an early childhood teacher educator, spoke about how society in Sri Lanka had changed because of the civil war, becoming more aggressive and self-centered:

> Another thing is that we are very quick in decision making. Not only young people but even our generation I would say . . . . they are looking for changes very fast and then their decisions are taken in a very rash way. They don't mind hurting others, crushing another person. We are too

self-centered. … When we go on the road, you can see that they are not thinking about each other, about the pedestrian, about the vehicle. I don't know what happened but I don't remember this in my childhood. Such strong kind of selfishness in the society. I don't remember this from times, from my school. … But now, even if you go to a preschool you see how they push each other. But even if you go to these places with big people, like go to a seminar, how they go for refreshments and things … it's ugly.

In Kamalika School, a slum-area school in India, some of the classrooms were no more than 6 feet by 7 feet holding at least 20 children, and the teachers were often young women who had not completed high school. In one classroom, the young teacher was using flash cards to enthusiastically teach English to 3-year-olds. There, within a crowded, impoverished local community, was evidence for the push to learn English, a language that is now being widely perceived in Asia as the language of communication and power in the global context. This was not an unusual phenomenon and has been spreading rapidly across the developing world, as described in Chapter 5. Both of these points—the use of flash cards as a formal instructional strategy and the teaching of 3-year-olds to memorize words in a foreign language—would be considered inappropriate and be viewed negatively by the proponents of progressive child-centered education. However, to me the significance of this observation lay in the pervasiveness of a high degree of love, the human interaction, the soft power of the school, and the teachers' dedication and commitment to the children of this economically impoverished community. The 3-year-olds in this classroom were chirpy, active, smiling, curious, and willingly participated in this floor activity chanting words like *mug, rug,* or *bug.* In this context, how much did it matter that the physical infrastructure and the qualification of the teachers did not meet Western standards of teaching?

Islamic spiritual beliefs seemed to influence educational decisions in the Maldives. Here the school hours are designed around Ramadan, which follows the lunar calendar. Although the academic school year is from January to November, during Ramadan the daily schedule changes and schools are open for shorter days. This calls for teachers and students to be able to live with a certain degree of uncertainty and changing schedules during each school year. Additionally, the notion of the extended family system is even more broadly defined in Muslim families as children may have two or three stepmothers each because their fathers are legally allowed to have four wives. Taking on extra wives is not considered unusual, and even children are used to the concept of multiple mothering and living with a large number of siblings and step-siblings. The ability to live harmoniously within a larger group, the willingness to put aside one's own interests and goals to accommodate those of other siblings are examples of skills and attitudes that would need to be promoted in an early childhood classroom, as opposed to a curriculum that promotes individuality, and the individual interests and choices of children, urging them to stand up for their rights within a group of peers.

Another characteristic feature of Malè schools is that each school offers three to four shifts during the day, mainly because space is a great commodity on this tiny island, permitting no scope for expansion. Urban expansion is impossible horizontally because of the island limits, and is impossible vertically because there is a restriction on how much weight these delicate coral islands can support. In order to ensure that all children in Malè can attend school daily, multiple shifts are necessary. As an Islamic society, there is a call to prayer five times a day, but because of the shorter duration of the school day many teachers and students can go home for their prayers. For others, prayer rooms are available in every school building. In most preschools on Malè, every classroom has three to four shifts per day, with each shift lasting about 2 hours. In each shift, there are approximately 30 children per classroom with one teacher, and each teacher works two shifts at a time. From the child-centered perspective, building classroom community is an important goal for early childhood education. It would seem challenging for young children to establish a sense of belonging and ownership in a classroom that is used by four different groups of children each day. This phenomenon would prevent children from leaving their artwork, bookbags, and extra clothing in the classroom, thus altering the concept of "my classroom" as it is understood in the West and viewed as crucial to creating a stable and consistent classroom space.

While conducting research on the islands of the Maldives, it was only with great difficulty that I found a street map of the capital, Malè, on the Internet, and was surprised at the map's unavailability in any of the tourist centers or hotels. The general outline map of Malè is commonly available but not a detailed street map. I soon realized that maps are not a way of life in Malè; moreover, street signs are not always displayed, and when they are, they are not easily visible. Street names did not seem to be very important to the local Maldivians. The people have a general sense of direction and know where buildings are, and they can take you there, but they are unable to give you directions in terms of specific street names when asked for a location. Their responses would include phrases such as "very far in that direction," or "two junctions more then turn left." Maldivians are island people and use boats for transportation the way we use land vehicles. At an early age they learn how to navigate the seas using only natural signs. This highlights the need for some individuals to be literate in a different kind of way. Spatial literacy rather than print literacy helps them navigate the ocean environment, and there is no need for maps. The West's early childhood curriculum is dominated by a social studies theme that includes mapping activities and construction of block buildings. This curriculum may not be very relevant in an island community where space is such a commodity that hardly any new construction takes place and maps are not commonly used.

In Sri Lanka, a large number of school experiences available to survivors of violence in the north, or those of a natural disaster in the south reflect a more traditional academic environment that is contrary to a Western early childhood discourse based on exploration and experimentation. For most of these children, however, structure, predictability, routine, and secure boundaries may bring a sense of comfort and stability that an open choice-based environment may not possess. The dominant Western discourse of progressive education, with its underlying assumptions of a choice-based classroom with plenty of materials, time, space, and teachers trained in a particular pedagogy, seemed a bit out of context here.

In the Jasmine PCF in Singapore, 4-year-old children were taught Chinese calligraphy in the Chinese Room by learning and practicing calligraphic techniques. The teaching of this fine motor skill as part of the writing curriculum would be considered developmentally inappropriate in a child-centered progressive curriculum for 4 year olds. But in Chinese-speaking societies where reading and writing depend on remembering and mastering hundreds of characters within a tonal language, the teaching of these skills does not seem inappropriate. As described earlier in Chapter 2, in traditional Chinese education repetition and imitation were instructional strategies widely used by kindergarten teachers where children were expected to listen closely to the teacher's instructions, pay close attention to the teacher's demonstration, "and then copy the teacher's work stroke by stroke, detail by detail, as best as they could" (Gu, 2006, p. 36). Perhaps this teaching method worked most effectively when children were expected to learn the highly complex writing system for the Chinese languages. The development of fine motor skills at an early age is further promoted in a society where young children learn to eat by regularly using chopsticks—a motor activity which requires the skill of deftly manipulating chopsticks with the fingers of one hand.

At the Dogwood Kindergarten in China, 30 four-year-old children sat in a circle with one teacher, who was leading them in an exercise to practice facial expressions and hand gestures from classical Peking Opera. Eventually, the children would be expected to perform stories from the opera on stage at the end of the year. This was a very teacher-directed activity, and the children seemed to follow the teacher quietly and patiently. This classroom curriculum and teacher-directed activity would not be viewed as child-centered teaching in the progressive education tradition. Within the context of many other child-friendly activities offered in the school curriculum, however, it seemed to strike the right balance in the school's overall educational goals.

Globalization and Pedagogical Hybridity

Policy makers at the periphery of global economics and politics are often caught between dealing with a colonial legacy and with the demands of being incorporated into a global, neoliberal capitalist economy (Crossley & Tikly, 2004). Because of the inevitable consequences of globalization, and/or the view that Western practices are the best practices, some schools consciously incorporated several Western elements. In Singapore the national emphasis on multiculturalism and unity underlying its diverse population is reflected in the kindergarten curriculum with regard to the linguistic, ethnic, and religious diversity of its students. There has also been an emphasis on teaching the academic skills of language and mathematics. The current national policy directions now echo the dominant Western discourse in steering the early childhood field away from academic goals and more toward learner-centered practices that highlight imaginative and creative play for children. With these changes in teaching strategies, the art and culture of the dominant West also seem to be creeping into the curriculum. A most interesting observation was the unit on the art of Keith Haring being studied in a local Singaporean community preschool, and the exploration of the art of Jackson Pollock in a private school in New Delhi as described in Chapter 5.

The culture of global economics and consumerism itself is a colonizing one inasmuch as the largest group targeted as consumers are young children. Numerous early childhood teachers and parents in the countries included in this study commented on the adverse effects of the commercial media on young children, and noted the uphill battle against the Western images of toys, fast foods, clothing, and lifestyles. A group of 12 private school teachers in New Delhi, who taught in early childhood classrooms ranging from Nursery through Grade 2, were asked to reflect on their perceptions of young children's behaviors and lifestyles in urban India. Many of these teachers, themselves being parents of young children, shared some of their frustrations at the habits and lifestyles young children had begun to develop in recent years. One teacher worried that "children are being exposed to a lot of animated media (games) which is making them more aggressive and their interest in reading books is being affected. With the Western culture being brought to India, the value system of respect and thoughtfulness is gradually disappearing." Another teacher highlighted the Westernization that was taking place: "Mainly our kids' eating habits have changed drastically, thanks to the media, for example all fast food and pizza joints that are so unhealthy for them. … Language has changed drastically as they are listening to all Western TV all the time." Several other teachers and teacher educators, in India and in other countries, expressed similar sentiments on the increasing evidence of cultural hybridity in children's lives.

An illustration of pedagogical hybridity was clearly evident in an earlier study that examined teaching practices in the early childhood classrooms of private schools in urban India. Classroom teaching appeared to be influenced by three different discourses coexisting in the educational climate in urban India:

> One dimension of this curriculum was highly structured, content-based, and had a formal academic aspect that was prescribed and mandated by the Indian government at the national level, and which had its roots in the colonizing influences of the British government on Indian education. Another dimension was the ongoing, parallel values-based curriculum inspired by the teachers' tacit knowledge and implicit beliefs resulting from their sociocultural-historical constructivist learning influenced by an all-pervasive Indian philosophy, and supported by the school administrators. A third dimension, although not specifically mentioned in the articulation of

educational objectives, was related to the school administrators' urgings of, and to the teachers' making sense of, the ideals of progressive early childhood pedagogy. (Gupta, 2006/2013, pp. 164–165)

This resulted in a unique kind of early childhood curriculum being enacted: the goal of teaching academics and developing academic proficiency in young children worked hand-in-hand with the goal of teaching values and developing good character, and at the same time there was also the intention for some child-centered practices as defined by the tradition of progressive education. Further, this curriculum was being implemented within a school environment that had large class-sizes and a high level of energy and engagement on the part of the students" (Gupta, 2006/2013).

In a similar manner, Zhu (2009, p. 54) notes that the occurrence of pedagogical hybridity in early childhood education in China reveals the three distinct cultural threads of traditional, communist, and Western cultures: the influence of the communist culture is evident in the practical aspects of the kindergarten curriculum, such as organization, administration, and curricular goals and content; the traditional influence is evident in the ideological and philosophical ideas such as views of the child, teacher–child interactions, and processes of teaching and learning; and finally, the Western influence has been introduced through exposure to diverse early childhood models such as Montessori, Reggio Emilia, Hi Scope, Project Approach, and Developmentally Appropriate Practices (DAP). But as classrooms begin to reflect changes from teacher-centered models to more child-centered and activity-based models, the process of transformation is not easy. The process reflects a "tension between traditional and modern cultures, Eastern and Western spirits, socialist and capitalist ideologies … the current educational ideas and practices reflect this cultural and ideological conjuncture in which changes and continuities co-exist" (Gu, 2006, p. 40). Dogwood Kindergarten in China placed a strong emphasis on traditional Chinese culture, specifically the Beijing (Peking) Opera. In every classroom, the curriculum was driven by the focus on traditional arts and culture, with young children learning to perform, paint, fold, cut, draw, and create, guided by the philosophy of the Chinese cultural arts. At the same time, the teachers and center director shared a deep desire to incorporate child-centered pedagogies in their goals. At the end of my tour, the director discussed this issue with me and asked me for my suggestions regarding activities and approaches in which Chinese traditional culture could be taught to young children in child-centered and learner-friendly ways. This is something that would be supported globally and would be a good example of how a traditional curriculum can be imparted in a learner-friendly manner.

These examples of hybridity may illustrate how, in these times of globalization, ideas from different worldviews may be combined to create a pedagogy that distances itself from an either/or approach and enables teachers and educators to embrace the local as well as the global in ways that make sense to those living in that reality. Globalization works in both ways, and there are a growing number of immigrants from Asia in the West whose lifestyles continue to reflect the cultural and spiritual philosophies of their native countries. In the face of rapidly increasing Asian diversity within the classrooms of Euro–American schools, educators have to think about how to creatively approach two critical issues: (1) ways in which teachers can learn to be more culturally empathetic toward children and families in their classrooms; (2) ways in which teachers, in turn, can prepare children in their classrooms to be more culturally intelligent. Ang & van Dyne (2008) define cultural intelligence as the capability to function effectively across various cultural contexts (as cited in Goh, 2013). But in order to teach children to be culturally intelligent teachers have to first learn how to teach with cultural intelligence. Goh (2013) clarifies that no teacher is prepared to teach in a culturally unintelligent manner, but in the increasingly complex cultural demographics of today's classrooms, value conflicts may easily occur, and teachers may unintentionally conduct themselves in a manner that may offend a child or family from another culture. Cultural intelligence and empathy may be nurtured by the use of culturally responsive pedagogy in teacher education programs.

Researchers and practitioners have suggested including culturally diverse traditions in schools, both locally and globally, as examples of practicing cultural responsiveness. Adair & Bhaskaran (2010) states that schools in India often include in their daily schedule traditional practices and customs such as silent sitting (an activity that may be viewed as a precursor to the ancient practice of meditation and that helps create a calmer inner and outer space for children in the classroom); the use of *rangoli* (the widely practiced Indian custom of decorating the threshold of one's home with a geometric or floral design that can be filled in with colored powders or flower petals and that develops a deeper awareness of respecting visitors to one's home, and a sense of pride in keeping one's space clean and beautiful); and eating meals on the floor (another traditional custom that is still practiced in rural India and during special ceremonies and celebrations such as weddings, funerals, and prayer gatherings). These practices in the curriculum of schools do not reflect unique school methods but rather are more reflective of social practices that are still widely observed in Indian society. Adair & Bhaskaran (2010) argues that including diverse cultural practices from around the world in a more global manner, in classrooms across many countries, would only help create a wider knowledge base and a deeper understanding of differences and similarities for both teachers and children.

Weijin Vun (2013) writes about the significance of Traditional Chinese Medicine (TCM), and the importance of being aware of the influence of biorhythms on our productivity and efficiency:

> In our competitive societies we are encouraged from a young age to be outstanding amongst our peers, to run the fastest on the track, to get the best grades, be the most creative artist, the most innovative entrepreneur. … This pushes us to be creative, productive, smart, fast and strong consistently throughout our waking hours. … While there's nothing wrong with

striving for achievement, unfortunately, sometimes in our rush to be the best, we think that needing rest is a sign of weakness and end up pushing ourselves beyond our limits on a daily basis.

With regard to schooling and the classroom environment, stress and fatigue can manifest in children when they become fidgety, start yawning or stretching or day dreaming, become restless and fidgety, start getting headache and tired eyes, making careless mistakes in spelling, reading, or writing, and begin to forget things they have just read. In attempting to apply the concepts of TCM to mitigate classroom challenges, Weijin Vun (2013) lists a number of relaxing activities designed to shift mental and physical energy to a restorative state, including: eating a healthy snack, listening to meditative music, doing a progressive muscle relaxation activity, taking a power nap, going for a short, relaxing walk, practicing abdominal breathing, and meditating. Each one of these activities can be easily incorporated into the curriculum of a pre-primary or primary program.

Another widely practiced custom in Asia is to remove one's shoes before entering a home. This custom was observed in many of the schools visited for this study, and children and adults were encouraged to take their shoes off before entering their classrooms. It's certainly a practice that we can all learn from with regard to teaching children about health and hygiene. It can only be beneficial for children to get into the habit of taking their shoes off, and it would also provide more opportunities for young children to practice and master self-help skills in the early childhood classrooms.

Being open-minded to diverse practices and routines from global cultures may be termed *borrowing*, but it can also enrich children's classroom experiences. During this process, however, *the key goal should be to implement a practice only while simultaneously understanding its underlying value and significance in the lives of those who do practice it*. It is the message rather than the practice itself, *why it is done in addition to how it is done*, that works to deepen our understanding of the "unfamiliar other."

Expanding the Early Childhood Education Research Base

These observations and experiences raise several questions about early childhood education: What do we understand of early childhood education? Who gets to determine the "acceptable" frameworks within which teachers are expected to position their early childhood practice? If it does not fit into any of the neatly labeled boxes that have been approved by the dominant early childhood education discourse, then is it deemed as unacceptable or inappropriate? The most important question, according to Brooker & Woodhead (2010), is how much are learning and development a factor of cultural processes within communities, and how much are they natural processes that occur with all children everywhere? By extension, how much of the "appropriateness" of pedagogy is culturally constructed and culturally applicable, and how much is generalizable?

The teaching and learning of the language and literacy of Indian languages is a good example based on research conducted by Nag et al. (2010). They report that most of the theorizing about how children learn to read has emerged out of the alphabetic scripts where symbol sets are typically between 26 and 34 symbols. Their research on early literacy shows that "when symbol sets are extensive there are particularities in the cognitive processes that are deployed. In the Indian *akshara* scripts for example, the pace of symbol learning is spread over the first four years in school. This is unlike in alphabetic languages where letter learning is rarely discussed as an issue beyond the first school year" (Nag et al., 2010, p. 49). Thus there are differences in theoretically explaining the cognitive underpinnings that support literacy acquisition as well as the delays and difficulties in the *akshara* languages as compared to the alphabetic languages. Similarly, the learning of thousands of Chinese characters comprised of ideas represented by calligraphic strokes would be another example in which the whole-language pedagogy widely promoted by child-centered educational approaches may not be as successful.

Another example of this dissonance may be found when definitions of terms that have been constructed in the West acquire a wide range of conceptualizations in diverse contexts. In a study conducted by Kubow (2007), teachers' construction of the notion of democracy was examined in countries in Africa. Their definitions were shown to be influenced by (1) a Western-oriented curriculum used in their school; (2) gender issues that impacted the lived experiences of teachers and students; (3) cultural beliefs and particular orientations to individualism and collectivism; and (4) the views that Westernization disrupted the African values of *ubuntu* that guide people in their interactions, and that individuality had come at the expense of communality.

A study by Sriprakash (2010) presents an analysis of child-centered teaching in rural India where the discourse of "child-centered, activity-based, joyful pedagogy" has been positioned as a national policy discourse to address issues of student retention and achievement in low-income rural areas of India. This study showed that using the democratic language of child-centered discourse did not necessarily hand over control to children, and that the teachers' interpretations were influenced by institutional systems, as well as by the hierarchy and social inequalities prevalent in rural India.

These examples of contextualized research are critical to making the early childhood education research base more reflective and inclusive of the majority world. There is clearly a need for a robust body of diverse early childhood theory that will allow for differences to be acknowledged as being appropriate within their own contexts rather than being inappropriate within a Western context. Viruru & Cannella wrote about making efforts that will "go beyond what common discourse describes as 'appropriate' early childhood education and look for other possibilities and ways of knowing" (2001, p. 145). More qualitative research across the non-West will help problematize the standard definitions and understandings of terms such as child-centric, citizenship, choice, motivation, teacher–child interactions, views on failure, and hard work. This research will also add new dimensions to their usage beyond the dominant Western perspectives, so that the West does not remain the sole norm against which educational systems measure each other. Blaise et al. (2013) urge educators to look toward the concepts of "Asia as method" (Chen, 2010) and "situated knowledges" (Haraway, 1991) as alternative paradigms for research to show how de-colonizing and de-imperializing methodologies can develop new practices that are potentially transformative.

Conclusion

At a very fundamental level, the concept of the child's well-being itself becomes nuanced relative to where it is defined and how much the definition of happiness is influenced by a sense of material well-being or by spiritual well-being, as well as by the particular developmental skills needed to successfully navigate life and society. So children might reach a state of well-being in different ways and through different experiences, depending on the larger cultures in which they live. In Chapter 1, I outlined the domains of learning specified for the goals of Education for All. It is important that teachers work toward certain goals, but it is even more critical that teachers receive the training that will enable them to implement these goals while recognizing children's circumstances and caregivers' and professionals' beliefs about children's development and learning (Brooker & Woodhead, 2010). Caution is advised for staying away from programs that offer parenting and teaching classes and workshops that draw directly from "standardized Anglo-European models and make assumptions about mother–child talk, mother–child control and direction, and time usage, which are culturally inappropriate" (Penn, 2010, p. 4). These world-class, global, and international programs look attractive and modern but fail to guide teachers in how to implement a contextually appropriate pedagogy. Teacher educators must support and encourage the preparation of teachers who will recognize the intimate connections between children's development and their cultural backgrounds, and truly believe that "rather as a background to children's emerging development, culture is … a foreground that leads to development" (Williams, 1999). The challenge lies in bridging the distance between the voice of the "familiar self" and the "unknown other" in recognizable and accessible ways (Williams, 1991). This bridging will lead to establishing a research base that is hybrid in nature, combining influences that are local and global, Western and non-Western, international and indigenous. Just as a third space can be created in actual practice (Gupta, 2006/2013), there can be the creation of a hybrid third space in theory as well that reflects and includes multiple perspectives and worldviews on the issues of children's development and education. This would be particularly helpful in complex and pluralistic societies in which conflicting values and expectations filtering down from the global and the local are often encountered. Finally, it is important to understand and emphasize that "the cultural appropriateness of any provision can only be assured by listening to local people as they explain their views of childhood" (Brooker & Woodhead, 2010, p. 36).

In a world that is so globalized, urban societies essentially reflect a cultural hybridity, just as classrooms may reflect pedagogical hybridity as was apparent in the two examples provided earlier in the chapter. In Chapter 2, I referred to another balancing act by teachers in China who need to juggle two pedagogical approaches in their practice: "loving children but not spoiling them; giving them more freedom but not abandoning discipline and order; being more democratic but not completely giving up centralism; meeting the needs and desires of individual children but not forsaking collectivism" (Gu, 2006, p. 38). In yet another illustration, an examination of globalization in three early childhood settings concludes with the advice that any early childhood approach needs to combine "traditional and modern, indigenous and transcultural approaches to create new preschool practices that are fitting to the particular children, parents and schools in a particular community" (Ball, as cited in Penn, 2010, p. 4). These instances underscore the importance of how teachers strive toward the practice of a hybrid pedagogy within the third space of cultural hybridity created by the interfacing of diverse worldviews, of the local and the global. *A pedagogy of the third space.*

This hybrid pedagogy, or pedagogy of the third space, is also the path to reconcile the two elements of pedagogy that have traditionally been positioned as a dichotomy but are often seen as emerging together in actual classroom practice—creativity and academics. In actuality, they are not mutually exclusive. Creativity does not just apply to arts and crafts, but it is really the ability to think outside the box. This kind of limitless thinking, or stretching of the imagination, can occur within any content area or field of study, whether it is drawing, dancing, or math and science. It is the thinking outside the box that led to many mathematical derivations and scientific inventions, as well as to innovative art techniques and dance forms. As a veteran Sri Lankan early childhood teacher and teacher educator said: "We need to teach our teachers how to be creative—not just how to do art and craft but how to think creatively. If I give them a paper clip, I want them to come up with ten ways in which this paper clip can be used differently."

The aim of this book has been to describe current trends in early childhood education policy and urban early childhood classroom practice in metropolitan cities across Asia, with the purpose of presenting educators everywhere with diverse images of early childhood education. As discussed in Chapter 1, this is not an in-depth study of early childhood education in any one of the five Asian countries. The fact that this book includes data from five different countries lends breadth rather than depth to the topic, and provides information with regard to broader trends that are emerging in early childhood education within this region. It is certainly helpful to know the future directions of policy and pedagogy in other parts of the world. In addition to the information in Chapter 2, the following examples of policy directions in Singapore, China, and India are provided by Singmaster (2011) from the Asia Society:

In 2010, Singapore's Ministry of Education identified 21st-century competencies essential for all its citizens, where each would be: (1) a confident person who has a strong sense of right and wrong, is adaptable and resilient, is discerning in judgment, thinks independently and critically, and communicates effectively; (2) a self-directed learner who questions, reflects, perseveres, and takes responsibility for his own learning; (3) an active contributor who is able to work effectively in teams, is innovative, exercises initiative, takes calculated risks, and strives for excellence; and (4) a concerned citizen who is rooted to Singapore, has a strong sense of civic responsibility, is informed about Singapore and the world, and takes an active part in bettering the lives of others around him (Singmaster, 2011).

China's 2020 education reform plan is projected to update the country's curriculum to meet real-world needs. For instance, math will no longer emphasize a student's response time and the need to memorize complex and seldom-used formulas. In science, calculations and drills will be replaced with student experiments in real-world applications, including an emphasis on new energy, health, and conservation (Singmaster, 2011).

In India, the government's plans for policy include less emphasis on memorization and more on analytic and communications skills, as well as a global focus in the curriculum. Further, students will be required to study three languages, as well as literature from around the world and world history. There will be less focus on textbooks, and an increased focus on project-based learning, service learning, discussions, and experiments as well as international business communication and technology skills (Singmaster, 2011).

In going through the descriptions in this book, readers might find images of early childhood classrooms that look similar to or different from their own. In the former instance it would strengthen their own views, and in the latter instance it would provide them with a challenge to grapple with a view different from their own. In either case, it is an opportunity for all to consider and reflect upon our own and others' ideas and to better understand how education is viewed and imparted in different parts of the world. In doing so perhaps, too, we will be inspired to rethink some aspect of our own practice or create our own unique plan for early childhood education.

REFERENCES

Abdullah, A.R.S. (1982). *Educational theory: A Quranic outlook*. Makkah, Saudi Arabia: Umm Al-Qura University.

Abhyadeva, C.M. (2003). *Early childhood care and development in Sri Lanka*. Colombo, Sri Lanka: National Education Commission.

Abhyadeva, C.M. (2010, 17 January). The next battle. *Sunday Observer*, p. 27.

Adair, J.K. & Bhaskaran, L. (2010). Practices from an urban preschool in Bangalore, India. *Young Children*, November 2010, pp. 48–55.

AFP (Agence France-Presse) (2007). *India passes law to punish children who abandon elderly parents*, December 6, 2007. Available at http://www.google.com/hostednews/afp/article/ALeqM5h-D8QxY-J5wpaNMshKiS2ouvHKLg

Alexander, R.J. (2000). *Culture and pedagogy: International comparisons in primary education*. Oxford, UK: Blackwell.

Ang, S., & van Dyne, L. (2008). Conceptualization of cultural intelligence: Definition, distinctiveness, and nomological network. In S. Ang & L. van Dyne (Eds.), *Handbook on cultural intelligence: Theory, measurement and applications* (pp. 3–15). Armonk, NY: M.E. Sharpe.

Anjum, Z. (2012). Microsoft launches educational research center in Singapore. *Computerworld Singapore*, June 5, 2012: Accessed on June 24, 2013 at http://www.computerworld.com.sg/print-article/20110/

Apple, M. (2001). *Educating the "right" way: Markets, standards, God, and inequality*. New York: Routledge Falmer Press.

Apple, M. (2011). Global crises, social justice, and teacher education. *Journal of Teacher Education* 62(2), 222–234.

Ashcroft, B., Griffiths, G., & Tiffin, H. (Eds.) (1995). *The post-colonial studies reader*. London, UK: Routledge.

Autin, F., & Croizet, J.C. (2012). Improving working memory efficiency by reframing metacognitive interpretation of task difficulty. *Journal of Experimental Psychology*, 141(4), 610–618.

BBC (2000, 25 September). China steps up one child policy. BBC News Report. Retrieved on 19 August 2013.

Ball, J. (2010). Afterword. In A. Cleghorn & L. Prochner (Eds.), *Shades of globalization in three early childhood settings: Views from India, South Africa and Canada*. Rotterdam: Sense Publishers.

Banks, J.A., & Banks, C.A.M. (Eds.) (2004). *Handbook of research on multicultural education* (2nd ed.). San Francisco, CA: Jossey-Bass.

Belfield, C.R., & Levin, H.M. (2002). The effects of competition between schools on educational outcomes: A review for the United States. *Review of Educational Research,* 72(4), 279–341.

Bhabha, H. (1994). *The location of culture.* London, UK: Routledge.

Bhabha, H. (2009, Winter). An interview with Homi Bhabha: Cultural translation and interpretation: A dialogue on migration, identity, and ethical responsibility: An argument against fixed identities. *Sangsaeng* (26). Asia-Pacific Center of Education for International Understanding, UNESCO.

Blaise, M., Leung, V.W.M., & Sun, C. (2013). Views from somewhere: Situated knowledges and partial perspectives in a Hong Kong kindergarten classroom. *Global Studies of Childhood.* www.wwwords.co.uk/gsch/content/pdfs/3/pdfs/3/issue3_1.asp

Bloch, M.N. (1992). Critical perspectives on the historical relationship between child development and early childhood education research. In S. Kessler & B.B. Swadener (Eds.), *Reconceptualizing the early childhood curriculum: Beginning the dialogue.* New York: Teachers College Press.

Bray, M., Adamson, B., & Mason, M. (2007). Different models, different emphases, different insights. In Mark Bray, Bob Adamson, & Mark Mason (Eds.), *Comparative education research: Approaches and methods.* CERC—The University of Hong Kong, Hong Kong: Springer.

Bray, M., Adamson, B., & Mason, M. (2007). Introduction. In Mark Bray, Bob Adamson, & Mark Mason (Eds.), *Comparative education research: Approaches and methods.* CERC—The University of Hong Kong, Hong Kong: Springer.

Bronson, P., & Merryman, A. (2013a). *Top dog: The science of winning and losing.* Twelve: New York: Hatchet Books Group.

Bronson, P., & Merryman, A. (2013b, 6 February). Why can some kids handle pressure while others fall apart? *New York Times.* Magazine Section, Available at http://www.nytimes.com/2013/02/10/magazine/why-can-some-kids-handle-pressure-while-others-fall-apart.html?pagewanted=all&_r=0

Brooker, L. (2011). Taking play seriously. In S. Rogers (Ed.), *Rethinking play and pedagogy in early childhood education: Concepts, contexts and cultures.* Oxford, UK: Routledge.

Brooker, L., & Woodhead, M. (2010). Early childhood programs and respect for diversity. In Liz Brooker & Martin Woodhead (Eds.), *Early childhood in focus: Culture and learning.* Milton Keynes, UK: The Open University.

Brooker, L., & Woodhead, M. (2010). Preface. In Liz Brooker & Martin Woodhead (Eds.), *Early childhood in focus: Culture and learning.* Milton Keynes, UK: The Open University.

Brown, C.P. (2009). Confronting the contradictions: A case study of teacher development in neoliberal times. *Contemporary Issues in Early Childhood,* 10(3), 240–258.

Burghardt, G.M. (2011). Defining and recognizing play. In A.D. Pellegrini (Ed.), *The Oxford handbook on the development of play,* pp. 9–18. New York: Oxford University Press.

Calman, L.J., & Tarr-Whelan, L. (2005). An early childhood investment for all: A wise investment: Recommendations arising from a conference "The Economic Impacts of Child Care and Early Education: Financing Solutions for the Future." Sponsored by Legal Momentum's Family Initiative and the MIT Workplace Center. Executive Summary retrieved from web.mit.edu/workplacecenter/docs/Executive%20Summary.pdf

Cannella, G.S. (1997). *Deconstructing early childhood education: Social justice and revolution.* New York: Peter Lang Publishing.

Chan, S. (1992). Families with Asian roots. In E. Lynch & M. Hanson (Eds.), *Developing cross-cultural competence: A guide for working with young children and their families,* pp. 181–257. Baltimore, MD: Paul H. Brookes.

Chen, K.H. (2010). *Asia as method: Toward deimperialization.* Durham, NC: Duke University Press.

Chong, K. (2007). The good life: Moral education in a consumerist society. In Charlene Tan & Kim-chong Chong (Eds.), *Critical perspectives on values education in Asia.* Singapore: Pearson Prentice Hall.

Cleverly, J. (1986). *The schooling of China: Tradition and modernity in Chinese education.* Sidney, Australia: Allen & Unwin.

Creel, H.G. (1949). *Confucius and the Chinese way.* New York: Harper & Row.

Crossley, M. (2000). Bridging cultures and traditions in the reconceptualization of comparative and international education. *Comparative Education,* 36(3), 319–332.

Crossley, M., & Tikly, L. (2004). Postcolonial perspectives and comparative and international research in education: A critical introduction. *Comparative Education,* 40(2), 147–156.

Cultural translation and interpretation: A dialogue on migration, identity, and ethical responsibility. (2009, Winter). Interview with Homi Bhabha. *Sang Saeng,* 32–35.

Dahlberg, G., & Moss, P. (2008). Beyond quality in early childhood education and care: Languages of evaluation. *New Zealand Journal of Teachers Work,* 5(1), 3–12.

Dave, I. (1991). *Indian personality in its developmental background.* Udaipur, India: Himanshu Publications.

Delpit, L. (1995). *Other people's children: Cultural conflict in the classroom.* New York: The New Press.

Dhillon Trivedi, H. (1993). *Colonial transactions: English literature and India.* Calcutta: Papyrus.

Dienstbier, R.A., & Pytlik Zillig, L.M. (2012). Toughness. *The Oxford handbook of positive psychology* (2nd ed.).

Dimmock, C. (2007). Comparing educational organizations. In Mark Bray, Bob Adamson, & Mark Mason (Eds.), *Comparative education research: Approaches and methods.* CERC—The University of Hong Kong, Hong Kong: Springer.

Dissanayake, W.K., & Gokulsing, M. (2004, May). *Indian popular cinema: A narrative of cultural change* (2nd ed.). Trentham Books.

Dockett, S. (2011). The challenge of play for early childhood educators. In S. Rogers (Ed.), *Rethinking play and pedagogy in early childhood education: Concepts, contexts and cultures.* New York, NY: Routledge.

Dube, S.C. (1990/2000). *Indian society.* New Delhi, India: National Book Trust.

Dweck, C. (1999, Spring). Caution: Praise can be dangerous. *The American Educator,* 1–5. American Federation of Teachers.

Dweck, C. (2007). *Mindset: The new psychology of success.* New York: Random House.

Earley, P.C., & Ang, S. (2003). *Cultural intelligence: Individual interactions across cultures.* Palo Alto, CA: Stanford University Press.

Education for Quality (1999). *The decision of the CPC Central Committee and the State Council on deepening education reform and promoting quality education in an all-round way (June 13, 1999).* Communist Party of China, 2000.

Edwards, S. (2013). Digital play in the early years: A contextual response to the problem of integrating technologies and play-based pedagogies in the early childhood curriculum. *European Early Childhood Education Research Journal,* 21(2), 199–212.

EFA National Action Plan, Sri Lanka (2004). Colombo, Sri Lanka: Ministry of Education.

EFA Plan of Action, Maldives: Follow up to Dakar Framework of Action. (2001). Male, Maldives: Ministry of Education.

Fafunwa, A.B. (1974). *A history of education in Nigeria*. London, UK: Allen & Unwin.

Fariq, F.Y., Farhath, A., Mufeed, A., & Rauffiya, A. (2010). University presentation in an Education Administration class in the Maldives, accessed on 4/15/2013 and available at www.slideshare.net/FaznaFariq/ece-maldives-final-7296428

Farrell, D., & Beinhocker, E. (2007, 19 May). Next big spenders: India's middle class. McKinsey & Company. Retrieved 17 September 2011.

Fisher, M.P. (1994). *Living religions* (2nd ed.). Englewood Cliffs, NJ: Prentice Hall.

Gallardo, C.G.C. (2009, June). Early childhood education: Toward sustainable peace education in Sri Lanka. Unpublished Master's thesis at Graduate Institute of Peace Studies, Kyung Hee University, Seoul, South Korea.

Gauld, J.W. (2011, 29 November). Strong parenting is key to America's future. *Education Week*.

Gay, G. (2002). *Culturally responsive teaching: Theory, research, and practice*. New York: Teachers College Press.

Genishi, C., & Dyson, A.H. (2009). *Children, language and literacy: Diverse learners in diverse times*. New York, NY: Teachers College Press.

Genishi, C., & Goodwin, A.L. (Eds, 2007). *Diversities in early childhood education: Rethinking and doing*. New York, NY: Routledge.

Gernet, J. (1962). *Daily life in China on the eve of the Mongol invasion*. Stanford, CA: Stanford University Press.

Giddens, A. (1991). *The consequences of modernity*. Stanford University Press. As cited in Arnove (2013). *Introduction: Reframing Comparative Education*. In Arnove, R.F., Torres, C.A. & Franz, S (Eds) *Comparative Education: The dialectics of the global and the local* (2013).

Goh, M. (2013). Teaching with cultural intelligence: Developing multiculturally educated and globally engaged citizens. *Asia Pacific Journal of Education*, 32(4), 395–415.

Goncu, A. (2010). Cultures of caregiving—mothers and others. In Liz Brooker & Martin Woodhead (Eds.), *Early childhood in focus: Culture and learning*. Milton Keynes, UK: The Open University.

Gonzalez-Mena, J. (2008). *Diversity in early care and education: Honoring differences*. New York: McGraw-Hill.

Grant, C.A., & Sleeter, C.E. (2007). *Doing multicultural education for achievement and equity*. New York: Routledge.

Green, C. (2005). *The privatization of state education: Public partners, private dealings*. Abingdon, Oxon UK: Routledge Falmer Press.

Grieshaber, S. (2008). Interrupting stereotypes: Teaching and the education of young children. *Early Education and Development*, 19(3), 505–518.

Gu, L. (2006, Fall). Chinese early childhood education in transition. *WINGSPAN Journal for Leadership, Learning, and School Development*, 16(1), 30–41.

The Guidance for Kindergarten Education (trial version, 2001). Ministry of Education in People's Republic of China. 2001. www.edu.cn/20011126/3011708.shtml (cited in Zhu, 2009).

Gupta, A. (2001). Implementing change at the pre-primary level in a school in India. *International Journal of Early Childhood*, 33(1), 34–42.

Gupta, A. (2004). The challenge of working with large class size: Dispositions of early childhood teachers in India. *Contemporary Issues in Early Childhood*, 5(3), 361–377.

Gupta, A. (2006). *Early childhood education, postcolonial theory, and teaching practices in India: Balancing Vygotsky and the Veda* (1st ed.). New York: Palgrave Macmillan Publishers.

Gupta, A. (2007). *Going to school in South Asia.* Westport, CT: Greenwood Press.

Gupta, A. (2008). Tracing global-local transitions within early childhood curriculum and practice in India. *Research in Comparative and International Education,* 3(3), 266–280.

Gupta, A. (2011). Play and pedagogy framed within India's historical, socio-cultural and pedagogical context. In S. Rogers (Ed.), *Rethinking play and pedagogy in early childhood education: Concepts, contexts and cultures.* Oxford, UK: Routledge.

Gupta, A. (2012). Neoliberal globalization and pre-primary teacher education policy and practice in India, Sri Lanka and the Maldives. In D. Kapoor, B. Barua, & A. Datoo (Eds.), *Globalization, culture and education in South Asia: Critical excursions.* New York: Palgrave Macmillan Publishers.

Gupta, A. (2013). *Early childhood education, postcolonial theory, and teaching practices and policies in India: Balancing Vygotsky and the Veda* (2nd ed.). New York: Palgrave Macmillan Publishers.

Haneef, S. (1995). *What everyone needs to know about Islam and Muslims.* Chicago, IL: Kazi Publications.

Haraway, D. (1991). Situated knowledges: The science question in feminims and the privilege of partial perspective. In D. Haraway, *Simians, Cyborgs and women: The reinvention of nature.* London: Free Association Books.

Hawkins, J.N. (2013). Education in the Asia-Pacific region: Some enduring challenges. In Robert F. Arnove, Carlos Alberto Torres, & Stephen Franz (Eds.), *Comparative education: The dialectic of the global and the local* (4th ed.). Plymouth, UK: Rowman & Littlefield.

Hirata, T., Morishita, M., Suzuki, K., & Kampeeraparb, S. (2005). A comparative study on citizenship education in Thailand and Japan: An analysis of questionnaire surveys and proposals for learning models. Paper presented at the 5th Comparative Education Society of Asia Biennial Conference held in Selangor, Malaysia on 30 May 2005.

Ho, W.K., & Gopinathan, S. (1999). Recent developments in education in Singapore. *School Effectiveness and School Improvement,* 10(1), 99–117.

Hsueh, Y., Tobin, J.J., & Karasawa, M. (2004). The Chinese kindergarten in its adolescence. *Prospects,* 34(4), 257–269.

Huntsinger, C.S., Huntsinger, P.R., Ching, W., & Lee, C. (2000, November). Understanding cultural context fosters sensitive caregiving of Chinese American children. *Young Children,* pp. 7–15.

Institute for a Competitive Workforce (2010). Why business should support early childhood education. Institute for a Competitive Workforce, U.S. Chamber of Commerce.

Irvine, J.J. (1992). Making teacher education culturally responsive. In M.E. Dilworth (Ed.), *Diversity in teacher education: New expectations* (pp. 79–82). San Francisco, CA: Jossey-Bass.

Irvine, J.J. (2003). *Educating teachers for diversity: Seeing with a cultural eye.* New York: Teachers College Press.

Issues regarding current development of early childhood education (2010). China State Council. www.gov.cn/zwgk/2010-11/24/content_1752377.htm (as cited in Zhou, 2011).

Jayaweera, S. (2007). Going to school in Sri Lanka. In A. Gupta (Ed.), *Going to school in South Asia.* Westport, CT: Greenwood Press.

Jiao, S., Guiping, J., & Quicheng, J. (1986). Comparative study of behavioral qualities of only children and sibling children. *Child Development,* 57, pp. 357–361.

Kakar, S. (1981). *The inner world: A psycho-analytic study of childhood and society in India.* New Delhi, India: Oxford University Press.

Katz, L. (1996). Child development knowledge and teacher preparation: Confronting assumptions. *Early Childhood Research Quarterly*, 11(2), 145–146.

Katz, L.G. (1999). International perspectives on early childhood education: Lessons from my travels. *Early Childhood Research and Practice*, 1(1). Available at eecrp.uiuc.edu/v1n1/katz.html

Kennedy, K.J., & Fairbrother, G.P. (2004). Asian perspectives on citizenship education in review: Postcolonial constructions of pre-colonial values. In W.O. Lee, D.L. Grossman, K.J. Kennedy, & G.P. Fairbrother (Eds.), *Citizenship education in Asia and the Pacific: Concepts and issues*, pp. 289–301. Hong Kong, Comparative Education Research Center, University of Hong Kong: Kluwer.

Kessler, S. (1991). Alternative perspectives on early childhood education. *Early Childhood Research Quarterly*, 6(2), 183–197.

Kessler, S., & Swadener, B.B. (1992). *Reconceptualizing the early childhood curriculum: Beginning the dialogue.* New York: Teachers College Press.

Kindergarten work regulations and procedures (1989). National Education Committee of the People's Republic of China. www.people.com.cn/item/flfgk/gwyfg/1996/206002199602.html (as cited in Zhu, 2010).

King, D. (2010). Failure of preschool education in Sri Lanka accessed at www.srilankaguardian.org/2010/01/failure-of-pre-school-education-in-sri.html) on 11/2/11.

Kluckhohn, F. (1961). Dominant and variant value orientations. In Florence Kluckhohn & Fred L. Strodtbeck (Eds.), *Variations in value orientations.* Westport, CT: Greenwood Press.

Kolucki, B. (2006). Program communication in early child development: A United Nations Children's Fund publication. New York: Early Child Development Unit, UNICEF.

Kristof, N.D. (2011, January 15). China's winning schools? *The New York Times.*

Kubow, P.K. (2007). Teachers' constructions of democracy: Intersections of Western and indigenous knowledge in South Africa and Kenya. *Comparative Education Review*, 51(3), 307–328.

Ladson-Billings, G. (1994). *The dreamkeepers: Successful teachers of African American children.* San Francisco, CA: Jossey-Bass.

Ladson-Billings, G. (1995, 21 September). Toward a theory of culturally relevant pedagogy. *American Educational Research Journal,* 32(3), 465–491.

Ladson-Billings, G. (2006). It's not the culture of poverty, it's the poverty of culture: The problem with teacher education. *Anthropology and Education Quarterly*, 37(2), 104–109.

Law, N. (2005). Comparing pedagogical innovations. In Mark Bray, Bob Adamson, & Mark Mason (Eds.) (2007). *Comparative education research: Approaches and methods.* CERC-University of Hong Kong, Hong Kong: Springer.

Learning Metrics Task Force (2013, February). Report No. 1. *Toward universal learning: What every child should learn.* Montreal, Canada: UNESCO Institute for Statistics, and Washington, DC: Center for Universal Education at Brookings.

Lee, T.Y. (2007). *Anyone can go to heaven: Just be good!* Singapore: KepMedia International, Pte. Ltd.

Li Wen (2008, 5 April). Four-two-one families, where is the road going? *Yunnan Daily Online.* Retrieved 19 August 2013.

Li, J., & Wang, Q. (2004). Perceptions of achievement and achieving peers in the US and Chinese kindergartners. *Social Development*, 13(3), 413–436.

Lim, S.M. & Lim, A.S.E. (in press). Govermentality of early childhood care and education in a global city. In N. Rao, J. Zhao and J. Sun (Eds.), *Early childhood education in Chinese societies.* Dordrecht. Netherlands: Springer

Lim, S.M., & Lum, C.H. (2013). Preschool teaching at its best. *Research in Education,* 9, p. 8. National Institute of Education, Singapore.

Lim, S.M., & Lum, C.H. (2012). Creating polyphony with exploratory web documentation in Singapore. *Autralasian Journal of Early Childhood,* 37(4), 123–126.

Lipman, J. (2013, 28–29 September). Tough teachers get results. *The Wall Street Journal.* Review Section, Saturday/Sunday.

Locust, C. (1988). Wounding the spirit: Discrimination and traditional American Indian belief systems. *Harvard Educational Review,* 58(3), 315–330.

Lomas, N. (2013, 26 June). India passes Japan to become third largest global Smartphone market, after China & U.S. *TechCrunch.* AOL Inc. Retrieved 19 August 2013.

Loomba, A. (1998). *Colonialsim/Postcolonialism.* London, UK: Routledge.

Macedo, D. (1999). Decolonizing indigenous knowledge. In L. Semali & J.L. Kincheloe (Eds.), *What is indigenous knowledge? Voices from the academy.* New York: Falmer Press.

Mahon, R. (2010). After neo-liberalism? The OECD, the World Bank and the child. *Global Social Policy,* 10(2), 172–192.

Marfo, K., & Biersteker, L. (2011). Exploring culture, play and early childhood education practice in African contexts. In S. Rogers (Ed.), *Rethinking play and pedagogy in early childhood education: Concepts, contexts and cultures.* Oxford, UK: Routledge.

Masemann, V.L. (2006). Afterword. *Current Issues in Comparative Education,* 8(2), 104–111.

Masemann, V.L. (2013). Culture and education. In Robert F. Arnove, Carlos Alberto Torres, & Stephen Franz (Eds.), *Comparative education: The dialectic of the global and local.* Plymouth, UK: Rowman & Littlefield.

Mason, M. (2007). Comparing cultures. In Mark Bray, Bob Adamson, & Mark Mason (Eds.) (2007), *Comparative education research: Approaches and methods.* CERC—The University of Hong Kong, Hong Kong: Springer.

Mayer, D., Luke, C. & Luke, A. (2008). Teachers, national regulations, and cosmopolitanism. In A. Phelan & J. Sumsion (Eds.), *Critical readings in teacher education: Provoking absences,* pp. 79–98. Rotterdam, The Netherlands: Sense Publishers.

Ministry of Child Development and Women's Empowerment (2006). *Starting right: Guidelines for child development centers.* Colombo, Sri Lanka: Ministry of Child Development and Women's Empowerment. www.childwomenmin.gov.lk/web/index.php?option=com_publication&Itemid=50

Ministry of Education of People's Republic of China (1996). *Regulations for kindergarten work.* Beijing.

Ministry of Human Resource Development, Education & Cultural Affairs (2004). Education for All National Plan Sri Lanka.

Ministry of Social Welfare (2003). National Policy on Early Childhood Care and Development Colombo, Sri Lanka. Retrieved from http://www.childwomenmin.gov.lk/web/index.php?option=com_publication&Itemid=5

Moffitt, T. E., Arseneault, L., Belskya, L., Dickson, N., Hancox, R.J., Harrington, H.L., et al. (2011). A gradient of childhood self-control predicts health, wealth, and public safety. *Proceedings of the National Academy of Sciences of the United States of America,* 108(7), 2693–2698.

Moll, L.C., Amanti, C., Neff, D., & Gonzalez, N. (1992). Funds of knowledge for teaching: Using a qualitative approach to connect homes and classrooms. *Theory into Practice,* 31(2), 132–141.

Mookerji, R. (1969). *Ancient Indian education.* Delhi, India: Motilal Banarsidas Publishers.

Morris, P., & Sweeting, A. (1995). *Education and development in East Asia.* New York: Garland.

Mukherjee, J.K. (2008). *Principles and goals of integral education: As propounded by Sri Aurobindo and the Mother.* Puducherry, India: Sri Aurobindo Ashram Publication Department.

Naftali, O. (2010). Recovering childhood: Play, pedagogy, and the rise of psychological knowledge in contemporary urban China. *Modern China,* 36(6), 589–616.

Nag, S., Treiman, R., & Snowling, M. (2010). Learning to spell in an Alphasyllabary: The case of Kannada. *Writing Systems Research,* 2(1), 41–52.

National Council for Teacher Education (2011). NCTE at a glance. New Delhi, India, NCTE. Retrieved from www.ncte-india.org/theintro.asp

National Council of Educational Research and Training (2006). Position paper: National Focus Group on early childhood education. New Delhi, India: NCERT.

National Curriculum Framework. (2005). New Delhi, India: NCERT.

National Institute of Education Press Release (2009, April 28): Available at https://www.nie.edu.sg/newsroom/press-release/2009/nan-chiau-primary-school-and-nie-set-first-research-centre-using-ict-teaching-and-learning-primary-s

National Policy and a Comprehensive Framework of Actions on Education for Social Cohesion and Peace (ESCP). (2008). Ministry of Education Sri Lanka, Social Cohesion and Peace Education Unit. Colombo: Ministry of Education Sri Lanka. Accessed on 10/31/2013, available at www.moe.gov.lk/web/images/stories/publication/peace_policy.pdf

National Policy on Education (1986/1992). Retrieved from Department of Education, Government of India home page at www.education.nic.in

Nieto, S. (2004). *Affirming diversity: The sociopolitical context of multicultural education* (2nd ed.). White Plains, NY: Longman Publishers.

Nieto, S. (2009). *The light in their eyes: Creating multicultural learning communities.* New York: Teachers College Press.

Organ, T. (1970). *The Hindu quest for the perfection of man.* Athens, OH: Ohio University Press.

The outline of China's national plan for medium and long-term educational reform and development (2010) China State Council. Available at www.gov.cn/jrgz/2010-07/29/content_1667143.htm (as cited in Zhou, 2011).

Ozmon, H., & Craver, S. (1995). *Philosophical foundations of education.* Englewood, NJ: Prentice Hall.

Penn, H. (2010). The universal and the particular. In Liz Brooker & Martin Woodhead (Eds.), *Early childhood in focus: Culture and learning.* Milton Keynes, UK: The Open University.

Perera, W.J. (2009, Winter). Walasbedda School: One individual makes a difference. *Sang Saeng,* 28–31. www.unescoapceiu.org/bbs/board.php?bo_table=sangsaeng&wr_id=462(77)

Philips, D., & Ochs, K. (2003). Processes of policy borrowing in education: Some explanatory and analytical devices. *Comparative Education,* 39(4), 451–461.

Pisa envy. (2013, 19 January). *The Economist,* pp. 61–62.

Rajendram, D. (2013, 10 March). The promise and peril of India's youth bulge. *The Diplomat.* Retrieved on 19 August 2013. Available at thediplomat.com/2013/03/10/the-promise-and-peril-of-indias-youth-bulge/

Reagan, T. (2005). *Non-Western educational traditions: Indigenous approaches to educational thought and practice.* London, UK: Lawrence Erlbaum Associates.

Richards, H.V., Brown, A.F., & Forde, T.V. (2006). Addressing diversity in schools: Culturally responsive teaching. Tempe, AZ: National Center for Culturally Responsive Educational Systems, Arizona State University.

Right of Children to Free and Compulsory Education (RTE) Act of 2009 accessed at mhrd.gov.in/rte on 10/31/2013

Rockstuhl, T., Hong, Y.Y., Ng, K.Y., Ang, S., & Chiu, C.Y. (2010). The culturally intelligent brain: From detecting to bridging cultural differences. *Neuro-Leadership Institute*, 3, 1–15.

Ross, E.W., & Gibson, R. (Eds.) (2007). *Neoliberalism and education reform*. New York: Hampton Press.

Rui, Y. (2007). Comparing policies. In Mark Bray, Bob Adamson, & Mark Mason (Eds.), *Comparative education research: Approaches and methods*. CERC—The University of Hong Kong, Hong Kong: Springer.

Saini, A. (2000). Literacy and empowerment: An Indian scenario. *Childhood Education, International Focus Issue*, 76(6), 381–384.

Sarva Shiksha Abhyaan. (2011). *A framework for implementation: Based on the right of children to Free and Compulsory Education Act, 2009*. Department of School Education and Literacy, Ministry of Human Development, Government of India.

Seery, M.D. (2011). Resilience: A silver lining to experiencing adverse life events? *Current Directions in Psychological Science, 20*, 390.

Seery, M.D., Holman, E.A., & Silver, R.C. (2010). Whatever does not kill us: Cumulative lifetime adversity, vulnerability, and resilience. *Journal of Personality and Social Psychology*, 99(6), 1025–1041.

Seery, M.D., Leo, R.J., Lupien, S.P., Kondrak, C.L., & Almonte, J.L. (2013, 14 May). An upside to adversity? Moderate cumulative lifetime adversity is associated with resilient responses in the face of controlled stressors. *Psychological Science*.

Semali, L., & Kincheloe, J.L. (Eds.) (1999). *What is indigenous knowledge? Voices from the academy*. New York: Falmer Press, p. 15.

Semel, S. (2006). Introduction. In S.F. Semel & A.R. Sadovnik (Eds.), *"Schools of tomorrow," schools of today: What happened to progressive education*. New York: Peter Lang Publishing.

Shanghai's People's Congress Standing Committee. (2004). Shanghai Municipality regulations on the protection of minors. www.shmec.gov.cn/xxgk/PubInfo/rows_content.php?article_code=201042005001 (as cited in Naftali, 2010).

Sin, C.H. (2002). The quest for a balanced ethnic mix: Singapore's ethnic quota policy examined. *Urban Studies, 39*(8), 1347–1374.

Singmaster (2011). How high-performing nations teach global skills. The Asia Society. Available at asiasociety.org/education/learning-world/how-high-performing-nations-teach-global-skills. Accessed on 1 October 2013.

Smith, P.K. (2010). *Children and play: Understanding children's world*. West Sussex, UK: Wiley-Blackwell.

Snarey, J. (2007). Foreword: Moral education and globalization. In Charlene Tan & Chong, Kim-chong (Eds.), *Critical perspectives on values education in Asia*. Singapore: Pearson Prentice Hall.

Spring, J. (2009). *Globalization and education*. New York: Routledge.

Sriprakash, A. (2010). Child-centered education and the promise of democratic learning: Pedagogic messages in rural Indian primary schools. *International Journal of Educational Development*.

Stewart, V., & Kagan, S.L. (2005 November). Conclusion. A new worldview: Education in a global era. *Phi Delta Kappan*, 87(3), 241–245.

Tibawi, A.L. (1972). *Islamic education: Its traditions and modernization into the Arab national systems.* London, UK: Luzac and Company.

Tikly, L. (1999). Postcolonialism and comparative education. *International Review of Education*, 45(5/6), 603–621.

Tobin, J., Hsueh, Y., & Karasawa, M. (2009). *Preschools in three cultures revisited.* Chicago: University of Chicago Press.

Tooley, J. (2009). *The beautiful tree: A personal journey into how the world's poorest people are educating themselves.* Washington, DC: Cato Institute.

Tooley, J., & Dixon, P. (2003). Providing education for the world's poor. A case study of the private sector in India. In B. Davies & J. West-Burnham (Eds.), *Handbook of educational leadership and management.* London, UK: Pearson Education.

Trawick-Smith, J. (2006). *Early childhood development: A multicultural perspective.* Upper Saddle River, NJ: Pearson Merrill Prentice Hall.

Trivedi, H. (1993). *Colonial transactions: English literature and India.* Calcutta: Papyrus.

Turning the key competencies into reality: A practical guide for teachers (2011). 2011 Draft National Curriculum Framework, Educational Development Center, Maldives.

UNESCO (2012). *EFA Global Monitoring Report 2012: Youth and skills—Putting education to work.* Paris, France: UNESCO.

UNESCO (2007). Maldives: Early childhood care and education (ECCE) programs. Strong foundations: Early childhood care and education. Compiled for Education for All Global Monitoring Report. Geneva, Switzerland: UNESCO International Bureau of Education.

UNICEF Statistics (2010). Sri Lanka statistics. Retrieved from www.unicef.org/infoby-country/sri_lanka_statistics.html

UNESCO (2011). World data on education. Retrieved from unesdoc.unesco.org/images/0021/002113/211312e.pdf

United Nations Millennium Development Goals available at www.un.org/millennium-goals/education.shtml

Van Oers, B. (2013). Is it play? Toward a reconceptualization of role play from an activity theory perspective. *European Early Childhood Education Research Journal*, 21(2), 185–198.

Vaughan, J. (1993). Early childhood education in China. Precious children. *Association for Childhood Education International.* www.pbs.org/kcts/preciouschildren/earlyed/read_vaughan.html accessed on 4/2/2013.

Villegas, A.M., & Lucas, T. (2002). Preparing culturally responsive teachers: Rethinking the curriculum. *Journal of Teacher Education*, 53(13).

Viruru, R. (2001). *Early childhood education: Postcolonial perspectives from India.* New Delhi, India: Sage Publications.

Viruru, R. (2005). The impact of postcolonial theory on early childhood education. *Journal of Education*, 35, 7–29.

Viruru, R., & Cannella, G.S. (2001). Early childhood education and postcolonial possibilities. In R. Viruru, *Early childhood education: Postcolonial perspectives from India.* New Delhi, India: Sage Publications.

Vong, K-I. (2012). Play—a multimodal manifestation in kindergarten education in China. *Early Years: An International Research Journal*, 32(1), 35–48.

Vygotsky, L.S. (1978). *Mind in society.* Cambridge, MA: Harvard University Press.

Wang, X.C., & Spodek, B. (2000). Early childhood education in China: A hybrid of traditional, communist, and Western culture. Paper presented at the annual meeting of the National Association for the Education of Young Children (NAEYC), Atlanta, Georgia.

Wang, J., Lin, E., Spalding, E., Odell, S.J., & Klecka, C.L. (2011). Understanding teacher education in an era of globalization. *Journal of Teacher Education*, 62(2), 115–120.

Weijin, V. (2013). Understanding bio-rhythms to enhance your students' schoolday. RED-STAR Education Guide, Qingdao, 2013/2014, The Hutong Education. May 10, 2013. Available at thehutong.com/enhance-your-day-with-tcm/

Why business should support early childhood education (2010) The Institute for a Competitive Workforce.

Williams, L.R. (1991). Curriculum making in two voices: Dilemmas of inclusion in early childhood education. *Early Childhood Research Quarterly*, 6, 303–311.

Williams, L.R. (1999). Determining the early childhood curriculum: The evolution of goals and strategies through consonance and controversy. In C. Seefeldt (Ed.), *The early childhood curriculum: Current findings in theory and practice.* New York: Teachers College Press.

Williams, L.R., & De Gaetano, Y. (1984). *ALERTA: A multicultural, bilingual approach to teaching young children.* Boston: Addison-Wesley.

Wittgenstein, L. (1953). *Philosophical investigations* (G. Anscombe translation). Oxford, UK: Blackwell.

The World Bank (2005). *Treasures of the education system in Sri Lanka*, p. 83. Colombo, Sri Lanka: The World Bank.

The World Bank (2006, 29 May). *Inclusive growth and service delivery: Building on India's success.* Retrieved on 19 August 2013.

The World Bank (2011). Why invest in early childhood development. Retrieved from web. worldbank.org/WBSITE/EXTERNAL/TOPICS/EXTCY/EXTECD/0,,content MDK:20207747~menuPK:527098~pagePK:148956~piPK:216618~theSitePK:344939,00. html

Yang, L. (2004, 28–29 August). Students get to sleep later: Primary classes shortened, lunch break extended. *Shanghai Daily*, p. 2.

Zhou, X. (2011). Early childhood education policy development in China. *International Journal of Child Care and Education*, 5(1), 29–39.

Zhu, J.X. (2003). Integrated theme-based curriculum. Paper presented at the meeting on Re-conceptualizing Early Childhood Education, 7 January 2003, Tempe: Arizona State University.

Zhu, J.X. (2009). Early childhood education and relative policies in China. *International Journal of Child Care and Educational Policies*, 3(1), 51–60.

Zhu, J.X. (2010). Curriculum implementation challenges and strategies in China. Paper written for the Eighth Meeting of the Organization for Economic Co-operation and Development (OECD) Network on Early Childhood Education and Care held 6–7 December 2010: Paris, France.

INDEX